Engaging Ideas

JOHN C. BEAN

FOREWORD BY
MARYELLEN WEIMER

Engaging Ideas

The Professor's Guide to Integrating Writing, Critical Thinking, and Active Learning in the Classroom

JOSSEY-BASS
A Wiley Imprint
www.josseybass.com

Published by Jossey-Bass
A Wiley Imprint
989 Market Street, San Francisco, CA 94103-1741   www.josseybass.com

Readers should be aware that Internet Web sites offered as citations and/or sources for further information may have changed or disappeared between the time this was written and when it is read.

Jossey-Bass books and products are available through most bookstores. To contact Jossey-Bass directly call our Customer Care Department within the U.S. at 800-956-7739, outside the U.S. at 317-572-3986, or fax 317-572-4002.

Jossey-Bass also publishes its books in a variety of electronic formats. Some content that appears in print may not be available in electronic books.

Library of Congress Cataloging-in-Publication Data
Bean, John C.
    Engaging ideas: the professor's guide to integrating writing, critical thinking, and active learning in the classroom / John C., Bean. — 1st ed.
        p.   cm.— (The Jossey-Bass higher and adult education series)
    Includes bibliographical references and index.
    ISBN 0-7879-0203-9
    1. English language—Rhetoric—Study and teaching. 2. Critical thinking—Study and teaching. I. Title. II. Series.
PE1404.B35   1996
808'.042—dc20   95-36265

Printed in the United States of America
FIRST EDITION
PB Printing   20 19 18 17 16 15 14 13 12

The Jossey-Bass
Higher and Adult Education Series

CONTENTS

WITHDRAWN

This book attempts to integrate two powerful recent movements in higher education—the writing-across-the-curriculum movement and the critical thinking movement. My purpose is to create a pragmatic nuts-and-bolts guide that will help teachers from any discipline design interest-provoking writing and critical thinking activities and incorporate them smoothly into their disciplinary courses. The goal of these activities is to transform students from passive to active learners, deepening their understanding of subject matter while helping them learn the thinking processes of the discipline: how members of the discipline ask questions, conduct inquiries, gather and analyze data, and make arguments.

A basic premise of the book, growing out of the educational philosophy of John Dewey, is that critical thinking—and indeed all significant learning—originates in the learner's engagement with problems. Consequently, the design of interesting problems to think about is one of the teacher's chief behind-the-scenes tasks. Equally important are strategies for giving critical thinking problems to students and for creating a course atmosphere that encourages inquiry, exploration, discussion, and debate while valuing the dignity and worth of each student. Teachers of critical thinking also need to be mentors and coaches, developing a range of strategies for modeling critical thinking, critiquing student performances, and otherwise guiding students toward the habits of inquiry and argument valued in their disciplines.

Unique Features of This Book

In keeping with these premises, therefore, this book has the following unique features:

- It takes a pragmatic nuts-and-bolts approach to teaching critical thinking, giving teachers hundreds of suggestions for integrating writing and other critical thinking activities into a disciplinary course.

- It integrates theory and research from the writing-across-the-curriculum literature with the broader pedagogical literature on critical thinking, intellectual development, active learning, and modes of teaching.

- It gives detailed practical assistance in the design of formal and informal writing assignments and suggests timesaving ways to coach the writing process and handle the paper load, including efficient ways to comment on student papers and various approaches to grading writing.

- It treats writing assignments as only one of many ways to present critical thinking problems to students; it shows how writing assignments can easily be integrated with other critical thinking activities such as use of small groups, inquiry discussions, cases, simulation games, classroom debates, and interactive lectures.

- It has separate chapters devoted to academic reading, small groups, various whole-class methods of active learning, essay exams, and research writing.

- It assumes that there is no one right way to integrate writing and critical thinking into a course; it therefore provides numerous options to fit each teacher's particular personality and goals and to allow flexibility for meeting the needs of different kinds of learners.

- It emphasizes writing and critical thinking tasks that focus on the instructor's subject matter goals for the course, thus reducing, and in some cases perhaps even eliminating, the conflict between coverage and process.

- It offers a wide array of ways to use writing in courses, ranging from short write-to-learn "microthemes" to major research papers and from formal academic writing to personal narratives; it also offers numerous ways to work exploratory writing into a course, including in-class freewrites, journals, practice exams, and e-mail conversations.

Link Between Writing and Critical Thinking

Although this book examines a wide range of strategies for promoting critical thinking in the classroom, it assumes that the most intensive and demanding tool for eliciting sustained critical thought is a well-designed writing assignment on a subject matter problem. The underlying premise is that writing is closely linked with thinking and that in presenting students with significant problems to write about—and in creating an environment that demands their best writing—we can promote their general cognitive and intellectual growth. When we make students struggle with their writing, we are making them struggle with thought itself. Emphasizing writing and critical thinking, therefore, generally increases the academic rigor of a course. Often the struggle of writing, linked as it is to the struggle of thinking and to the growth of a person's intellectual powers, awakens students to the real nature of learning.

Readers dismayed by what one of my colleagues calls the "abysmal awfulness" of student writing may be comforted to know that we seldom see our students' best work when we read their prose. Many of our students, unless we establish a classroom environment that alters their behavior, write their papers too quickly and submit to us what are essentially first drafts. When students do their writing the night before a paper is due, they insulate themselves from the intellectual struggle of revision where the true craft of writing is learned. Part of the problem, surely, is the discouraging lack of motivation and interest that we witness in many of today's students. But part of the problem, too, is the way we design and give assignments. When we create interesting and challenging writing assignments—tailored to the developmental needs of our students in an atmosphere that encourages and facilitates revision—we can engage students in a sometimes transforming intellectual experience. It is surprising, in fact, how good undergraduate writing can be when students are effectively coached and when they devote to it the time and effort it requires.

Intended Audience

Engaging Ideas is intended for busy college professors from any academic discipline. Many readers may already emphasize writing, critical thinking, and active learning in their classrooms and hope to find in this book ways to fine-tune their work such as additional approaches or strategies, more effective or efficient methods for coaching students as writers and thinkers, or tips on managing the paper load. Other readers may be attracted to the ideas in this book yet held back by nagging doubts or fears that they will be buried in paper grading, that the use of writing assignments does not fit their disciplines, or that they will have to reduce their coverage of content. This book tries to allay these fears and help all faculty find an approach to integrating into their courses writing and critical think-ing activities that help each student meet course goals while fitting their own teaching philosophies and individual personalities.

It may be helpful to realize that this book is aimed primarily at improving students' engagement with disciplinary subject mat-ter and *not* at improving student writing. Whenever I conduct writing-across-the-curriculum workshops, I always stress that a teacher's purpose in adding writing components to a course is *not* to help English departments teach writing. In fact, improvement of student writing is a happy side effect. Rather teachers should see writing assignments and other critical thinking activities as useful tools to help students achieve the instructor's content and process goals for a course. The reward of this book is watching students come to class better prepared, more vested in and motivated by the problems or questions the course investigates, more apt to study rigorously, and more likely to submit high-quality work. A serendipitous benefit for teachers may be that their own writing gets easier when they develop strategies for helping students. Many of the ideas in this book—about posing problems, generat-ing and exploring ideas, focusing and organizing, giving and receiving peer reviews of drafts, and revising for readers—can be applied to one's own scholarly and professional writing as well as to the writing of students.

General Structure of the Book

Chapter One, designed for the busy professor, gives the reader a nutshell compendium of the whole book and provides handy cross references enabling readers to turn to specific parts of the book that concern their immediate needs. It also addresses four misconcep-tions that tend to discourage professors from integrating writing and critical thinking assignments into their courses.

Part One (Chapters Two through Four) presents the general theoretical background and pedagogical principles on which the book is based. Chapter Two examines the principles that relate writing to critical thinking and argues that good writing is both a process and a product of critical thought. Chapter Three introduces readers to the debate in the writing-across-the-curriculum litera-ture between professional and personal writing and argues that students need to practice both kinds. In Chapter Four, I focus on the problem of error in student writing, examine the debate among linguists and others over the role of grammar in writing instruc-tion, and offer concrete suggestions about ways to reduce the inci-dence of error in students' writing.

Part Two (Chapters Five and Six) focuses on the design of problem-based writing assignments. Chapter Five focuses entirely on the design of formal writing assignments, and Chapter Six concerns ways to use informal, exploratory writing both inside and outside of class to enhance learning and promote critical thinking.

Part Three (Chapters Seven through Twelve) examines a wide variety of strategies for stimulating active learning and for coaching writing and critical thinking through the way teachers design courses, structure assignments, use class time, critique student performance, and model critical thinking themselves. Chapter Seven provides a heuristic for designing critical thinking problems and illustrates them with examples from across the disciplines. These problems can then be used in a wide variety of ways—as formal or informal writing assignments, as problems for small groups, as topics for class debates, and so forth. Chapter Eight, which focuses on the teaching and coaching of academic reading, explores the causes of students' difficulty with academic texts and suggests coaching strategies to help students improve their skills in comprehending and responding to difficult readings. Chapters Nine and Ten together discuss ways to use class time for active inquiry and critical thinking. Chapter Nine focuses on the use of small groups in the classroom, and Chapter Ten suggests ways to make lectures more interactive and whole-class discussions more productive. It also offers suggestions for teaching critical thinking through cases, simulations, classroom debates, "cold-calling," and other methods. Chapters Eleven and Twelve examine ways to increase the levels of critical thinking and learning in two of the most common writing assignments across the curriculum—the essay exam and the "term paper." The strengths and weaknesses of essay exams as writing assignments are explained in Chapter Eleven, which also offers ways to improve their effectiveness. Chapter Twelve, on term papers, opens with a discussion of students' alienation from research writing—an alienation that often results in uninspired cut-and-paste writing or even plagiarism—and offers suggestions for engaging students in undergraduate research that is truly productive and inquiry-based.

The final section of the book, Part Four (Chapters Thirteen through Fifteen), concerns strategies for coaching the writing process and for marking and grading student papers. Chapter Thirteen offers ten timesaving strategies for coaching the writing process while avoiding burnout. Chapter Fourteen focuses on ways to write revision-oriented comments that guide students toward significant revision of their work. Chapter Fifteen offers ideas for grading student writing using analytic or holistic scales or other kinds of scoring guides tailored to the individual teacher's needs and subject matter.

Thanks and Acknowledgments _____

Many people have helped shape this book. My first thanks go to all my colleagues at the College of Great Falls (Montana), Montana State University, and Seattle University, who have taught me about their disciplines and formed learning communities that nurtured my work. Many of their assignments and teaching strategies have found their way into the pages of this book. For their warm friendships and for their lengthy discussions with me about writing and critical thinking in their disciplines, I wish to thank especially W. Daniel Goodman in the Department of Chemistry at the College of Great Falls; Dean Drenk in the School of Business at Montana State University; Joanne Kurfiss Gainen, director of the Center for Teaching and Learning at Santa Clara University; Linda Shohet, director of the Centre for Literacy in Montreal, Canada; Terri Hasseler, former assistant director of the Writing Center at Seattle University; and Larry Nichols, director of the Writing Center at Seattle University. I would like to thank also the many students who have served as consultants in the Seattle University Writing Center; through their observations and research, they have taught me much about the writing experiences of today's college students. And special thanks go to two gracious and capable administrators at Seattle University who have encouraged and facilitated my work: David Leigh, the chair of the English Department and director of the core curriculum, and Stephen Rowan, dean of the College of Arts and Sciences.

I am especially grateful to the Jossey-Bass Higher and Adult Education Series editor, Gale Erlandson, for her patience, encouragement, and support. The chief reviewer for the manuscript, Maryellen Weimer of Pennsylvania State University, was unusually diligent and perceptive in her detailed commentary. She will recognize her influence throughout. I also thank her for her gracious willingness to write the foreword for the book.

My deepest thanks and love go to my family: Kit, Matthew, Andrew, Stephen, and Sarah.

Vashon, Washington   John C. Bean
January 1996

FOREWORD

One of the most successful movements to sweep through American higher education is known as writing across the curriculum, now more than a decade old. Among its successes can be counted a new level of awareness and appreciation for the power of writing as a means of both engaging students and developing their thinking skills. In addition, we faculty now know and understand that the writing competence of our students is a shared responsibility, not one to be held over the heads of English departments.

And we have all pretty much accepted the basic tenets of the movement. We must have our students write more. Practice makes them better writers and, even more important, better *thinkers*. This movement has taught us about the kind of writing that benefits students. Writing to learn identifies a process whereby writing itself leads to greater understanding. And most of us now realize that not all student writing needs to be graded or done for credit—which fact exonerates those of us who worry about our own qualifications to judge the writing skills of others. It is comforting to know that students will benefit from all the writing we make them do, no matter what.

However, even though the writing-across-the-curriculum movement has changed the way most college teachers think about writing, it has not significantly altered what goes on in their classrooms. In other words, despite the fact that we faculty know what we ought to be doing, we aren't doing it. This result the writing-across-the-curriculum movement shares with many other reform efforts: collaborative and cooperative learning, assessment, curricular transformation, science education reform, total quality management, and instructional technology come to mind. Some of these movements have produced more change than others, but overall, the much-needed reform of higher education is still a marginal effort. Why? There are lots of reasons, and the most serious impediments to change have nothing to do with the movements themselves.

The waning years of the twentieth century mark higher education's winter of discontent, a bleak time of scarce resources and few bright days. Survival is most on our minds, not doing extras that help our students learn more and better. The quest for students, external funding, and ways to save money saps most of our institutional energy while faculty busily sandbag against rising teaching loads and class sizes.

Admittedly, there has been a lot of interest in teaching of late, but at too many institutions, it remains a second-class, intellectually inferior, unrewarded, devalued activity. It does need to be improved. We know why and how, but all that has been proposed and in some places partially implemented requires more work, institutional commitment, and a faith that many faculty have lost. Missing motivation, low morale, and declining salary dollars engender cynicism about the likelihood of imminent pedagogical change.

In this deteriorating climate, the roots of the writing-across-the-curriculum movement have tried to take hold. That they have survived and in some cases even thrived is remarkable. That so many faculty have been persuaded to accept responsibility for the development of students' writing skills stands as credible testimony to the power of this reform movement. However, given the bleak realities of higher education despite the intellectual readiness of faculty to address writing skills, is there something else that might advance the cause of a curriculumwide focus on writing?

I propose that what faculty need most, what would help those convinced but not taking action, what has been missing from the literature on writing across the curriculum, is quite simply an *owner's manual*—a book that every faculty member turns to when efforts to develop writing and critical thinking skills need support. The owner's manual would include written guarantees—all the promises about outcomes and descriptions of what will happen to and for students once faculty have the product in hand. More important, the manual would have all the necessary directions and even some insights beyond the basics. It would answer the fundamental questions of how to do it, what kinds of activities you can put together to fit into the unique fabric of your course and content, what kinds of exercises promote what kinds of thinking skills, how to operate a class with such an agenda, how to make it work throughout the life of a course without detracting from all the other goals and objectives you have to accomplish, and what to do when it doesn't work.

Good owner's manuals come complete with troubleshooting guides. They suggest possible sources of the problem and then lay out lots of solutions to try. And a truly useful owner's manual is written so that people who lack expertise and technical background in the areas can still run and maintain the device they now own.

What you have in your hands is the definitive owner's manual for the writing-across-the-curriculum movement. It is written for any faculty member convinced that this cause has merit but in need of the ready array of ideas and information necessary to ensure smooth operation. And an awesome manual it is—comprehensive and detailed in its coverage—describing how writing activities and assignments can be woven into and around virtually every aspect of instruction. The focus here is on the writing-thinking connection, and the validity and ultimate value of that relationship is established here so thoroughly that it stands beyond debate.

This manual may be the best-organized one you will ever encounter. Amazingly, what you need to know is here to be found, easily, when you need it and where you would expect to find it. It is a book that keeps good track of itself, referring the reader back to, forward to, and around content chunks related to the matter under discussion at any given point.

Best of all, this manual is written by someone who knows the subject inside and out. John Bean has been there through all the development phases of this movement, during its implementation, and now as the analysis of its impact begins. He writes from first-hand experience. He knows what kinds of writing activities best develop thinking skills because he has used them in his classes. But Bean writes as a reflective practitioner: he builds on his experiences and uses them to explore, extrapolate, and refine suggestions for faculty in a variety of instructional and institutional settings. Beware: you are about to embark on a book that will overwhelm you with good ideas.

In the rarefied and often elitist atmosphere of higher education, perhaps it demeans a scholarly work to refer to it as an owner's manual. It absolutely should not. We lack a number of crucial manuals in higher education, especially ones that would allow the less technically able among us to enter into and work effectively with the finer points of instructional technology. That these reference works are missing adversely affects the pace at which change occurs in every domain where they are absent. We suffer seriously without them.

Higher education is all but drowning in a sea of isolated research reports. We frequently wander aimlessly in the fog of complex theoretical constructs. Granted, research and theory both add a certain richness to the life of the mind; but we live in a world of action, a place where what we know and believe gets transformed into tangible things, the things we do for and with our students. Books like this one are bridges that connect the currently wide interstices between thought and action. Bridging those gaps requires considerable intellectual engineering, as you will discover as you wander through this fine owner's manual. Explore it appreciatively, and keep it on your nearest shelf, alongside the other dog-eared references that put essential information easily within reach.

Howard, Pennsylvania   Maryellen Weimer, Ph.D.
January 1996

THE AUTHOR

John C. Bean is a professor of English at Seattle University, where he directs the writing program and chairs the University Task Force on Teaching and Learning. He holds a B.A. degree from Stanford University (1965) and a Ph.D. degree from the University of Washington (1971). Active in the writing-across-the-curriculum movement since 1975, he has conducted numerous faculty workshops at colleges and universities across the United States and Canada. He has helped develop cross-disciplinary writing programs at the three institutions where he has taught: at the College of Great Falls (Montana) under a grant from the Lilly Endowment, at Montana State University under a grant from the Fund for the Improvement of Postsecondary Education, and at Seattle University under a grant from the Consortium for the Advancement of Private Higher Education.

Bean is coauthor (with John D. Ramage) of *Form and Surprise in Composition: Writing and Thinking Across the Curriculum* (1986) and *Writing Arguments: A Rhetoric with Readings* (3rd ed., 1995). He has also published numerous articles on writing and on Renaissance literature. He is a former member of the executive board of the Conference on College Composition and Communication and has been active as a consultant and evaluator for the Council of Writing Program Administrators.

His most recent work, as chair of Seattle University's Task Force on Teaching and Learning, is the joint development with colleagues of the four-day Institute on Teaching and Learning for new faculty members at Seattle University.

Using Writing to Promote Thinking

A Busy Professor's Guide to the Whole Book

The premise of this book is that integrating writing and other critical thinking activities into a course increases students' learning while teaching them thinking skills for posing questions, proposing hypotheses, gathering and analyzing data, and making arguments. Professors who successfully integrate writing and critical thinking tasks into their courses often report a satisfying increase in their teaching pleasure: class discussions are richer, students are more fully engaged in their learning, and the quality of their performance improves.

But the use of writing and critical thinking activities to promote learning does not happen through serendipity. Teachers must plan for it and foster it throughout the course. This chapter suggests a sequence of steps that teachers can take to integrate writing and critical thinking into their courses. It then addresses four negative beliefs that often discourage teachers from taking these steps—the belief that integrating writing into a course will take time away from content, that writing assignments are not appropriate for some disciplines or courses, that assigning writing will bury a teacher in paper grading, and that assigning writing requires specialized expertise. Because these beliefs raise important concerns, I seek to supply reassuring responses at the outset.

This chapter provides, in effect, a brief overview of the whole book; subsequent chapters treat in depth each of the suggestions or issues introduced briefly here. Teachers who are pressed for time can read this chapter and then, using the cross-references provided, turn directly to the other chapters that address their most immediate concerns.

Steps for Integrating Writing and Critical Thinking Activities into a Course

This section surveys seven steps teachers can take to integrate writing and critical thinking activities into a course.

Step 1: Become Familiar with Some of the General Principles Linking Writing to Learning and Critical Thinking

To appreciate how writing is linked to learning and critical thinking, we can begin with a brief discussion of how we might define critical thinking.

Critical Thinking Rooted in Problems. Although definitions in the pedagogical literature vary in detail, in their broad outlines they are largely elaborations, extensions, and refinements of the progressive views of John Dewey (1916), who rooted critical thinking in the students' engagement with a problem. "The most significant question which can be asked," says Dewey, "about any situation or experience proposed to induce learning is what quality of problem it involves" (p. 182). Problems, for Dewey, evoke students' natural curiosity and stimulate both learning and critical thought. "Only by wrestling with the conditions of the problem at first hand, seeking and finding his own way out, does [the student] think" (p. 188).

Part of the difficulty of teaching critical thinking, therefore, is awakening students to the existence of problems all around them. Meyers (1986), who agrees with Dewey that problems are naturally motivating, argues that teachers ought to begin every class with "something that is a problem or a cause for wonder" (p. 44). Meyers quotes philosopher and chemist Michael Polanyi, who claims that "as far down the scale of life as worms and even perhaps amoebas, we meet a general alertness of animals, not directed towards any specific satisfaction, but merely exploring what is there: an urge to achieve intellectual control over the situations confronting [them]" (p. 41). Presenting students with problems, then, taps into something natural and self-fulfilling in our beings. As Brookfield (1987) claims, critical thinking is "a productive and positive" activity. "Critical thinkers are actively engaged with life" (p. 5). This belief in the natural, healthy, and motivating pleasure of problems—and in the power of well-designed problems to awaken and stimulate the passive and unmotivated student—is one of the underlying premises of this book.

The Special Nature of Academic Problems. Not all problems, however, are *academic* problems—the kinds of problems that we typically present to students in our classrooms or that we pose for ourselves in doing scholarly research. To grow as critical thinkers, students must develop the mental habits that allow them to experience problems phenomenologically, to dwell with them—to understand, in short, what makes a problem problematic. To a large extent, these mental habits are discipline-specific, since each discipline poses its own kinds of problems and conducts inquiries, uses data, and makes arguments in its own characteristic fashion. But some aspects of critical thinking are also generic across all disciplines. For Brookfield (1987), the two "central activities" of critical thinking involve "identifying and challenging assumptions and exploring alternative ways of thinking and acting" (p. 71). Similarly, Paul (1987) argues that critical thinking involves entering imaginatively into opposing points of view to create "dialogic exchange" between our own views and those whose thinking differs substantially from our own. Kurfiss (1988) likewise believes that critical thinkers pose problems by questioning assumptions and aggressively seeking alternative views. For her, the prototypical academic problem is "ill-structured"; that is, it is an open-ended question that does not have a clear right answer and therefore must be responded to with a proposition justified by reasons and evidence. "In critical thinking," says Kurfiss, "all assumptions are open to question, divergent views are aggressively sought, and the inquiry is not biased in favor of a particular outcome" (p. 2). Kurfiss's formal definition of critical thinking, which emphasizes that its outcome is *both* a tentative solution to the problem and a justifying argument, is particularly helpful. For Kurfiss, critical thinking can be defined as "an investigation whose purpose is to explore a situation, phenomenon, question, or problem to arrive at a hypothesis or conclusion about it that integrates all available information and that can therefore be convincingly justified" (p. 2).

The Link Between Writing and Critical Thinking. Given this view of critical thinking, what is its connection with writing? Quite simply, writing is both a process of doing critical thinking and a product communicating the results of critical thinking. As I show in Chapter Two, writing instruction goes sour whenever writing is conceived primarily as a "communication skill" rather than as a process and product of critical thought. If writing is merely a communication skill, then we primarily ask of it, "Is the writing clear?" But if writing is critical thinking, we ask, "Is the writing interesting?

Does it show a mind actively engaged with a problem? Does it bring something new to readers? Does it make an argument?" Academic writing, as Chapters Two and Three explain, begins with the posing of a problem. The writer's thesis statement is a tentative response to that problem, a "solution" that must be supported with the kinds of reasons and evidence that are valued in the discipline. Writers produce multiple drafts because the act of writing is itself an act of discovery or, in Dewey's terms, of "wrestling with the conditions of the problem" at hand. Behind the scenes of a finished product is a messy process of exploratory writing, conversation, discarded drafts, midnight agony. Chapter Two deals with this issue in depth.

Step 2: Plan Your Course with Critical Thinking Objectives in Mind

Once teachers are convinced of the value of critical thinking, the next step is to design a course that nurtures it. What is such a course like? In her comprehensive review of the literature on critical thinking, Kurfiss (1988) examined a wide range of successful disciplinary courses devoted to the teaching of both subject matter and critical thinking. In each case, she explains, "the professor establishes an agenda that includes learning to think about subject matter. Students are active, involved, consulting and arguing with each other, and responsible for their own learning" (p. 88). From this review, she derives eight principles for designing a disciplinary course that supports critical thinking:

1. Critical thinking is a learnable skill; the instructor and peers are resources in developing critical thinking skills.
2. Problems, questions, or issues are the point of entry into the subject and a source of motivation for sustained inquiry.
3. Successful courses balance challenges to think critically with support tailored to students' developmental needs.
4. Courses are assignment centered rather than text and lecture centered. Goals, methods, and evaluation emphasize using content rather than simply acquiring it.
5. Students are required to formulate and justify their ideas in writing or other appropriate modes.
6. Students collaborate to learn and to stretch their thinking, for example, in pair problem solving and small group work.
7. Several courses, particularly those that teach problem-solving skills, nurture students' metacognitive abilities.
8. The developmental needs of students are acknowledged and used as information in the design of the course. Teachers in these courses make standards explicit and then help students learn how to achieve them [pp. 88–89].

This book aims to help teachers develop courses that follow these guidelines. Of key importance are principles 2, 4, and 5: a good critical thinking course presents students with "problems, questions, and issues" that make a course "assignment centered, rather than text or lecture centered" and holds students responsible for "formulating and justifying" their solutions orally or in writing. This book particularly emphasizes writing assignments because they are perhaps the most flexible and most intensive way to integrate critical thinking tasks into a course and because the writing process itself entails complex critical thinking. But much attention is also given to class discussions, small group activities, and other teaching strategies that encourage students to work collaboratively to expand, develop, and deepen their thinking. Attention is also given throughout to the design of problems at appropriate levels of difficulty, to the developmental needs of students, and to the importance of making expectations and criteria clear (principles 1, 3, and 8).

Step 3: Design Critical Thinking Tasks for Students to Address

A crucial step in teaching critical thinking is to develop good problems for students to think about. Tasks can range from major disciplinary issues down to tiny questions about the meaning of a key passage in a course reading. The kinds of questions you develop for students will depend on the nature of question asking in your own discipline and on your own emphases in teaching critical thinking.

When I conduct workshops in writing across the curriculum, I like to emphasize a disciplinary, content-driven view of critical thinking by asking faculty to write out one or two final examination essay questions for one of their courses—questions that they think require both subject matter knowledge and critical thinking. We then discuss the kinds of critical thinking needed and the relative difficulty of each question, sometimes offering suggestions on ways to improve questions to elicit the kinds and levels of critical thinking the teacher seeks. When we have appreciated the value of these questions for promoting critical thinking, I suggest that it is a shame to waste them on a timed exam, where students spend only an hour or so on task. Such questions and dozens more like them can be integrated into the fabric of a course where they can stimulate curiosity, drive inquiry, and promote learning. Chapters Five, Six, and Seven focus specifically on the design of critical thinking tasks to serve as formal or informal writing assignments or as starting points for other critical thinking activities.

Step 4: Develop a Repertoire of Ways to Give Critical Thinking Tasks to Students

Once you have developed a stockpile of critical thinking problems based on your course's subject matter, you can choose from dozens of ways to integrate them into your course. This book presents numerous options for giving critical thinking problems to students. These include the following:

1. *Problems presented as formal writing assignments.* Formal writing assignments, which require revision and multiple drafts, keep students on task for extended periods and are among our most powerful tools for teaching critical thought. They can range in length from one-paragraph "microthemes" (see Chapter Five) to major research papers (see Chapter Twelve). As these chapters show, good academic assignments usually require that the student formulate and support a thesis in response to a problem. Such assignments are far more effective for developing critical thinking than traditional topic-centered assignments ("Write a paper on a topic of your choice").

2. *Problems presented as thought-provokers for exploratory writing.* Although students normally write only a few formal papers for a course, they can do behind-the-scenes exploratory writing on a daily basis. Chapters Two, Three, and Six provide a rationale for this kind of writing, which is a seedbed for critical thought. Exploratory writing records the actual process of critical thinking while simultaneously driving it forward. Perhaps more than any other instructional tool, exploratory writing transforms the way students study for a course because it can make active critical thinking part of each day's homework. Chapters Six and Eight give numerous suggestions for ways to integrate exploratory writing into a course, ranging from various kinds of journals to e-mail conversations.

3. *Problems presented as tasks for small group problem solving.* One of the most effective ways to use critical thinking problems in class is as collaborative learning tasks for small groups. Groups are given a set time to debate alternative solutions to a problem and to arrive at either a consensus or a reasoned "agreement to disagree." In a plenary session, groups report and justify their solutions to the whole class. The instructor usually critiques the groups' solutions and often explains how experts in the discipline (for whom the teacher is spokesperson) might tackle the same problem. During plenary sessions, the instructor becomes a powerful role model and coach of critical thinking. Chapter Nine focuses on the uses of small groups to promote critical thinking.

4. *Problems presented as starters for inquiry-based class discussions.* Discussion classes can begin with one or two critical thinking prob-

lems written on the chalkboard as "questions of the day." The teacher guides the discussion, encouraging students to appreciate and manage complexity. (If students have addressed the same questions the night before in a journal entry or some other form of exploratory writing, they will be both eager and prepared for class discussion.) Chapter Ten suggests techniques for leading class discussions that promote critical thinking.

5. *Problems presented as think-on-your-feet questions for in-class "cold calling."* The teacher calls on one person at a time to think aloud, systematically following one question with another, Socratic style. Professor Kingsfield, in the 1973 film *The Paper Chase*, is many persons' nightmare example of the cold-calling professor. Chapter Ten offers suggestions for softening Kingsfield's cold-calling strategy to make it a supportive yet challenging way to encourage students to use course material rather than just memorize it.

6. *Problems presented as focusing questions for in-class debates, panel discussions, cases, or fishbowls.* Other ways to get students actively addressing critical thinking problems in class include classroom debates, panel discussions, cases, and fishbowls. All of these techniques are described in detail in Chapter Ten.

7. *Problems presented as practice exam questions.* Chapter Eleven suggests ways to coax more student learning and critical thinking out of essay exams. One of the best approaches is to give practice exams that students write for homework on a self-timed basis. Feedback is provided through in-class discussion of representative essays.

The point of all these strategies is to model for students a view of knowledge in which inquirers must develop and support provisional answers to disciplinary problems. By actively using new concepts and information, students engage course material on a deeper level.

Step 5: Develop Strategies to Include Exploratory Writing and Talking in Your Courses

Good writing, I like to tell my students, grows out of good talking—either talking with classmates or talking dialogically with oneself through exploratory writing. A key observation among teachers of critical thinking is that students, when given a critical thinking problem, tend to reach closure too quickly. They do not suspend judgment, question assumptions, imagine alternative answers, play with data, enter into the spirit of opposing views, and just plain linger over questions. As a result, they often write truncated and underdeveloped papers. To deepen students' thinking, teachers need to build into their courses time, space, tools, and motivation for exploratory thinking. Chapters Six, Eight, Nine, and Ten suggest numerous ways to make exploratory writing and talking a habit of students in your courses.

Step 6: Develop Effective Strategies for Coaching Students in Critical Thinking

Besides giving students good problems to think about, teachers need to critique students' performances and to model the kinds of critical thinking they want students to develop. According to Meyers (1986), teachers of critical thinking will often spend much of their class time as "referees, coaches, and mentors rather than as lecturers and purveyors of the truth. . . . For most of us," he continues, "this is a worthwhile but difficult shift" (p. 39). This book suggests numerous ways that teachers can coach critical thinking, including guiding discussions, critiquing solutions developed by small groups, writing comments on student drafts, holding conferences, sharing autobiographical accounts of their own thinking and writing processes, discussing strengths and weaknesses of sample papers, breaking long assignments into stages, and stressing revision and multiple drafts. An equally important aspect of coaching is providing a supportive, open classroom that values the worth and dignity of students. Suggestions for coaching writing and critical thinking are integrated throughout the book but occur especially in Chapter Thirteen. Chapter Eight focuses specifically on coaching students as critical readers of academic texts, and Chapter Fourteen focuses entirely on ways to comment on student papers to promote critical thinking.

Step 7: When Assigning Formal Writing, Treat Writing as a Process

In most kinds of courses, the student "product" that most exhibits the results of critical thinking is a formal essay or technical report. Often, however, what the student submits as a finished product is in effect an early draft, the result of an undeveloped and often sterile writing process. No matter how much we exhort students to write several drafts and to collaborate with peers, most of our students will continue to write their papers on the night before they are due unless we structure our courses to promote writing as a process.

Teachers can get better final products, therefore, if they design their courses from the outset to combat last-minute writing, to promote exploratory writing and talking, and to encourage substantive revision. Chapter Thirteen deals with this problem in detail.

Four Discouraging Beliefs and Some Encouraging Responses

The steps just described can help teachers integrate writing and critical thinking activities into their courses. However, many teachers who are tempted to do so may be held back by negative beliefs or misconceptions about what happens when a teacher begins developing a pedagogy using writing and critical thinking. It will be helpful, therefore, to address these beliefs at the outset. Based on discussions with faculty from across the disciplines, I find the following four misconceptions the most pervasive and potentially discouraging.

Misconception 1: Emphasizing Writing and Critical Thinking in My Courses Will Take Time Away from Content

Many faculty, understandably concerned about coverage of material, do not want to shift class time away from content. In my experience, however, emphasizing writing and critical thinking in a course increases the amount of subject matter that students actually learn and in many cases can actually *increase total coverage* of content. My assertion may seem counterintuitive until one realizes that the primary effect of adding writing and critical thinking components to a course is the restructuring and transforming of students' study time outside of class. Critical thinking tasks—which require students to *use* their expanding knowledge of subject matter to address disciplinary problems—motivate better study habits by helping students see their learning as purposeful and interesting. If tasks are designed to improve academic reading (see Chapter Eight), students often learn to read textbooks more powerfully and interact more critically with supplemental readings, reducing the teacher's need to explain readings in class. Students come to class better prepared, ready to ask questions, and looking forward to discussions. More confident that students can acquire "coverage" from assigned readings, teachers can, if they choose, redirect some class time away from explaining readings toward critical discussions, small group problem solving, or other critical thinking activities. To ensure that courses accomplish both the instructor's content and coverage goals for a course and the process goals of inquiry, analysis, and argument, instructors should first establish content goals and then develop critical thinking problems that will help students achieve those goals. Throughout, the emphasis of this book is on helping students learn the subject matter of a course at a deeper and more intellectually mature level. Chapter Five includes some suggestions for identifying both content and process goals for a course.

Misconception 2: Writing Assignments Are Unsuitable in My Course

Most teachers believe that writing applies naturally to English courses, to liberal arts courses, and to certain specialized courses in their fields. They may not, however, believe that writing is equally appropriate in their own courses. These doubts are frequently expressed by teachers of quantitative or technical courses or ones that focus on basic facts, concepts, or algorithmic procedures that according to the teacher must be "committed to memory" before the student can move on to problem solving and analysis. If we apply some conceptual blockbusting, however, we see that writing assignments can be used profitably in any course. (My point is exemplified by the wide range of disciplines represented in this book—accounting, physics, chemistry, all levels of mathematics, nursing, business, education, and engineering, as well as the humanities and social sciences.) By conceptual blockbusting, I mean primarily rethinking what constitutes a "writing assignment." Many of the assignments in this book are nongraded or are very short formal tasks designed to help students understand an important course concept. Others have a metacognitive aim—helping students reflect on their own thinking processes or productively altering their methods of studying or reading. Still others have a procedural aim—helping students learn disciplinary methods of inquiry and analysis. Whatever a teacher's goals for a course, writing assignments can be designed to help students meet them.

Misconception 3: Adding More Writing to My Course Will Bury Me in Paper Grading

Many teachers would gladly require more writing in their courses if it were not for marking and grading all those papers. If teachers do not currently assign any writing in their courses, adding a writing component will admittedly require extra work, although not necessarily more total time devoted to teaching if some of the teacher's current preparation or conference time is shifted toward responding to writing. If teachers already require writing in their courses (say, a couple of essay exams and a term paper), following the suggestions in this book might *reduce* the total time they spend on student writing while simultaneously making that time more rewarding for themselves and more productive for students.

There are many ways to work writing into a course while keeping the paper load manageable. Some methods require no teacher time (for example, in-class freewriting), some minimal time (perusing a random selection of entries from a guided journal), and some very modest time (assigning write-to-learn microthemes using models feedback). Even when you require several formal essays or a major research paper, you may employ any number of timesaving strategies to reduce the paper load (see Chapter Thirteen). The key is to decide how much time you are willing to spend on student writing and then to plan your courses to include only what you can handle—always remembering that you do not have to read everything a student writes.

Misconception 4: I Am Not Knowledgeable Enough About Writing and Grammar to Help Students with Their Own Writing

Many teachers across the curriculum will admit that English was not their favorite subject. Although they produce competent professional writing in their own fields, they believe that because they struggle with their own writing and because they do not know grammatical terminology or composition theory, they lack the skills to help students. This book aims to allay these fears. Because the best teacher commentary focuses primarily on ideas and development, no special terminology is needed. Teachers simply need to be honest readers, making comments like these:

"I got lost in this part."

"You need more evidence here."

"You seem to be overlooking Baker's research on this problem. Can you summarize and respond to Baker's views?"

"Excellent point!"

A main key to teaching writing, as Chapter Two argues, is teaching students how to revise. The more teachers struggle to revise their own writing, the more they can serve as role models for students. In short, you should discover that your own experience as an academic writer and reader, combined with your expertise in how scholars in your field inquire and argue, should be all the background you need to help your students with their writing.

Conclusion: Engaging Your Students with the Ideas of Your Course _____

The steps suggested here for integrating writing and critical thinking assignments into a course can increase students' engagement with subject matter and improve the quality of their work. Moreover, these suggestions do not call for rapid, complete makeovers of a course. It is possible to make changes in a course gradually, trying a few new activities at a time, looking for strategies and approaches that fit your discipline and subject matter, that work for your students, and that accord with your own personality and teaching philosophy.

Some teachers make only minimal changes in their courses. I know of one teacher, a brilliant lecturer, who has changed nothing in his courses except for adding a series of nongraded "practice essay exams." He collects the exams (written out of class, self-timed by students), keeps a record of who submits them, reads randomly selected ones in search of representative problems as well as models of excellent exams, and then holds class discussions of what constitutes a good answer. He is very happy with this minimalist approach and offers persuasive anecdotal evidence that this practice has improved students' study habits as well as the quality of their actual essay exams.

But I know of other teachers who have radically transformed their classrooms, moving from a teacher-centered to a student-centered pedagogy, from lecture-based courses to inquiry-based courses using exploratory writing, collaborative learning, lively discussions, and other strategies for engaging students in inquiry and debate.

In the pages that follow, I invite readers to find what works for them and for their students.

PART ONE

Understanding Connections Between Thinking and Writing

CHAPTER 2

How Writing Is Related to Critical Thinking

The writing-across-the-curriculum movement (or the language-across-the-curriculum movement, as it is known in Canada and Great Britain) is largely a reaction against traditional writing instruction that associates good writing primarily with grammatical accuracy and correctness and thus isolates writing instruction within English departments, the home of the grammar experts. The problem with traditional writing instruction is that it leads to a view of writing as a set of isolated skills unconnected to an authentic desire to converse with interested readers about real ideas.

A recent nationally syndicated "Shoe" cartoon will illustrate my point. Skyler, a bright young bird of a student, sits at his school desk writing essays—an activity that he apparently relishes. "They give me an opportunity to perfect a verbal skill I can use all my life," he says with a self-satisfied smile. In the last frame of the cartoon, his smile turns to a triumphant grin as he discloses the skill he has in mind: "the ability to disguise total ignorance with good writing."

To the general public this is a funny cartoon; to me it is a symbol of what has gone wrong with traditional writing instruction. Skyler believes that the act of writing can be separated from the interior life of the writer, that writing is merely packaging and thus a separate thing from "content," which he assumes exists independently, apart from language. To put it another way, writing is like the box and wrapping paper into which we put our already formulated ideas. Our schools and colleges are now awash with students who view writing in this bifurcated way—students who complain that a writing teacher has no business criticizing one's ideas ("This is a *writing* class!") just as a history or science or philosophy teacher has no business criticizing one's writing ("This is *not* a writing class!").

Once writing is imagined as "packaging," students find little use for it. Separated from the act of thinking and creating, writing becomes merely a skill that can be learned through grammar drills and through the production of pointless essays that students do not want to write and that teachers do not want to read. This is the view of writing possessed by many first-year students when they show up at our gates to begin their college careers. It is the challenge of faculty across the disciplines to show them other ways of imagining writing.

Another View: Metaphors for Writing in French Versus English

Before turning directly to a better way to imagine writing, let's see what writing looks like through the metaphors of a different language. In French, the word for a rough draft is *brouillon,* derived from a verb meaning "to place in disorder, to scramble" and related etymologically to the words for *cauldron* and *vortex.* This metaphor suggests a writing process that begins as a journey into disorder, a making of chaos, out of which one eventually forges an essay. Perhaps driven by their awareness of disorder in the term *brouillon,* the French place an equally strong emphasis on a *plan* (roughly equivalent to the English *outline*), which is the principle of order that the mind must impose on the scrambled *brouillon.* Together the metaphors *plan* and *brouillon* reveal a creative tension between order and disorder. In English, we have no equivalent word for a *brouillon.* Our phrase "rough draft" suggests something that must be smoothed and polished but not something deliberately scrambled, something placed in disorder, something that must be wrestled into form. Nor is our word *outline*—suggesting an inert structure—exactly equivalent to *plan,* which like the English word *plan* implies a sense of human purpose and intention.

Viewed in the light of the metaphorical *brouillon* and *plan,* traditional writing instruction seems impoverished indeed. Traditionally, we have seldom suggested to students that writing has a *brouillon* stage, a creative period of confusion and disorder; rather, we have taught that writing begins with an outline (which we dutifully correct for proper indentation and placement of periods and capital letters). Without the *brouillon*, we have eliminated from our writing classes the rich, creative source of ideas and substituted instead a sterile order that leaves us obsessed with correctness, neatness, and propriety. The message from our schools has been that writing is a joyless activity, an opportunity mainly for displaying errors for teachers to red-pencil. The social cost is incalculable: when writing gets separated from what the writer really thinks, the experience of "really thinking" can be quickly lost from the curriculum.

The writing-across-the-curriculum movement is thus rooted in a radical revisioning of what it means to be a writer. It is the purpose of the three chapters in Part One to sketch in for the reader a general overview of the theory, principles, and rationale that underlie a revised approach to writing, one that can transform a student's view of learning and thinking in the disciplines. The present chapter discusses how writing can be best understood as a process of critical thinking, Chapter Three focuses on the relationship between professional and personal writing, and Chapter Four examines current thinking about the best way to respond to grammatical problems and error in student writing. Together, these chapters provide a theoretical background for the pragmatic focus in the rest of the book on classroom strategies for improving students' writing and critical thinking.

This present chapter, in its focus on writing as a thinking process, discusses the dialogic view of knowledge that underlies academic writing, explores various theories explaining why students have difficulty composing thesis-based prose, and concludes with an examination of the writing processes through which experienced writers, in a series of drafts, discover, complicate, and clarify their ideas.

Writing, Thinking, and a Dialogic View of Knowledge

Before our friend Skyler can appreciate the connection between good thinking and good writing, he needs to see knowledge as something other than discrete bits of information to be studied and stored in memory. Asking a first-year student to write a college-level essay is really asking for a baffling new way of imagining knowledge itself.

The View of Knowledge Underlying Academic Writing

For the most part, formal academic writing requires analytical or argumentative thinking and is characterized by a controlling thesis statement and a logical, hierarchical structure. By a thesis state-ment, I mean a one-sentence summary of the writer's argument, a main point to be supported by good reasons and evidence. Thesis-governed writing entails a complex view of knowledge in which differing views about the nature of truth compete for alle-giance.

However, as William Perry (1970) has shown in his influential study of students' cognitive growth through college, most of our students do not come to college seeing the world this way. Perry shows that most beginning college students view education dualis-tically, imagining knowledge as the acquisition of correct informa-tion and right answers. They see themselves as empty buckets being filled with data by their professors. To dualists, the only aca-demic use of writing is to demonstrate one's knowledge of the cor-rect facts—a concept of writing as information rather than as argument or analysis. Students in Perry's middle stages of multi-plicity are beginning to accept the notion of opposing views, but they see these simply as "opinions"; since "everyone has a right to his or her own opinion," they see little purpose in defending any particular view and thus are not compelled through the process of rigorous thinking that intellectually mature writing demands. It is not until they reach Perry's highest stages of development that a real need for reasoned argument begins to emerge.

What our beginning college writers do not understand, there-fore, is the view of academic life implied by writing across the cur-riculum, where writing means joining a conversation of persons who are, in important ways, *fundamentally disagreeing*. In other words, they do not see that a thesis implies a counterthesis and that the presence of opposing voices implies a view of knowledge as dialogic, contingent, ambiguous, and tentative.

It follows that teaching thesis-governed writing means teach-ing students an unfamiliar way of looking at their courses and at knowledge itself. For a brief glimpse of a student being initiated into this uncomfortable world, consider for a moment the follow-ing transcript of a writing center conference in which the student had been asked to support one of two opposing theses: "The U.S. involvement in Central America is or is not imperialism."

Tutor: If I said, "Tell me whether or not this is imperialism," what's your first gut reaction?

Writer: There are very strong arguments for both. It's all in how you define it.

Tutor: Okay, who's doing the defining?

Writer: Anybody. That's just it—there's no real clear definition.

Over time, it's been distorted. I mean, before, imperialism used to be like the British who go in and take Hong Kong, set up their own little thing that's their own British government. That's true imperialism. But the definition's been expanded to include indirect control by other means, and what exactly that is I guess you have to decide. So I don't know. I don't think we really have control in Central America, so that part of me says no, that's not imperialism. But other parts of me say we really do control a lot of what is going on in Central America by the amount of dollars and where we put them. So in that sense, we do have imperialism. . . . So the other big question on that, and why I brought in the balance of power, is, where are we allowed to cross the line and where are we not?

Tutor: Okay then, if you're going to ask that question—where are we allowed to cross the line?—it implies that a line is drawn. So what I guess I'm trying to get you to say is . . .

Writer: Whether I'm for or against.

Tutor: Yes!

Writer: The reason why I'm undecided is because I couldn't create a strong enough argument for either side. There are too many holes in each side. If I were to pick one side, somebody could blow me out of the water.

The student writer, obviously engaged with the assignment, is keenly aware of the tentativeness of both positions, either of which can be "blown out of the water" by the other side. Both the facts of the case and, more troublingly, the definition of imperialism are open-ended problems. The student longs for a "right answer," resisting the frightening prospect of having to make meanings and defend them. Good writing assignments produce exactly this kind of discomfort: the need to join, in a reasoned way, a conversation of differing voices.

We thus need to help our students see that academic writing involves intellectual and often emotional *struggle:* it begins with the writer's awareness that a problem exists—often dimly felt, unclarified, and blurry—and that the writer's thesis is a tentative, risky proposition in response to that problem, a proposition that competes for readers' allegiance with other differing propositions.

Teaching Writing as a Thinking Process

Fortunately, the writing process itself provides one of the best ways to help students learn the active, dialogic thinking skills valued in academic life. Students need to understand that even for the most skilled writers, composing an essay is a tortuous process because, as writing theorist Peter Elbow (1973) has argued, "meaning is not what you start out with but what you end up with. . . . Think of writing then not as a way to transmit a message but as a way to grow and cook a message" (p. 15). Thus, the elegance and structure of thesis-governed writing—as a finished product— evolves from a lengthy and messy process of drafting and redrafting. An across-the-curriculum emphasis on multiple drafts encourages the messy process whereby writers become engaged with a problem and, once engaged, formulate, develop, complicate, and clarify their own ideas. Thesis-governed writing is thus the exterior sign of an interior thinking process that we as faculty need to help our students develop. Teaching this process is itself a slow developmental task. The habit of problem posing and thesis making does not come naturally to beginning college students, who write more clearly when given assignments that do *not* challenge them as thinkers. The next section explores this phenomenon in more detail.

Avoiding a Thesis: Three Cognitively Immature Essay Structures

To see more clearly the relationship between a dialogic view of knowledge and the approach to writing instruction advocated here, let's examine several cognitively immature organizational structures that students often resort to when unable to produce thesis-governed prose.

"And Then" Writing, or Chronological Structure

By "and then" writing I mean a chronological narrative in which the writer tells what happens between time point A and time point B without focus, selection, pacing, or tension. Students produce "and then" structures whenever they resort inappropriately to chronological organization. A typical example is writing a summary instead of an argument when asked to review an article or producing a straight chronological narrative instead of a causal analysis when asked to write about an interpretive problem in history. The same tendency is exhibited in research papers when the writer presents data in chronological order rather than using the data to support points or when the writer recounts the story of his or her particular research process rather than arranging material to meet the needs of readers.

"And then" writing can be illustrated by the following student's difficulty with a two-paragraph problem-solution assignment in a first-year English course. The first paragraph is supposed to introduce the reader to a problem, and the second paragraph is supposed to explain the writer's solution to the problem. (Typical problems posed by students include "How do you keep grasshoppers out of your garden?" and "How do you bleed the most money out of a car insurance adjuster?")

Example of "And Then" Writing

Last Fall and Winter I was living in Spokane with my brother, who during this time had a Platonic girl friend come over from Seattle and stay for a weekend. Her name was Karen, and we became interested in each other and I went over to see her at the first of the year. She then invited me to supposedly, the biggest party of the year, called the Aristocrat's Ball. I said sure and made my way back to Seattle in February. It started out bad on Friday, the day my brother and I left Spokane. We left town an hour late, but what's new? Then my brother had to stop along the way and pick up some parts; what a bitch—we stayed there for an hour trying to find this guy. It all started out bad because we arrived in Seattle and I forgot to call Karen. We were staying at her brother's house and after we brought all our things in, we decided to go to a few bars. Later that night we ran into Karen in one of the bars, and needless to say she was not happy with me. When I got up the next morning I knew I should of stayed in Spokane, because I felt bad vibes. Karen made it over about a hour before the party. By the time we reached the party, which drove me crazy, she wound up with another guy, so her friends and I decided to go to a few bars. The next morning when I was packing, I could not find my watch and decided that someone had to of taken it. We decided that it had to of been the goon that Karen had wound up with the night before, because she was at her brother's house with him before she went home. So how was I going to get my watch back?

We decided that the direct and honest approach to the problem would work out the best. We got in contact and confronted him. This turned out to be quite a chore. It turned out that he was visiting some of his family during that weekend and lived in Little Harbor, California. It turned out that Karen knew his half brother and got some information on him, which was not pretty. He had just been released by the army and was trained in a special forces unit, in the fields of Martial Arts. He was a trained killer! This information did not help matters at all, but the next bit of information was just as bad, if not worse. Believe it or not, he was up on charges of attempted murder and breaking and entering. In a way, it turned out lucky for me, because he was in enough trouble with the police and did not need any more. Karen got in contact with him and threatened him that I would bring him up on charges, if he did not return the watch. His mother decided that he was in enough trouble and sent me the watch. I was astounded, it was still working and looked fine. The moral of the story is don't drive 400 miles to see a girl you hardly know, and what ever you do, don't leave your valuables out in the open.

The problem this writer addresses seems to be something like "How do you get your watch back from a trained killer?" and the solution—potentially humorous if handled effectively—seems to be "Go tell the killer's mother." But the writer is unable to focus the essay on the problem of recovering stolen property from a trained killer, so instead he resorts to a chronological retelling of the whole trip.

It must be noted, however, that it is not just inexperienced writers who produce chronological structures. Flower and Hayes (1977) and Flower (1979) have shown that long passages of chronological writing characterize the early drafts of expert writers. In fact, they argue that chronological thinking provides a natural way of retrieving ideas and details from long-term memory. But experienced writers convert "and then" material into hierarchically focused material as they revise, whereas novice writers seem satisfied with the draft at the "and then" stage.

"All About" Writing, or Encyclopedic Order

Whereas the "and then" paper strings details on a chronological frame, the "all about" paper tries to say a little bit of everything about a topic. When well written, such papers may seem organized hierarchically because the writer usually groups data by category. But the categories do not function as reasons in support of a thesis. Rather, like the headings in an encyclopedia article or the numeral categories in the Dewey Decimal System, they are simply ways of arranging information that do not add up to an argument.

Unfortunately, educators in America have a long tradition of rewarding "all about" writing. We encourage such writing when we assign a "report on North Dakota" in fifth-grade social studies, a "library paper on General Rommel" in eleventh-grade history, or "a term paper on schizophrenia" in college psychology. Assignments like these have endured because they have one major virtue: they increase students' general store of knowledge about North Dakota, General Rommel, or schizophrenia. But they often do little to increase students' maturity as writers and thinkers.

Consider the difference between a student who is asked to write a traditional "term paper" on, say, Charles Darwin versus a student who is asked to write a research paper on Darwin that must begin with the presentation of a problem or question that the writer will investigate and try to resolve.

Without guidance, the first student will tend toward "all about" writing, perhaps producing an initial outline with headings like these:

I. Early childhood
II. How Darwin became interested in evolution
III. The voyage of the *Beagle*
IV. An explanation of Darwin's theory
V. Darwin's influence

This paper promises to be encyclopedic and surpriseless. But when the student is guided toward a focus on a significant question that grows out of the writer's interests and that demands critical thinking, undergraduate research writing can spring to life. Flower (1993, p. 299) describes a successful undergraduate term paper on Darwin written at Carnegie Mellon University for a course in cognitive psychology. Flower's student Kate, a sophomore, posed the following problem about Darwin at the end of her introduction:

> In this paper I will look at the creativity of Charles Darwin by asking two questions. Does Darwin's work support or contradict current psychological definitions of creativity? And secondly, what is the best way to account for Darwin's own kind of creativity? Which of the major theories best fits the facts of Darwin's life and work?

Within her paper, Kate presented different theories of creativity and examined Darwin's work in the light of each theory. She proposed that Darwin was indeed creative and that his creativity could best be accounted for by the "problem-solving theory" of creativity, as opposed to the "romantic imagination theory," the "Freudian sexual energy theory," or "Wallis's four-stage theory."

Kate's essay reveals how successful undergraduate writing can be when students are actively engaged in posing and exploring questions. Emphasizing inquiry and question asking is thus a promising antidote to "all about" writing.

Data Dump Writing, or Random Organization

Both "and then" writing and "all about" writing have discernable organizational plans—chronological in the former case and encyclopedic in the latter. Data dump writing, by contrast, has no discernible structure. It reveals a student overwhelmed with information and uncertain what to do with it. Commonly encountered in research papers, data dump writing patches together quotes, statistics, and other raw information without a thesis or a coherent organizational plan. It takes all the data the writer gathered about topic X and dumps it, as it were, on the reader's desk.

As writers ourselves, we can empathize with data dumpers, for we know how it feels to be overwhelmed with information, to have to sort through it, classify it, and decide what is and is not relevant. We recognize data dumping as a kind of frustrated defense strategy against information overload. Because data dump writing is familiar to all teachers, it needs no special illustration here.

What Causes These Organizational Problems?

The "and then" paper, the "all about" paper, and the data dump paper all reveal a retreat, in some manner, from the kind of reasoned analysis and argumentation that we value in academic writing. Why do these problems occur? Is there some underlying thinking impairment that prevents students from producing thesis-governed writing? Are students not yet developmentally ready for academic writing? Are they simply the victims of poor instruction? Writing theorists have proposed a number of different but overlapping answers to these questions. What follows are three explanations that I find particularly illuminating and helpful.

Piagetian Explanations

The influence of the Swiss psychologist Jean Piaget has been felt nearly as extensively in composition studies as in science education. To Piagetians, the immature organizational patterns just described are symptomatic of concrete operational reasoners, who tend to focus on data, objects, or things as opposed to propositions or forms (Lunsford, 1979; Bradford, 1983). In writing, concrete operational reasoners can string details together chronologically ("and then" writing) or arrange them in simple informational categories ("all about" writing). But creating the kinds of nested hierarchical structures required in propositional writing requires the abstract thinking that characterizes formal operations.

Piagetian explanations offer hope that students, given the right kind of academic environment, will gradually develop the formal capacity to work effectively with abstractions. The pedagogical literature on critical thinking often takes a Piagetian perspective and suggests ways in which writing assignments can be integrated into a Piagetian learning cycle (see particularly Meyers, 1986, chaps. 2 and 6). Instructors operating from this perspective stress the importance of developing short writing assignments that challenge students without overwhelming them. Often they give students lists of data, statistical tables, charts, opposing quotations, and similar materials and ask them to write short pieces that use these data in different ways (Lunsford, 1979; Bean, Drenk, and Lee, 1986). Many of the critical thinking tasks illustrated throughout this book (generally short problems suitable for overnight journal entries, microthemes, or small group tasks) are influenced by Piagetian insights.

Explanations Based on Theories of Intellectual Development

Another interpretation of students' difficulty with thesis-governed writing focuses on theories of intellectual development. The most influential of these has already been mentioned—William Perry's developmental theory (1970) based on extensive research with Harvard students. Because Perry's scheme focuses primarily on the intellectual development of men, it has been modified by the work of Belenky, Clinchy, Goldberger, and Tarule (1986) to take into account significant differences between men and women in typical patterns of intellectual growth. For a schema that integrates Perry with Belenky and her associates, see Kurfiss (1988) and Erickson and Strommer (1991).

Although they use somewhat different terms to describe the stages of students' intellectual growth—Perry's terms for the four major stages are *dualism, multiplicity, relativism,* and *commitment in relativism,* whereas Belenky and colleagues' terms are *received knowledge, subjective knowledge, procedural knowledge,* and *constructed knowledge*—in both schemas, students come to college imagining knowledge as the acquisition of correct information rather than the ability, say, to stake out and support a position in a complex conversation. Eventually, students develop a complex view of knowledge, where individuals have to take stands in the light of their own values and the best available reasons and evidence.

Composition scholars using these theories have hypothesized that students will produce cognitively immature prose as long as their attitude toward knowledge remains in the early stages of intellectual growth (Hays, 1983; Lunsford, 1985). "In terms of Perry's scheme, the transition from . . . multiplicity to relativism appears to be the most difficult shift for these student writers," Hays observes. "Once they have made it, their writing becomes more elaborated, more qualified, more concessionary, and yet at the same time more committed to a position" (pp. 140–141).

Like Piagetian explanations, explanations based on intellectual development are hopeful. We need not despair, says Hays (1983), when "our freshman students do not write like mature adults, for we can reasonably hope that by the time they are seniors they will be considerably further along the road to discursive maturity" (p. 141). But, she warns, this maturity does not occur automatically; it is the "experience of a liberal arts education that produces this development" (p. 141). The kinds of writing assignments and critical thinking tasks most frequently recommended by these developmental theorists ask students to consider multiple points of view, to confront clashing values, and to imagine, analyze, and evaluate alternative solutions to problems. Many of the assignments used as illustrations throughout this book have these aims.

Novice Versus Expert Explanations

Much cognitive research has focused on the differences in behaviors between novices and experts when confronting a cognitive task (Kurfiss, 1988). The resulting pedagogical strategy is to teach novices to approximate in increasingly successful stages the thinking procedures of experts. In this view, students simply have not been taught the kind of writing admired in the academy. "And then" structures, "all about" structures, and data dumping are the result of badly designed writing assignments and ineffective, uncoordinated teaching. In this view, students are capable of producing what we want, but we need to develop effective methods of teaching and coaching. The pedagogical approach from this perspective is to study the thinking and writing strategies used by experts (see, for example, Flower and Hayes, 1977; Sommers, 1980; Flower, 1979, 1993; Voss, 1989) and then to guide students toward approximating similar thinking processes and habits of mind. This is perhaps the most hopeful of all the theories because it implies fairly quick results derived from improved teaching practices. Many reports in the literature suggest that using insights from novice versus expert research can often produce dramatic improvements in the quality of some students' writing. (See, for example, Cohen and Spencer, 1993, who systematically explain to undergraduates how experts in economics produce arguments.)

Implications of These Theories for Teachers

Although each of these theories explains cognitive development somewhat differently, they all point toward similar teaching strategies. If we are to create a pedagogy truly aimed at the development of thinking skills, we should consider adopting the following teaching principles.

1. Our Pedagogy Should Create Cognitive Dissonance for Students

According to Meyers (1986), "Students cannot learn to think critically until they can, at least momentarily, set aside their own visions of the truth and reflect on alternatives" (p. 27). A good way to foster such reflection is to undermine students' confidence in their own settled beliefs or assumptions by creating what psychologists call cognitive dissonance. For example, a math teacher could give an assignment like this:

In class yesterday, 80 percent of you agreed with this statement: "The maximum speed of a sailboat occurs when the boat is sailing in the same direction as the wind." However, that intuitive answer is wrong. Sailboats can actually go much faster when they sail across the wind. How so? Using what you have been learning in vector algebra, explain why sailboats can sail faster when the wind blows sideways to their direction of travel rather than from directly behind them. Make your explanation clear enough for the general public to understand. You can use diagrams if that helps.

Another strategy is to create "decentering" tasks that encourage students to see a phenomenon from an unfamiliar perspective. A typical approach might ask students to create an argumentative dialogue between persons on opposite sides of a controversial issue, to summarize fairly the views of a person with whom the student disagrees, or to enter imaginatively into someone else's world view by writing a monologue from that person's perspective. Still another strategy is to teach what Peter Elbow calls the "believing and doubting game" (1973, p. 147) (which I explain in Chapter Eight, pages 142–143).

The point of these strategies, all of which are developed in more detail in later chapters, is to present students with conflicting interpretations of material and to encourage them to confront the inadequacies and contradictions lying dormant in the views they bring to college.

2. Our Pedagogy Should Present Knowledge as Dialogic Rather Than Informational

As a corollary to creating cognitive dissonance for our students, we need to show them that our course readings (and our lectures) are not "information" but arguments. In many academic disciplines—particularly the humanities and social sciences—introductory courses often initiate students into disciplinary examples of opposing views (Plato versus the pre-Socratics in philosophy, variant interpretations of *Hamlet* in literature, behaviorism versus humanism in psychology). In other disciplines—particularly the physical sciences and engineering—introductory courses must build up a disciplinary knowledge base presented largely as information. But much of what is now "known" in the sciences—and passed on to students as current knowledge—was once unknown and subject to theory, hypothesis, and empirical study. If science teachers can promote awareness of the historical development of knowledge—the original questions that gave rise to the currently accepted facts—they will be foregrounding what I mean by a dialogic or questioning epistemology.

To dramatize the difference between information and argument, teachers can situate readings and lectures within a dialogic structure. A master of this approach is a historian at my own institution who, in advance of a unit of lectures, gives his students a series of controversial theses that bring the course's subject matter into problematic focus. The students know in advance that they must use what they learn from lectures and readings to attack or defend each thesis in a short writing assignment. Typical theses used by my colleague include the following:

> The *essential* theme of the French Revolution was human freedom; Napoleon Bonaparte killed the French Revolution by reversing its thrust toward freedom.
> The industrial revolution created unprecedented wealth at the expense of brutalizing European labor and colonial producers.
> The ultimate victors in the English Revolution of 1688, the American Revolution, and the French Revolution were the economically conservative property-owning classes.

In all cases, the writing assignment is the same: "Present an argument that supports, rejects, or modifies the given thesis, and support your response with factual evidence." My colleague's goal is to help students see the difference between history as one damn thing after another and history as a complex interplay between data and interpretation.

3. Our Pedagogy Should Create Opportunities for Active Problem Solving that Involve Dialogue and Writing

Homework and other activities for a course should engage students in complex thinking about significant problems. To accomplish this end, teachers need to structure activities to help students become personally engaged with questions addressed by the course. As we have seen, teachers can do so by designing good problems for students to think about—problems that cause students to reflect on course readings and to use course concepts and data actively in writing assignments and in class discussions and debate. (Recall that by "writing assignments," I mean anything from formal term papers to one-minute freewrites.) The rest of the chapters in this book discuss numerous strategies for integrating teacher-designed problems into a course.

Teaching Thinking Through Teaching Revision

Composition research over the past two decades confirms that most students do not revise their essays, as the term *revise* is understood by expert writers (see, for example, Beach, 1976; Sommers, 1980; Faigley and Witte, 1981). Of course, students *think* they are revising, but usually they are merely editing— cleaning up spelling, tinkering with sentences, playing with punctuation. What they submit to us for grades, by and large, are first drafts that exhibit the problems typical of most first drafts, even those of expert writers: confused purpose, inadequate development, rambling organization, uncertain audience, lack of clarity. (I like to tell my students that a C essay is an A essay turned in too soon.)

What our students need to understand is that for expert writers, the actual act of writing causes further discovery, development, and modification of ideas. If one examines the evolving drafts of an expert writer, one sees the messy, recursive process of thinking itself. Early drafts, in the language of Flower (1979), are "writer-based" in that writers are struggling to clarify their meanings for themselves without yet worrying about clarity for audiences. Later, writers reshape their original drafts extensively in order to create "reader-based" prose, which aims to meet readers' needs for effective organization, adequate development, and clarity. Expert writers often go through three or four—and sometimes dozens—of drafts. Typically, the final product is substantially different from the first draft.

The foregoing description differs considerably from the older "positivist" model of the writing process that many of us were taught in school. The old model looks like this:

A Positivist Model of the Writing Process

1. Choose a topic.
2. Narrow it.
3. Write a thesis.
4. Make an outline.
5. Write a draft.

6. Revise.

7. Edit.

This description presupposes what Elbow (1973) calls the "think, then write" model of composing in which writers discover and clarify their ideas before they start to write. But it seriously misrepresents the way most academic writers actually compose. For example, few scholars report starting an article by choosing a topic and then narrowing it. Rather, academic writers report being gradually drawn into a conversation about a question that does not yet seem resolved. The writer-to-be finds this conversation somehow unsatisfactory; something is missing, wrongheaded, unexplained, or otherwise puzzling. Similarly, having focused on a problem, only rarely does a skilled academic writer write a thesis statement and outline before embarking on extensive exploration, conversation, correspondence with colleagues, and even, on some occasions, writing one or more drafts. A thesis statement often marks a moment of discovery and clarification—an "aha!" experience ("So *this* is my point! Here is my argument in a nutshell!)—not a formulaic planning device at the very start of the process.

Compare the positivist description of the writing process with the following "new rhetorical" or problem-driven description, which more accurately represents the thinking processes used by most academic writers. (I have adapted and abridged this model from Freedman, 1982.)

The Composing Processes of Expert Academic Writers

1. *Starting point: perception of a problem.* Expert writers feel an uncertainty, doubt a theory, note a piece of unexplained data, puzzle over an observation, confront a view that seems mistaken, or otherwise articulate a question or problem.

2. *Exploration.* The expert writer gathers data through library or laboratory and field research and through probing of memory; explores ideas in a journal or research log, in the margins of texts, or on note cards or the backs of envelopes; analyzes, compares, puzzles, talks with others, writes to self; focuses intensely on problem. The expert writer often explores ideas by rapid drafting of potential pieces of the essay or by making notes, doodles, or tentative outlines.

3. *Incubation.* The writer takes time off from the problem, does other things, and lets ideas cook in the subconscious. These first three stages are all recursive—as writers alternate between exploration and incubation, their perception of the problem may change.

4. *Writing the first draft.* Expert writers try to get ideas down on paper in preliminary form. Some writers make an informal outline prior to writing; others discover direction as they write, often pursuing different branches of ideas without worrying about coherence. To avoid writer's block, expert writers lower expectations. They do not try to make first drafts perfect as they go.

5. *Reformulation or revision.* Having gone once through the territory, expert writers take another look at the problem and think it through again. Many writers report dismantling their first drafts and starting afresh, often discovering their true thesis at the conclusion of their first draft. At this point, writers often make new outlines; they begin considering audience; they clarify their rhetorical purpose; they try to make the essay work for readers. Several drafts are often necessary as writer-based prose is gradually converted to reader-based prose.

6. *Editing.* At this point, craftsmanship takes over from initial creativity. Writers worry about unity, coherence, paragraphing, sentence structure. Finally, writers begin to polish by correcting spelling and punctuation. Often, the recursive nature of the process is again felt as a writer, working on sentence structure, discovers new meanings or new intentions that require the rethinking of minor or even major parts of the essay.

This description of the writing process emphasizes the fact that expert academic writers are driven by their engagement with questions or problems and by their need to see their writing as a contribution to an ongoing conversation. Presenting students with this problem-driven model of the writing process has a distinct advantage for teachers. It allows them to link the teaching of writing to their own interests in teaching the modes of inquiry and discovery in their disciplines. Their goal is to get students personally engaged with the kinds of questions that propel writers through the writing process. Thus, the writing process itself becomes a powerful means of active learning in the discipline.

Why Don't Students Revise?

If one of our major goals is to teach thinking through revision, we need to understand more clearly why students do not revise. Our first tendency may be to blame students' lack of motivation or their ineffective time management. They do not revise because they are not interested in their work or do not care about it or simply put off getting started until the night before a paper is due. But other explanations should also be considered.

For example, Piagetians propose that revision requires the ability to "decenter," which is a trait of formal operations (Kroll, 1978; Bradford, 1983). Piaget demonstrated that concrete operational reasoners have trouble imagining other people's viewpoints. If sitting in the back of a classroom, for example, concrete reasoners have trouble drawing a picture of the room from the perspective of a lecturer standing in front. By analogy, such persons cannot imagine their drafts *from a reader's perspective.* If a passage seems clear to the writer, he or she believes that it ought to be immediately clear to the reader also.

Related theories also emphasize a writer's difficulty in adopting a reader's point of view but see the problem related to intellectual growth or accumulated experience rather than Piagetian formal operations. What drives revision for mature writers, as we have seen, is their awareness of the complex conversation that a piece of writing must join—how its argument must accommodate opposing views, for example, while also contributing something new to the conversation. Thus, mature writers need multiple drafts because, in the face of many different goals and rhetorical constraints, they can concentrate on only one or two problems at a time. From still another perspective, before writers can revise effectively, they must learn to appreciate what readers expect and need within a given genre. To write academic prose, in other words, students need to read academic prose and to have teachers point out the writing strategies that experts use.

Teachers often ask whether the advent of word processing has increased students' tendency to revise. Word processors have had a curiously ambiguous effect on students' revising habits. Several researchers (Daiute, 1986; Hawisher, 1987) have shown that word processing facilitates sentence-level revision as well as some larger-scale revisions such as additions, deletions, and block moves of text but that it may actually discourage major reconceptualizing of a text—the kind of global revision that leads to substantial dismantling and rewriting. Perhaps because students have invested so much time typing the draft into the computer, they do not like to make changes that require complete deleting of large blocks of text and starting over. Or perhaps, because they tend to revise off the screen rather than off a hard copy, they see only narrow windows of their text rather than the whole.

Whatever the cause of students' failure to revise, teachers need to create an academic environment that encourages revision. Fortunately, it is relatively easy to do so. I offer fifteen suggestions that can help turn the tables, making revision an expected way of life.

Fifteen Suggestions for Encouraging Revision

1. *Profess the "new rhetorical" or problem-driven model of the writing process.* Instead of asking students to choose "topics" and narrow them, encourage students to pose questions or problems and explore them. Show how inquiry and writing are related.

2. *Give problem-focused writing assignments.* Students are most apt to revise when their essays must be thesis-governed responses to genuine problems. See Chapter Five for advice on creating writing assignments that guide students toward a problem-thesis structure.

3. *Create active learning tasks that help students become posers and explorers of questions.* Students need to be seized by questions and to appreciate how the urge to write grows out of the writer's desire to say something new about a question or problem. Through classroom activities that let students explore their own responses to questions, students rehearse the thinking strategies that underlie revision. Chapters Eight through Thirteen focus on strategies for active learning.

4. *Incorporate nongraded exploratory writing into your course.* Chapter Six suggests numerous ways to incorporate exploratory writing into a course. Exploratory writing gives students the space, incentive, and tools for more elaborated and complex thinking.

5. *Build adequate talk time into the writing process.* Students need to converse among themselves, to bounce ideas off each other, to test arguments, and to see how audiences react. In this regard, consider having students talk through their ideas in small groups, or reward them for visits to a writing center if one is available on your campus. Perhaps the most important service offered by writing centers is the opportunity for students to talk through their ideas in the early stages of drafting.

6. *Intervene in the writing process by having students submit something to you.* Take advantage of the summarizable nature of thesis-based writing by having students submit to you their problem proposals, thesis statements, or self-written abstracts. Use these brief pieces of writing to identify persons who need extra help. See Chapter Thirteen for further details.

7. *Build process requirements into the assignment, including due dates for drafts.* If students are going to stay up all night before a paper is due, make that an all-night session for a mandatory rough draft rather than for a finished product.

8. *Develop strategies for peer review of drafts, either in class or out of class.* After students have completed a rough draft, well in advance of the final due date, have students exchange drafts and serve as "readers" for each other. See Chapter Thirteen for advice on conducting peer reviews.

9. *Hold writing conferences, especially for students who are having difficulty with the assignment.* Traditionally, teachers in American universities spend more time writing comments on finished products than on holding conferences earlier in the writing process. As a general rule, time spent "correcting" finished products is not as valuable as time spent in conference with students at the rough draft stages. See Chapter Thirteen for suggestions.

10. *Require students to submit all drafts, notes, and doodles along with final copies.* Have students staple their final copies on top of draft material arranged chronologically like geological strata. Not only will you have evidence of your students' writing process, but you will also set up a powerful defense against plagiarism.

11. *Allow rewrites of final drafts, or make comments on typed next-to-final drafts and make your comments revision-oriented rather than editing-oriented.* Many students are motivated toward revision by the hope of an improved grade. If students have an opportunity to revise an essay after you have made your comments, you will strike a major blow for writing as a process. See Chapters Four, Thirteen, and Fourteen for advice on writing marginal and end comments that encourage revision rather than cosmetic editing.

12. *Bring in examples of your own work in progress so that students can see how you go through the writing process yourself.* Students like to know that their teachers also struggle with writing. The more you can show students your own difficulties as a writer, the more you can improve their own self-images.

13. *Give advice on the mechanics of revising.* If students compose at a computer, explain the advantages of revising off a double-spaced hard copy rather than on the screen. If they compose by hand or use conventional typewriters, explain the advantage of writing double-spaced on one side of the page to provide plenty of room for revision and to facilitate cutting and pasting. Many students simply do not leave enough room on the page to make revisions.

14. *Don't overemphasize essay exams.* Symbolically, essay exams convey the message that writing is a transcription of already clear ideas rather than a means of discovering and making meaning. They suggest that revision is not important and that good writers produce acceptable finished copy in one draft. Although essay exams obviously have an important place in liberal education, they should not substitute for writing that goes through multiple drafts. See Chapter Eleven for further discussion of essay exams.

15. *Hold to high standards for finished products.* Teachers are so used to seeing edited, patched-up drafts that they often forget how good an effectively revised essay can be when teachers demand excellence. Students do not see much point in revision if they can earn A's or B's for their edited first drafts.

Conclusion: The Implications of Writing as a Means of Thinking in the Undergraduate Curriculum

As this chapter has tried to show, teaching thesis-based analytical and argumentative writing means teaching the thinking processes that underlie academic inquiry. To use writing as a means of thinking, teachers need to make the design of writing assignments a significant part of course preparation and to adopt teaching strategies that give students repeated, active practice at exploring disciplinary questions and problems. Additionally, it is important to emphasize inquiry, question asking, and cognitive dissonance in courses and, whenever possible, to show that scholars in a discipline often disagree about answers to key questions. By teaching a problem-driven model of the writing process, teachers send a message to the Skylers of the world that good writing is not a pretty package for disguising ignorance. Rather it is a way of discovering, making, and communicating meanings that are significant, interesting, and challenging.

CHAPTER 3

Engaging All Learners
Valuing Professional
and Personal Writing

This chapter asks an apparently innocuous question: what kind of writing should be assigned in undergraduate courses? I say "apparently innocuous" because, when pushed, this question often discloses deep-seated differences among faculty. Consider, for example, the love-hate relationship many of us have with academic writing. Here's what a colleague wrote to me not long ago: "I'm blanching a little at holding up academic writing as any kind of exemplar—what with its jargon, excessive reliance on the passive voice, excessive qualification of conclusions, nonstylized redundancy. The last thing I want to teach my students is how to write a 'scholarly' article." And yet, recently, several colleagues and I coached students who were preparing papers for the National Conference on Undergraduate Research. We tried to help students sound exactly like professionals in their field, including—especially—using the passive voice, getting the jargon right, qualifying the conclusions, and so forth.

So it is not always a simple matter deciding what kind of writing to assign in an undergraduate course. I invite you here, at the start of this chapter, to rate the importance you place on different kinds of writing for one of your courses.

For any one of your undergraduate courses, rate the following statements on a scale of 1 (not important) to 5 (very important):

1. For this course, I prefer essays with a top-down organizational structure: explicit thesis statement near the beginning;

fully developed paragraphs with topic sentences; clearly mapped argument with transitions. _____

2. For this course, I prefer essays that vary from a top-down structure—stories, myths, dialogues, letters, "detective" essays with the thesis delayed until the end, exploratory papers, personal reflection papers. _____

3. For this course, the writing assignments should stress logical thinking and argumentation of the sort required in my discipline and should be written in an appropriate academic voice and professional format. _____

4. For this course, I want students to become engaged with course content through short write-to-learn assignments including exploratory writing in journals and learning logs. _____

If you rate questions 1 and 3 highly, you strongly value professional writing. If you rate 2 and 4 highly, you value what I broadly call "personal writing." What I hope to show in this chapter, however, is that these kinds of writing are not mutually exclusive—that personal writing, in fact, enriches professional writing and that we engage more students in our courses when we include several different kinds of assignments.

This chapter's focusing question—"What kind of writing assignments should I use in my undergraduate courses?"—needs to be examined from two perspectives: (1) what kinds of assignments will most benefit students, and (2) what kinds of assignments will best fit each teacher's own values, teaching style, and available time. Embedded in this second perspective is teachers' need to sort out their own perhaps ambivalent feelings about academic prose. Throughout this chapter, my purpose is to emphasize the freedom teachers have to experiment with the design of writing assignments.

Perspective 1: What Kinds of Writing Assignments Will Most Benefit Our Students?

At perhaps no time in history have college professors faced a more diverse group of students than at present. At many institutions, students have such a wide range of backgrounds, aptitudes, and academic preparation that teachers hardly know where to pitch instruction. At my own institution, for example, a typical undergraduate class includes—in addition to traditionally aged full-time residential students—a number of international or recently immigrated students, U.S. students from nonmajority cultures, harried commuters, part-timers, older students trying to squeeze in college between family and full-time jobs, and any number of students undergoing personal crises. The range of academic preparation also varies enormously; the same course can mix high-GPA students heading for graduate or professional school with at-risk students whose lack of academic skills puzzles and dismays us. To complicate teachers' lives, many students seem passive and unmotivated; often these same students vociferously resent homework assignments yet expect high grades. How can anyone possibly develop writing assignments that will stimulate learning in such a diverse group of students?

The Challenge of Different Personality Types and Cognitive Styles

One helpful approach comes from research on the various ways in which students prefer to gather, interpret, organize, and think about new concepts or information. Often students do their best work when instructional methods and assignments match the way they like to learn. Although it is beyond the scope of this book to survey the extensive research on learning styles, I will look briefly at two representative examples—research using the Myers-Briggs Type Indicator and Kolb's Learning Style Inventory—because they help explain otherwise puzzling differences among students and offer insights into how to design writing assignments that engage different kinds of learners.

Of particular interest to composition researchers has been Jung's theory of personality types as refined and modified in personality inventories such as the Myers-Briggs Type Indicator (Myers and McCaulley, 1985). This inventory situates persons along four different continua: introversion/extroversion, thinking/feeling, sensing/intuition, and perceiving/judging. Jensen and Di Tiberio (1989) have used the Myers-Briggs inventory to reveal fascinating differences among writers that throw valuable light on assignment design.

For example, along the thinking/feeling continuum, "thinkers" excel at writing logical, well-organized essays requiring analysis and argumentation. They prefer academic assignments dealing with ideas that can be treated intellectually and abstractly, and they are often uninterested in issues of style or audience appeal. They like assignments in which they can support a thesis through reasons and evidence; like classic debaters, they often stay personally detached from an issue and are able to argue opposing theses with equal vigor. In contrast, "feelers" prefer assignments that allow for personal voice, conviction, and emotion. They are unlikely to be motivated by an assignment unless they can relate to it personally, and they are attuned to a reader's desire for lively, interesting prose. They like to put their own personal experiences into a paper and often prefer autobiographical or narrative approaches rather than an abstractly reasoned approach.

Differences across other continua reveal other insights into assignment design. "Sensing" types, for example, want writing assignments with very detailed instructions and guidelines and find comfort in teacher-prescribed organizational patterns such as the "five-paragraph theme." In contrast, "intuitive" types rebel against prescribed patterns and like open-ended assignments that give them room for their own unique or creative personal touches. Along the perceiving/judging scale, "judgers" tend to arrive quickly at a thesis and are often bored with personal exploratory writing such as journals, which they dismiss sneeringly as "busy-work." In contrast, "perceivers" like to play with ideas endlessly, have trouble deciding on a thesis, and will explore ideas forever in their journals unless a deadline forces them to quit. Finally, along the extrovert/introvert continuum, "extroverts" prefer to explore ideas through class discussions or small groups, whereas "introverts" like solitude, preferring a journal for exploration rather than group conversation. When assigned journals, extroverts like to read their entries to classmates, whereas introverts are reluctant to do so, protecting their privacy.

The point of Jensen and Di Tiberio's research is clear: students vary widely in the ways they approach writing and in the kinds of writing they prefer to do. By including several different kinds of assignments in a course, teachers give students more opportunity to find one or two that are particularly effective for them; likewise, students get to discover that they can learn significantly from doing an assignment that is not, by nature, their preferable way of operating. (For example, it is important for judgers to learn how to delay closure—hence the value of journal tasks asking them to explore alternative views.)

Teachers should also note that the majority of today's students have personality types and learning styles very different from those of their professors. One study (Schroeder, 1993) analyzed the Myers-Briggs personality types of the first-year class and of representative samples of faculty members at the University of Missouri. On the sensing/intuition scale, approximately 60 percent of students were sensing types, whereas fewer than 10 percent of the faculty members fit that style. Thus, the kinds of writing assignments that most appealed to teachers when they were in college (open-ended, analytical, theoretical) differ from the kind that over half of today's students prefer (structured and concrete rather than theoretical, accompanied by detailed explanation of what the teacher wants and lots of help with what to say). Such students make the most progress, says Schroeder, when instruction and assignments are sequenced to move students gradually from concrete experiences into theory and abstraction.

From a somewhat different perspective, Kolb's study of cognitive styles recommends a similar mix of assignments. Kolb (1985) plots an individual's cognitive style along four axes: concrete experience (feeling), reflective observation (watching), abstract conceptualization (thinking), and active experimentation (doing). Predominant learning styles are indicated in the quadrants between each adjacent pair of axes: "convergers" like to reach closure quickly by finding concrete solutions to problems; "divergers" enjoy brainstorming and imagining alternative solutions; "assimilators" like to take in lots of information, compare approaches, and build theories and models; and "accommodators" like to teach themselves through trial and error by taking risks and plunging into problems. Kolb recommends that for each learning unit in a course the instructor cycle through activities that focus on each of these learning styles, thus helping learners find at least one approach that most appeals to them while giving all students practice at thinking in less natural ways. Each phase of the cycle suggests a different kind of writing assignment, as shown in Table 3.1.

Kolb's research in cognitive styles thus recommends a mixture of personal writing (in the form of exploratory, reflective, or creative pieces) and professional writing (in the form of mainstream academic papers, proposals, lab write-ups, and so forth).

Accommodating At-Risk Students and Second-Language Speakers

Although at-risk students and second-language speakers have very different needs, they often manifest themselves to teachers in the same way—papers so loaded with errors or so underdeveloped or so off-target from the assignment that teachers throw up their hands in dismay. I treat the problem of error in considerable detail in the next chapter, so here I will focus only on the kinds of assignments that bring the most benefit to these populations.

Because there is no magic solution for the problem of error (unfortunately, as I will show in Chapter Four), teachers can make more progress with at-risk and second-language students if they focus on the content, organization, and development of papers, aiming to teach the kind of writing and critical thinking skills that the instructor values. Awareness of a student's cultural background is particularly helpful in dealing with both at-risk students

Table 3.1. Assignments Throughout the Learning Cycle.

Learning Cycle Phase	Suggested Writing Assignments
Concrete experience phase. Learners are introduced to new concepts and issues through watching a film or demonstration, playing a game, doing field observations, and so forth.	• Nongraded personal writing that records the learner's personal observations, thoughts, and feelings during the initial experience and that raises questions and expresses puzzlement
Reflective observation phase. Learners consider the concepts and issues again after doing readings, listening to lectures, participating in class discussions, and hearing different points of view.	• Personal exploratory writing such as journal entries that allow the students to connect new material to their personal experiences and previous knowledge • Personal pieces based on autobiographical experiences with a topic or concept • Personal reflection papers that encourage a questioning, open-ended, thinking-aloud-on-paper approach rather than thesis-with-support writing
Abstract conceptualization phase. Learners try to achieve abstract understanding of the concepts and issues by mastering and internalizing their components and seeing the relationship between new material and other concepts and issues.	• Formal academic papers calling for thesis-based analyses and arguments
Active experimentation phase. Learners actively use the new concepts to solve problems by applying them to new situations.	• Position papers based on cases that use the new concepts • Write-ups of a student's laboratory or field research using the concepts • Proposals applying new concepts and knowledge to solve real-world problems • Creative pieces demonstrating understanding of new material

and second-language speakers because both groups are generally unfamiliar not only with the disciplinary discourse of specific fields but also with academic discourse in general. In her study of international students struggling with writing in American academies, Fox (1994, p. xxi) concludes that "the dominant communication style and world view of the U.S. university, variously known as 'academic argument,' 'analytical writing,' 'critical thinking,' or just plain 'good writing,' is based on assumptions and habits of mind that are derived from western—or more specifically U.S.—culture. . . . This way of thinking and communicating is considered the most sophisticated, intelligent, and efficient by only a tiny fraction of the world's peoples." Fox then shows how cultural differences explain most of the characteristic difficulties that second-language speakers have with academic prose—reluctance to come to a point, digression and irrelevancies, a tendency to transmit the wisdom of others rather than do original critical analysis, and bafflement about the sin of plagiarism (that is, about Western writers' peculiar notion that individuals can "own" words and ideas and that this ownership must therefore be acknowledged). Fox's analysis applies similarly to at-risk students from U.S. minority cultures—based either on ethnicity or class—where academic modes of communication are not valued or practiced in the home.

Fortunately, the best way to reach both populations is through the kinds of writing and critical thinking activities recommended throughout this book. As we saw in Chapter Two, most of our students—not just at-risk or second-language students—come to college baffled by academic discourse. An academic argument is nearly as alien to a "dualist" on Perry's scale of intellectual development as it is to a student from Nairobi or Qui Nhon. What we need to remember is that we are teaching not simply a way of writing but a style of thinking. When we develop assignments to teach the thinking processes we value, we help all our student populations simultaneously.

Recommendations Based on Issues of Student Diversity

What advice about writing assignments can we draw from our knowledge about students' diversity and their general unfamiliarity with academic discourse? To stimulate the most learning of course content and the most growth in writing and critical thinking skills, we should be guided, I think, by the following general principles of assignment design:

- For most of our students, especially in lower-division courses, a series of short assignments is better than one long one.

- Long assignments (research papers, term papers) will be more successful if teachers break them into stages (see Chapter Twelve).

- A mixture of different kinds of assignments (exploratory writing such as journals, learning logs, and freewrites; formal academic assignments; reflective or creative pieces stressing personal voice) are better than a single monolithic type.

- For most of our students, structured assignments (rather than open-ended ones) lead to greater growth: the instructor specifies the problem to be addressed; clarifies expectations about content, structure, and length; and makes grading criteria explicit. (See Chapter Five for advice on structuring assignments to promote thesis-based writing.)

- Opportunities for group work and for experiential learning should be provided whenever possible.

- Assignments should be sequenced to promote a gradual increase in difficulty level with plenty of opportunities for early success; the purpose of each assignment should be explained.

- Frequent and timely feedback should be provided to encourage students, to give helpful guidance for improvement, and to reduce anxiety.

Perspective 2: What Kinds of Assignments Will Best Fit Each Teacher's Values, Teaching Style, and Available Time?

Additional factors influencing the design of assignments are the teacher's own values, teaching style, and available time.

The Problem of Teacher's Time

I have often seen teachers emerge from workshops excited about writing, vow to require more of it, and then quickly burn themselves out in their struggle to read and comment on everything their students write. Teachers can sustain the use of writing and critical thinking activities over the long haul only if they develop strategies for keeping the workload manageable. Many such strategies exist, as this book tries to show, ranging from the use of very short writing assignments to exploratory writing that the teacher does not read to timesaving ways to coach longer papers. The key, then, is to find an approach to using writing and critical thinking that fits one's schedule, teaching values, and curricular goals. To this end, many of the chapters in this book enumerate a wide variety of options. My intention is not to overwhelm teachers with detail but rather to provide numerous possibilities for consideration. Teachers are invited to skim these sections, looking for approaches that might work for them.

Understanding Teachers' Love-Hate Relationship with Academic Discourse

As we saw at the beginning of this chapter, teachers vary widely in the kinds of prose models they choose for their undergraduate students to emulate. Some choose professional models (scholarly articles, technical proposals), while others choose alternative forms that give greater voice to the individuality and creativity of the writer. To help teachers sort through their own feelings about academic prose, let's look first at its strengths and then examine some of the arguments against it in the literature on writing across the curriculum.

The Heuristic Structure of Academic Prose. To begin an examination of academic prose, let's consider first how such prose can advance students' thinking skills. A perusal of scholarly journals will show that most academic articles follow a thesis-based structure, in which the writer places an explicit thesis statement in the introduction of the essay. Essential to this structure is the presence of a guiding question or problem that usually precedes the thesis. This basic structure provides a simple and powerful heuristic of great value for students to learn. Thus, we can explain to students that the academic writer typically begins an article by engaging the reader's interest in a question, problem, or issue. The writer usually explains why the question is significant and why it has not yet been solved, often by reviewing the relevant literature. Following the presentation of the problem, the writer presents his or her thesis, which is the writer's tentative solution to the problem. (See Chapter Twelve for further elaboration on the generic pattern of academic introductions.)

The advantage of teaching this pattern to undergraduates is that it reflects the "deep structure" of academic thinking, which is rooted in questioning and problem posing. As we saw in Chapter Two, the presence of a true problem is at the heart of academic writing; it is what drives critical thinking and sends the writer through multiple drafts in search of conceptual clarity. The thesis statement that the writer places confidently in the introduction of a finished product may have been discovered late at night in the conclusion of an earlier draft.

Moreover, traditional academic writing teaches students valuable skills of organization and clarity. For the most part, academic prose is arranged in conceptual hierarchies to support a summarizable main point or thesis statement. In a prototypical case of thesis-based writing—which I call "top-down"—the writer both places the explicit thesis statement in the introduction of the essay and, in the body, regularly reminds the reader of the thesis through transitions and paragraph topic sentences that refer to it. Closely related to thesis statements are two other kinds of focusing devices: "purpose statements" ("The purpose of this article is . . . ," or, "In what follows, my intention is . . . "), and "blueprint statements," which forecast the article's structure ("First I show that . . . ; the second section argues that . . ."). Placing a thesis statement (and perhaps also a purpose statement or blueprint statement) in the introduction creates an obvious, self-announcing structure in which the writer summarizes the whole of the essay before presenting the parts. In aiming at maximum clarity for readers, top-down writing requires maximum clarity from writers, who must be able to put their meaning, their purpose, and their structure in a nutshell in order to write an introduction.

The effect of top-down writing is to stress meanings up front. By summarizing the whole before presenting the parts, top-down writing produces a cognitive framework for readers that according to much recent research in cognitive psychology, eases the reader's processing of information and the storage of it in memory (Colomb and Williams, 1985). It is an especially effective form for creating logical arguments in which reasons and evidence are brought to bear on a thesis. It is also effective for reaching readers quickly in busy and noisy environments (hence its importance in business and technical communication and other professional settings).

Traditional academic writing, then, reflects a characteristic pattern of thinking that tries to advance a particular thesis or proposition in response to a problem or question. Although such thesis-based prose is clearly valued by most academics, there is no universal agreement that teaching this kind of propositional thinking and writing should be the only goal, or even the primary goal, of writing-across-the-curriculum programs or of undergraduate education in general.

Interrogating Academic Prose: Insights from Expressivism and Social Construction. The literature on writing across the curriculum interrogates academic prose from a variety of perspectives, two of which can be broadly identified as expressivism and social construction (see Mahala, 1991, for an overview of the expressivist and social constructionist movements in writing across the curriculum).

Perhaps the most influential critique of academic discourse comes from expressivism, a neo-Platonic pedagogy that has its roots in the language-across-the-curriculum movement in British secondary schools. Emphasizing the worth of students' individual voices and the value of their own cultures, this movement aims to revolutionize an alienating curriculum. The movement has been popularized in the American academy by James Britton's influential book *The Development of Writing Abilities (11–18)* (Britton and others, 1975) and is often associated in the United States with the work of Toby Fulwiler and his colleagues from Michigan Technological University and more recently from the University of Vermont (see Fulwiler and Young, 1982; Fulwiler, 1987b).

The term *expressivism* comes from Britton's classification scheme, which identifies three categories of prose: the "expressive," the "transactional," and the "poetic." The latter two categories are generally familiar. Transactional writing, which includes most academic or scholarly discourse, refers to writing that "transacts" the world's business by conveying messages from writer to reader. It is usually thesis based and aimed at informing, explaining, analyzing, or persuading. Poetic writing, in contrast, is what Americans call "creative writing" (fiction, drama, poetry, literary nonfiction).

Britton's first category—expressive writing—is much less familiar. Britton calls it writing that is close to the self. One of its main functions is to help the individual assimilate new ideas by creating personal contexts that link new, unfamiliar material to what one knows or has experienced. It is writing to discover and explore, to mull over, to ruminate on, to raise questions about, to personalize. It is often fragmentary and disorganized, done in private code, like talking to oneself on paper. Although intended for the self, it seems to be the seedbed for ideas that later emerge in products written for others. Britton noticed how characteristic it is of professional writers to explore ideas in notebooks, journals, day-books, memoranda to themselves, and letters to colleagues about ideas in progress. He further noticed how extensively expert writers revise their ideas through multiple drafts in which the earliest drafts have the characteristic inchoateness of expressive writing.

Britton's work has strongly influenced contemporary composition practice by emphasizing expressive writing across the curriculum in the form of journals, in-class freewriting, thought letters to classmates, and so forth. The effect of this emphasis can be startling in the classroom in terms of the changed nature of learning, in the increased validation of the personal experience of the individual writer, and in the increased creativity and elaboration of ideas that can emerge in students' writing. (See, for example, the collection of articles in Fulwiler and Young, 1982; Fulwiler, 1987a; Belanoff, Elbow, and Fontaine, 1991; Herrington and Moran, 1992; and Connolly and Vilardi, 1989.) Expressive writing gives students an opportunity to think on paper and to connect their learning to their own experiences and concerns. (Chapter Six discusses expressive writing in detail and offers numerous suggestions for incorporating it into courses across the curriculum.)

Although expressivism is often associated with "behind-the-scenes" journals and other kinds of exploratory writing, at its heart is the value it places in the phenomenological experience of the individual. When Stanford political science professor Richard Fagen (1990) was asked why he switched late in his career from writing academic articles to writing a novel, he explained that a key motive was "frustration born of more than thirty years of trying to express myself within the constraints of the language of the academic social sciences." He goes on to explain, "Lest I be misunderstood, when I speak of this language I am not talking about turgid prose, vapid topics, twisted logic, or banalities paraded as breakthroughs. These are the sins of third-rate scholarship, and although they abound in the academy, they are not intrinsic to the enterprise. No. My frustration stems from canons of propriety and evidence, from rules of the game that outlaw satire, indignation, passion, love, hate—in short, most of the feelings that are at the heart of our humanity." Later Fagen observes that the centrality of academic prose (both reading it and writing it) "suggests a very widespread problem of undergraduate education in the social sciences: How to get the human beings, warts and all, back into a curriculum that emphasizes abstraction, generalities, methods, and theory at the expense of people." He turned to fiction, he says, because "I wanted a different voice, an uninhibited voice, a voice that spoke from the heart without being filtered through the screens and cautionary devices that are part and parcel of scholarly writing" (p. 41).

Fagen's concern for lost "voice"—the sound of an individual human being, warts and all, with a life and passions—is at the heart of what we might call the "expressivist" critique of traditional academic prose.

A related but somewhat different critique of academic discourse comes from social construction, which is related in complex ways to the whole nexus of critical theory associated with postmodernism. For social constructionists, meanings inhere neither in data nor in metaphysical universals but are created by humans and sustained in human communities. Knowledge is "known" through the discourse of the community that creates it— a multivocal conversation of differing perspectives seeking consensus. In this view, academic disciplines are constituted by their discourse, and it is one of the tasks of writing across the curriculum to initiate students into the particularized discourse communities of the academy (Maimon, 1979; Bazerman, 1981; Bizzell, 1982; Bruffee, 1983, 1984, 1993; Bartholomae, 1985; Williams, 1989). Learning to write as a sociologist or a historian or a biochemist means learning how to pose questions, gather and weigh evidence, and construct arguments as members of that discipline. An example of social construction in action is Professor Kingsfield's classroom in the classic 1973 law school movie *The Paper Chase.* His students come to him, so he says, with heads full of mush and leave thinking like lawyers.

Composition scholars studying the social construction of knowledge are interested in what happens to students when they are initiated into new discourse communities. To these scholars, many problems of student writers stem not from cognitive or linguistic inadequacies but from their unfamiliarity with the thought processes of the disciplines they are trying to join. What looks like a skull full of mush is actually an intelligent mind struggling to learn what counts or does not count as an argumentative "move" within the discipline's discourse system. Students begin by mimicking the sound of a discipline—its jargon, tonal patterns, and sentence structures—before they begin controlling the language and making sense.

One of the concerns raised by social constructionists is the personal, social, ethical, and political costs of being socialized into an academic community. One might note Professor Kingsfield's unexamined assumption that it is a good thing to "think like a lawyer" and his concomitant contempt for his students' prior knowledge and experience (they come to him mush skulled) and his disregard for their personal lives (he drives one student to suicide). But social constructionists recognize the limitedness of any particular discourse community. They ask to what extent it is a net gain or a net loss for a person to think like a lawyer (or a chemist or an art critic or a sociologist or an engineer). They stress the importance of respecting and valuing the different discourse communities to which students belong and show that no single discourse system has a lock on truth.

As teachers, we can appreciate the questions raised by social constructionists, for they grow out of the tension between our own desire (which we share with Professor Kingsfield) to teach our students as expeditiously as possible to think like professionals in our fields and our awareness of a potential sterility, narrowness, limitedness of vision—even pointlessness—at the heart of much of our disciplinary discourse.

Other Reservations About Academic Discourse. Reservations about academic prose also come from several other quarters. For some people, the problem with academic prose is mainly stylistic—a complaint that academic writing is needlessly voiceless, jargon-ridden, and dull. But others raise philosophical objections to the whole enterprise of what Bridwell-Bowles (1992) calls "the standard academic essay" (p. 350). Acknowledging that she had to write "in conventional language, in traditional rhetorical patterns, using accepted research methodologies" (p. 366) in order to get published and achieve tenure, Bridwell-Bowles now seeks to write in "alternative" or "experimental" forms, which give her "a more personal voice, an expanded use of metaphor, a less rigid methodological framework, a writing process that allows me to combine hypothesizing with reporting data, to use patterns of writing that allow for multiple truths, what Dale Spender has called a 'multidimensional reality,' rather than a single thesis, and so on" (p. 350). Part of what drives Bridwell-Bowles to experiment is her postmodern awareness that what we can know and say and think is shaped by the discourse in which we write. (See, for example, Myers, 1985, 1986b; Brodkey, 1987, 1994; Bazerman, 1981, 1987). The point here is that writing in different genres creates different ways of thinking. Thus, essayist Chris Anderson (1993, pp. 165–166) argues that a forestry engineer's orientation toward forests would be altered if foresters occasionally wrote personal essays about nature in the tradition of Thoreau, Barry Lopez, or Loren Eiseley as well as academic forestry articles.

Objections to thesis-based writing are particularly common among feminist critics, who have argued that such writing reflects a Western, patriarchal, and ultimately distorting way of knowing (see Meisenhelder, 1985, and Flynn, 1988). In marginalizing traditional academic writing, many feminist critics hope that their emphasis on journals, personal essays, experimental writing, and other nonconventional genres can facilitate ways of thinking that push against the rigidity of patriarchal forms and their concomitant modes of thinking. Thus, the writing-across-the-curriculum movement, rather than being a monolithic attempt to enculturate students into academic writing, raises profound questions about the nature of the academy itself and about the epistemological assumptions that shape our teaching.

Establishing One's Own Goals and Values. Thus, in deciding what kinds of assignments to give in their courses, teachers need to articulate where they stand with regard to traditional academic writing. At the beginning of Chapter Five, on the design of formal writing assignments, I provide a list of questions that will help teachers establish their learning goals for a course. A wide range of assignment types can then be used to help students achieve these goals. (As an example, I show how a single learning goal—evaluating the argument of a scholarly article—can be achieved through four different assignment options, ranging from a highly structured academic option to a highly personal creative option; see pages 75–78.) The key here is to develop approaches that balance the teacher's perception of students' needs with the teacher's own values, goals, and teaching style.

Conclusion: Integrating Professional and Personal Writing _____

Based on the issues we have examined in this chapter—the needs of students balanced against teachers' own values and educational philosophy—it is easy to see why teachers vary so much in the kinds of writing they assign. In a fascinating exchange of letters among a chemical engineer, a sociologist, a philosopher, and a professor of health and physical education (Abbott, Bartelt, Fishman, and Honda, 1992), we see the extent of these differences. Sociologist Bartelt's natural instinct is toward mainstream academic writing: "In the advanced courses I teach within the sociology major, I place a heavy emphasis on writing. . . . Few of these students will go on to graduate school, yet I require them to write in formal academic language, using appropriate footnoting and bibliographic entries" (p. 105). In contrast, philosopher Fishman focuses first on the personal: "There are many reasons why I use writing in my courses. The most important is to help students see the relevance of philosophy to their own lives and to help them gain control over their own learning. For example, in my introduction to philosophy class I push students to start with personal problems. I urge them to give me as much detail as possible and to use a narrative form. What I want to do is engage students in philosophic reflection rather than merely introduce them to the canonic or influential theories" (p. 109). But it is not necessary to set up a Hobson's choice here—an either-or decision between professional and personal writing. In fact, what emerges from the exchanges among Abbott, Bartelt, Fishman, and Honda is a recognition that both kinds of writing are important and that, in fact, the personal underlies and nourishes the professional. Health and physical education professor Honda talks about her own past insecurities with writing and her disappointment in the quality of term papers she received from her students. Then she explains how she switched her assignments from academic term papers to personal journals in which students reflected on a "question of the day." She describes her enjoyment reading the journals, noting that one of her satisfactions is the way the "journal writings sensitize me to individual student differences that I overlooked before" (p. 108). The other correspondents agree, and in exploring the role of personal writing in their own lives, they begin articulating their discovery that the "commitment" needed for high-level professional work grows out of personal writing in which, in Fishman's words, "students write to find out what they care about. . . . Without sufficient work at this first [personal] stage students run the risk of writing 'uncommitted' papers, papers they do not care enough about to do the necessary reworking and editing. I also [believe in personal writing] because of its implied ideology. Students are the silent ones in American education, yet students learn best when they have a personal stake in the classroom. I believe that personal writing is a crucial step in education, no matter the discipline or field" (p. 113).

The value of personal writing, which emerges as a kind of revelation in the letter exchange of Abbott, Bartelt, Fishman, and Honda, is also widely confirmed throughout both the writing-across-the-curriculum literature and the critical thinking literature. To the question posed at the beginning of this chapter—what kind of writing should we assign our students?—we can now sense the emergence of a consensus answer: a mixture of professional and personal writing that can be achieved through three different categories of assignments:

1. Nongraded exploratory writing: journals, in-class freewrites, thought letters, e-mail conversations, and so forth. This is the seedbed of personal writing out of which committed professional writing can emerge.

2. Thesis-governed academic writing: analyses, arguments, research studies, and other forms of mainstream academic discourse.

3. Essays written in other styles and forms that stand against conventional academic writing and create different ways of "seeing": autobiographical essays, interviews, experimental pieces, personal reflection pieces, dialogues, magazine articles for popular audiences, satires, short stories or poems, and the like.

Although no one course is likely to require the full range of these assignment types, students, as they pass through a curriculum, should have an opportunity to experience as many of them as possible. Individual teachers need to find a balance that works for their students and for them.

CHAPTER 4

Dealing with Issues of Grammar and Correctness

For many persons, when they think of poor writers, sentence-level errors come first to mind. The horror stories we hear of college graduates who cannot spell or who make sentence errors on job application letters make us all cringe. One of the goals of any writing program ought to be the reduction of the number of college graduates who embarrass themselves and their alma maters through careless editing errors or through unfamiliarity with the usage conventions of standard edited English. As an example of many teachers' passionate concern for error, I quote here a memorandum from a colleague on my own campus. It addresses the provost, who had asked teachers for their "top three academic priorities" for long-range budget planning and mentions me in my role of director of writing. I retain the writer's emphatic use of capital letters.

> *Priority 1:* ADDRESS THE MISERABLE STATE OF THE UNDER-GRADUATE CONTROL AND USAGE OF ENGLISH, BOTH ORAL AND WRITTEN. *Priorities 2 and 3:* There is no Second Choice and, to me, all other possibilities rank a distant Third.
>
> ANYONE IN THE UNIVERSITY WHO FEELS THAT THIS SUGGESTION IS MERELY IDLE SHOULD SPEND A FEW DAYS CORRECTING PAPERS OR EXAMINATIONS.
>
> WE NEED AN EXTENDED COURSE IN ENGLISH STRUC-TURE AND GRAMMAR, A CONSISTENT EFFORT TO IMPROVE SPELLING, AND A STAFF OF ASSISTANTS WHO WILL PATIENT-LY GO OVER THE WORK OF OUR STUDENTS AND EXPLAIN TO THEM HOW ENGLISH—A MAGNIFICENT TOOL—WORKS.

THEY SIMPLY DO NOT KNOW (unless they come from the bloc of lucky ones whose parents and teachers constantly and carefully corrected and guided their efforts to learn to use English).

DR. JOHN BEAN HAS RIGHTFULLY CAUTIONED US AGAINST BEING SO OVERLY CRITICAL THAT WE DISCOURAGE THE STUDENTS AND I AM SYMPATHETIC TO THAT POINT OF VIEW: HOWEVER, the student's work can be discouraging to the instructors and the only way they seem to pay attention is to have every error pointed out and to be told to correct every error and TOLD WHY THERE IS AN ERROR AND HOW TO GO ABOUT CORRECTING IT. FAR TOO MANY OF OUR STUDENTS SIMPLY DO *NOT HAVE A GOOD 8TH GRADE KNOWLEDGE OF ENGLISH.*

My colleague's frustration with student writing (and with my own caution against overemphasizing errors) extends to our whole first-year composition program, which does not provide an "extended course in English structure and grammar." Consequently, writing teachers at my own institution—and I am sure these politics are played out on other campuses across the country—are often seen as "soft on error" and perhaps even professionally remiss in not teaching the basics of grammar. There is a genuine conflict here between what composition teachers do and what many disciplinary instructors wish they would do. The purpose of this chapter is to examine the problem of error in enough depth so that non-English faculty can appreciate the reservations that many composition teachers have about teaching grammar in a writing course. At the same time, I hope to assure faculty across the curriculum that composition teachers are not "soft on error" and to suggest strategies that faculty in all disciplines can use to reduce the incidence of error in their own students' writing.

The Difficulty of Teaching Sentence Correctness

For reasons no one fully understands, improvement of students' grammatical competence in writing is a difficult goal to achieve. Weak writers seem to make more progress in generating ideas, improving fluency, and organizing and developing arguments than they do in sentence correctness. It may well be, in fact, that competence in editing and correctness is a late-developing skill that blossoms only after students begin taking pride in their writing and seeing themselves as having ideas important enough to communicate.

Whatever the cause, it is a slow and difficult process to eliminate error from students' prose. Partly as a response to this difficulty, contemporary composition theory has changed the way writing teachers approach sentence correctness. The old model was to teach formal grammar, which students then applied to writing through workbook exercises in punctuation, usage, sentence construction, and so forth. Teachers supplemented this workbook approach by dutifully red-penciling all errors on student essays.

Although this model may have helped relatively skilled writers improve their control of the fine points of punctuation and usage, it has been largely discredited as a method of teaching composition to most writers. In a landmark research review that helped change the direction of composition studies in the mid-sixties, Braddock, Lloyd-Jones, and Schoer (1963) concluded that teaching grammar does not improve writing: "In view of the widespread agreement of research studies based upon many types of students and teachers, the conclusion can be stated in strong and unqualified terms: the teaching of formal grammar has a negligible or, because it usually displaces some instruction and practice in composition, even a harmful effect on the improvement of writing" (pp. 37–38). To teachers outside of composition, this statement may seem perplexing and counterintuitive, but it corroborated what many veteran composition teachers secretly felt and had a profound influence on the emergence of the process movement described in Chapter Two. (It should be noted here that not all composition scholars are swayed by the research summarized by Braddock and colleagues and that debates about grammar still occur in the literature. For a pro-grammar critique of the anti-grammar research, see Kolln, 1981. For a critique of Kolln and a passionate anti-grammar argument from a variety of linguistic perspectives, see Hartwell, 1985. For an attempt to synthesize the views of the pro- and anti-grammarians, see Noguchi, 1991.)

What Does It Mean to Know "Grammar"?

When my colleague complained that today's students "simply do not have a good 8th grade knowledge of English," he opens up a complex question: what does it mean to "know" a language?

Linguists distinguish between a tacit, preconscious "knowing how"—the unfathomably complex ability to produce language by internalizing the rules for word formation, inflection, and ordering that all native speakers of a language learn as toddlers—and a conscious "knowing about" that provides a nomenclature for describing and analyzing the structural features of an utterance. It is the difference between being able to throw a curve ball and being able to explain the physics of the ball's motion.

To appreciate the complexity of the internal grammar (the "knowing how" knowledge) that native speakers learn as toddlers, consider the following two exercises. The first is a little quiz I give my first-year composition students on the following sentence:

> Flobbing sallably, glotty yofs sambolated in the wickersnacks.

Here is my quiz, with the answers in brackets:

> What were the yofs doing? [They were sambolating.]
> Were the yofs norgy or glotty? [These yofs were glotty.]
> Do we have one yof or more than one? [There were at least two yofs.]
> What else were they doing besides sambolating? [They were flobbing sallably.]

I have yet to encounter any group of students, including students in remedial writing classes, who could not easily pass this test. They evidently know how the English language works, even if most of them could not label *glotty* as an adjective or *flobbing sallably* as a participial phrase.

For a second exercise, you might try your hand at a problem we give writing center consultants at my institution as part of their training:

> Explain to a native speaker of Japanese when English speakers use the articles *a*, *an*, and *the* in front of nouns and when they don't. Consider utterances such as these: *Here is a cookie. Here is the cookie. Where are the cookies? I think I smell cookies. I like sugar. He brought the sugar* (but not *He brought a sugar*).

Native speakers know instinctively how to use these articles, but unless they are trained as linguists, they are baffled when they try to formulate rules that can accurately describe their performance, just as speakers of most Asian languages are baffled in trying to learn the rules.

When we talk about knowing grammar, therefore, it is important to understand as precisely as possible what we mean by both "knowing" and "grammar." To help clarify these matters, Hartwell (1985) identifies five different meanings for the word *grammar*, which I summarize as follows:

Grammar 1. The internalized, preconscious knowledge of word arrangement and inflectional endings shared by all native speakers of a language. Hartwell calls grammar 1 the "grammar in our heads" (p. 111). It is this grammar that allows us to talk, listen, read, and write.

Grammar 2. Scientific attempts to understand and describe the preconscious rules of grammar 1. The cumulative work of linguists—whether structuralists, generative transformationalists, or whatever—gradually increases our conscious knowledge of grammar 1 through increasingly improved models (grammar 2). Hartwell argues persuasively that expertise in grammar 2 does not increase one's ability to use grammar 1.

Grammar 3. The grammar of linguistic etiquette. Grammarians in this third sense are on the lookout for *ain't, brung, he don't,* and other dialectical features that signal class or social distinctions. To linguists, these are issues of usage rather than grammar. Grammar 2 calls "he brung the luggage" a grammatical utterance (a non-grammatical utterance would be "brung the he luggage"); grammar 3 calls it "bad grammar." (I will deal with this issue in greater length shortly.)

Grammar 4. Traditional school grammar associated with the "8th grade" and perpetuated in textbooks and college handbooks. It analyzes language into eight parts of speech, identifies various kinds of clauses and phrases, and describes function slots in sentences as subjects, verbs, objects, complements, modifiers, and so forth. Based on ill-fitting Latin categories, traditional school grammar has very little explanatory power as a scientific grammar (grammar 2) and is used largely in the service of grammar 3.

Grammar 5. Stylistic grammar. This grammar studies language beyond the sentence level and is concerned with such matters as coherence, gracefulness, and rhetorical effectiveness. Strunk and White's *Elements of Style* or the style chapters of college handbooks are examples of grammar 5. When used in the service of grammar 3, grammar 5 introduces such "errors" as wordiness, weak verbs, and lack of emphasis.

My purpose in summarizing Hartwell's five kinds of grammar is to emphasize two points: (1) the ability to use language flexibly and fluently is a function of grammar 1, which grows out of our participation in a rich language environment and is independent of our ability to describe language either with scientific grammars or traditional school grammar, and (2) the common meaning of the concept "bad grammar" (as in *he brung it*) has nothing to with grammar itself but with conformity to social conventions and is properly called a usage matter rather than a grammar matter. To this issue we turn next.

The Politics of Grammar and Usage

The sentence *He brung it,* though grammatical, is produced in a nonstandard dialect of English. The speaker speaks this dialect because, probably, that is the dialect of his parents and peers. Unfortunately for his success in college and professional life, his parents and peers do not speak the prestige dialect of our culture— a sociological and political issue, not an issue of intelligence or verbal skill.

Some persons, such as those seeking higher social status, want to expurgate all vestiges of their home dialects in order to speak (and write) standard English. Others resist standard English as a badge of pride, defiance, and social identity. Consider Black Panther Stokely Carmichael's ([1968] 1970) "Declaration of War," published in the *San Francisco Express Times:* "Take the English language. There are cats who come here from Italy, from Germany, from Poland, from France, in two generations they speak English perfectly. We have never spoken English perfectly, never, never, never. And that is because our people consciously resisted a language that did not belong to us. . . . Anybody can speak that simple honkey's language correctly. Anybody can do it. We have not done it because we have resisted, resisted" (p. 180). As Carmichael makes vividly clear, to change usage is to change one's social identity. The linguist Noguchi (1991) explains:

> Like other primates of the animal kingdom, humans seek, in one way or another, to signal, enhance, and, ultimately, protect status. . . . Language partakes in these activities insofar as linguistic form conveys not just cognitive meaning but often social status as well—high, low, in between, insider, outsider. People usually gauge the status of speakers (and writers) by socially and culturally determined surface criteria. Japanese speakers, for example, gauge it principally by the presence of polite forms; British English speakers, principally by pronunciation; American English speakers, principally by "grammar." Whether we care to admit it or not, American English speakers employ various grammatical shibboleths (e.g., use of *ain't, brung,* double negatives) not only to affirm their current status within a social group but sometimes also to distance themselves from other social groups [p. 114].

As a general rule, middle-class Americans (especially those with upwardly mobile desires) strive to avoid any grammatical shibboleths that would identify them as poorly educated. They explain their behavior as a desire for "good grammar," unaware of the distinction Hartwell makes between grammars 1 and 3. To appreciate the underlying issues of etiquette and class, consider the most common grammar 3 error made by middle-class college professors: using a nominative pronoun in compound constructions requiring the accusative (for example, saying "between John and I" rather than "between John and me"). Linguists call this error "hypercorrection," stemming from the middle-class fear of usage mistakes (grammar 3). Having been reprimanded for saying "Sally and me are playing marbles" in grade school, we now overcorrect by always saying "Sally and I": "The dean wants Sally and I to serve on this committee" or "The dean wants to see Sally and I first thing in the morning." Upon reflection, we all know that these are grammar 3 errors, but that knowledge does not stop our brains from generating the wrong forms. To change, we do not need grammar lessons so much as behavior modification, perhaps by enlisting a grammar 3 friend to stop us each time we make the error. But what drives us to change is not the innate demands of grammar 1; we want to change to avoid social embarrassment (grammar 3).

Where one stands on social embarrassment is, of course, a political issue. My own personal stance is conservative: I want to avoid grammar 3 errors in my own speech and writing. My stance as a composition teacher is to empower students to make their own decisions about social embarrassment by describing very clearly those language practices that cause embarrassment in different rhetorical contexts and by giving them the power to avoid unintentional errors in whatever dialect their audience expects. This stance obviously leads to a conservative position on error in academic, business, or professional writing where audiences expect standard edited English that obeys the rules of grammar 3.

What Teachers Across the Curriculum Need to Know About Recent Studies of Error

Teaching students to avoid errors in standard edited English is, of course, more easily said than done. Many of our students' errors are of the grammar 3 variety, but many are also grammar 1 errors—the production of truly tangled, incomprehensible sentences. What can be done to help students avoid errors of both types?

Although most contemporary theorists doubt the value of teaching school grammar (at least in the traditional diagramming-sentences way) as a strategy for avoiding error, the study of error remains an important branch of research in composition studies. (For a detailed review of the research on error, see Hull, 1985.) Drawing on work from a number of related disciplines including speech communications, cognitive psychology, linguistics, brain research, sociology, early childhood development, and first- and second-language acquisition, this branch of the discipline addresses a number of puzzling questions about error. Some of the findings of this research, which I review in this section, may prove useful to faculty across the curriculum in developing effective strategies for dealing with error in their own students' writing.

College Teachers Have Always Railed Against Errors in Student Writing

It might be comforting to know that teachers have a long tradition of complaining about errors in their students' writing and that the frequency of error has not risen appreciably. Connors and Lunsford (1988) have compared the types and frequency of errors of today's students with earlier studies from 1917 and 1930. Basing their study of today's students on a random sample of three thousand student essays collected nationwide in 1986, they found surprising consistency in the frequency of error across time. The error frequency rate in 1917 was 2.11 errors per hundred words; in 1930, it was 2.24 errors per hundred words; and in 1986, it was 2.26 errors per hundred words. Their conclusion: "College students are not making more formal errors in writing than they used to" (p. 406).

There are interesting differences in the kinds of errors observed, however. For one thing, what is perceived as an error shifts as the language evolves. Connors and Lunsford report that two Harvard professors, writing in 1901, identified confusion about the rules for *shall* and *will* as the most common grammatical error in their first-year students' papers. The most significant difference discovered by Connors and Lunsford is that today's students make substantially more errors in spelling and in confusing of homonyms *(to, two, too; it's, its)*, a phenomenon they attribute to "declining familiarity with the visual look of the written page" (p. 406). Thus, the poor spelling of today's students, according to this hypothesis, reflects a decline in the amount of time spent reading.

Students' Prose Contains Fewer Mistakes Than Teachers Sometimes Perceive

Even in an error-laden essay, an actual count of the errors reveals that there are many more correct sentences than flawed ones and many more correctly spelled words than misspelled ones. When we throw up our hands at a "miserable" student essay, therefore, we need to acknowledge that at least some of our own perception of error is shaped by our psychology of reading. Williams (1981), writing about the phenomenology of error, notes that many teachers read student essays with the primary purpose of finding errors, whereas they read their own colleagues' drafts-in-progress for ideas. When Williams secretly embedded errors in a professional essay, readers noticed far fewer of them than they noticed when the same errors occurred in a student essay. Moreover, Williams points out as an illustration that the renowned essayist E. B. White unwittingly violates in his own essays various "rules" from his own *Elements of Style* (written with William Strunk). "Now I want to be clear," says Williams; "I am not at all interested in the trivial fact that E. B. White violated one or two of his own trivial rules. That would be a trivial observation. . . . What I am interested in is the fact that no one, E. B. White least of all, seemed to notice that

E. B. White had made an error" (p. 156). Williams's point here is that we are less apt to notice errors if we are not looking for them.

Moreover, readers vary widely in the kinds of errors that bother them. Some teachers mark every instance of an apostrophe error but do not notice comma splices; others rail at fragments but apparently do not notice dangling modifiers. Some teachers get livid over "Everyone in the room raised their hands," while others prefer this form over the sexist "his hand" or the unwieldy "his or her hand." Thus, if we are looking for certain errors, they leap out at us, even though another reader might not notice any of the errors that bothered us.

Finally, we should note that much of what constitutes "error" really involves stylistic choices—issues of rhetorical effectiveness and grace rather than right-or-wrong adherence to rules. For purposes of definition, we might label as an error any unintentional violation of a stable convention of standard edited English, such as a wrong pronoun case, a comma splice, or an awkwardly dangling participle. However, it is less helpful to think of wordiness or choppy sentences or excessive use of the passive voice as errors in the same sense. Yet many teachers lump all violations of their own stylistic pet peeves into the "error" category.

Our Students Have More Linguistic Competence Than the Surface Features of Their Prose Sometimes Indicate

Our tendency, when we see an error-ridden student paper, is to consider the student hopelessly lacking in skills. Composition researchers, however, in studying the etiology of error, have discovered that often students have far more linguistic competence than the surface features of their texts might indicate. In this section, I offer three signs of an encouraging competence beneath the surface tangle.

1. *At least half of student errors result from inattentive editing and proofreading.* Haswell (1983) discovered that students found and corrected approximately 60 percent of their own sentence errors (misspellings, comma splices, dangling modifiers, and so forth) when he quit circling mistakes and simply marked an X in the margin next to lines that contained errors. Haswell's system of "minimal marking," which I describe more fully later in this chapter and again in Chapter Fourteen, withholds a grade on an essay until students have found and corrected as many of their own errors as possible. Haswell thus creates a classroom environment that motivates better habits of editing and proofreading. This system can easily be implemented across the curriculum and will go a

long way toward teaching students to take personal responsibility for the surface features of their prose.

2. *When asked to read their drafts aloud, students unconsciously correct many of their mistakes.* Bartholomae (1980) discovered that when developmental writers read their drafts aloud, their oral rendering of the text unconsciously corrected most of their written errors, even though the students were often unaware that their spoken version differed from their written version. Here is an example based on Bartholomae's research (pp. 261–262):

What the Student Wrote

The school suspense me for being late ten time. I had accummate ten dementic and had to bring my mother to school to talk to a conselor and Princicable of the school what when on at the meet took me out mentally period.

What the Student Said When Reading Aloud

The school *suspended* me for being late ten *times.* I had *accumulated* ten *demerits* and had to bring my mother to school to talk to a counselor and *the Principal* of the school (full stop) what *went* on at the *meeting* took me out mentally (full stop) period (with brio).

Bartholomae's work helps us keep faith in the tacit power of Hartwell's grammar 1. When reading aloud, this student pronounced correctly all his misspelled words (the student did not stumble over the unfamiliar nonword *dementic* but simply said "demerit"); he also corrected past tense formations (by adding *-ed*), punctuation (through intonation—coming to a full stop between sentences), and wrong-word errors (*when* for *went* and so forth). What Bartholomae puzzles over is why the student does not notice or "see" the differences between the oral sounds and the written symbols on the page.

Whatever the cause—and surely this student's lifetime of nonreading is an essential factor—the pedagogy that emerges is hopeful. Teachers can help struggling writers rely more trustingly on the preconscious grammar that generates their speech—to talk their writing, as it were. Bartholomae's strategy with developmental writers is to teach students to "hear" their own voices and to master gradually the skills of transcribing oral language into the written code. The strategy of reading drafts aloud also helps more skilled writers and has widespread application across the curriculum. Students should be asked to read their drafts aloud—both to themselves and to peer audiences—and to note places where their oral reading differs from what they have written. Often the simple act of reading a draft aloud can clear up a large number of errors. (See the discussion of peer review workshops in Chapter Thirteen.)

3. *Student errors are systematic and classifiable.* The late Mina Shaughnessy, who founded modern research into the problems of developmental writers, discovered that students seldom make random errors. Shaughnessy (1977) demonstrated that many of the errors in a typical student's essay are reiterations of a few consistent mistakes, often stemming from a misunderstood, misapplied, or idiosyncratic rule or from second-dialect or second-language interference. By helping students classify their errors and understand their causes, teachers can make order out of tangled texts and teach the specific skills needed to overcome each student's particular pattern of errors. Thus, Bartholomae (1980), using Shaughnessy's strategy, analyzes a student's error-laden text as follows: "The passage contains 41 verbs; only 17 of them are used incorrectly. With the exception of four spelling errors, the errors are all errors of inflection and, furthermore, these errors come only with regular verbs. There are no errors with irregular verbs. This would suggest, then, that when John draws on memory for a verb form, he gets it right; but when John applies a rule to determine the ending, he gets it wrong" (p. 260). Chapter Fourteen describes ways that teachers across the curriculum can use a nonspecialist version of this strategy to make their comments on student papers more helpful and productive.

Errors in Student Writing Increase with Greater Cognitive Difficulty of the Assignment

A particularly illuminating discovery of composition research is the extent to which students' apparent skill level varies according to the cognitive complexity of the writing task. Schwalm (1985) has noted the relationship between error production and the difficulty level of a communication task in the examinations used by government language schools to categorize students' skill levels. An examinee might seem totally fluent in a foreign language when making small talk; however, grammatical competence begins to drop off as the tasks become more complex and decreases dramatically when the examinee is asked to advance arguments, hypothesize, or handle abstractions. The more cognitively difficult the task, the more an examinee's sentence structure breaks down. Using insights from second-language examination procedures, Schwalm designed an experiment in which sixty developmental writers who could produce error-free prose when writing descriptions or personal narratives were given a simple academic task requiring the analysis of new information. Almost all the students, reports Schwalm, "experienced partial or total linguistic collapse. . . . Grammatical, lexical, and syntactic skills that they *seemed* to have mastered disintegrated. The papers were nearly incomprehensible. . . . *Their skills developed in personal writing, especially sentence level skills, were not adequate to simple academic writing tasks*" (p. 633, emphasis in the original). In a recent workshop presentation, Joseph Williams of the University of Chicago noted a similar phenomenon in his study of the writing of first-year law students, where grammatical problems, supposedly eliminated in undergraduate work, begin cropping up again in their first attempts to write legal briefs. Williams's finding accords with my own experience with students who wrote well for me in first-year English going on to produce poorly written papers the next term in philosophy or political science.

This research points to a relationship between grammatical competence and a writer's control over the ideas being expressed. Since each new course immerses students in new, unfamiliar ideas, the quality of students' writing, predictably, degenerates. Teachers can help counter this phenomenon by building requirements for multiple drafts into their assignments so that students can use early drafts to clarify their thinking. This last suggestion leads to the next point.

Errors Often Disappear in Students' Prose as They Progress Through Multiple Drafts

Here is a common scenario. A student writes a paper loaded with sentence errors. The teacher, treating the paper as a draft rather than a finished product, notes that the paper is also confusingly organized, unfocused, and thinly developed. Instead of working on errors, teacher and student focus on clarifying the ideas in the paper. The writer leaves the conference with a newly formulated thesis and an improved organizational plan. On the next draft, many of the grammatical errors disappear. This phenomenon suggests that the early error-laden draft is a necessary step toward the writer's eventual mastery of the ideas and that once the ideas have become clearer, the sentence structure begins to clear up also. In our desire for students to produce correct sentences, then, we must trust the writing process and not ask for premature editing.

Teachers Can Expect to See Sentence Problems in First Drafts and on Essay Exams

Based on my own experience, I can classify students loosely into four skill categories with regard to error production. Writers in category 4—my top category—come to college blessed with the ability to write error-free prose at both the rough-draft and finished-product stages. Whatever accounts for their skill at correctness—heredity, home environment, early reading habits, a tough old bird of an eighth-grade grammar teacher—they show few sentence problems, and the errors they do make are often the result of lack of knowledge about a specific rule, not a deficient level of skill. A brief explanation from a handbook clears up the errors. (Category 4 students may or may not be good writers with regard to ideas and argumentation: there is little correlation between correctness and other measures of good writing.)

Students in my categories 3 and 2 write rough drafts marred by numerous sentence-level errors, often serious ones. Looking at their rough drafts (or their essay exams), one might be dismayed at their lack of sentence-level competence. Category 3 students, however, can usually edit these problems out of their drafts without assistance (if they have the time and the motivation to do so). Category 2 students, by contrast, need guidance—often the patient editing help of a tutor or teacher. The most severe writing problems occur with category 1 students, who need the intense extra help provided by developmental courses in basic writing.

It follows, then, that unless a student is consistently a category 4 writer, we can expect to see sentence-level problems in early drafts. We will see even more problems on essay exams—the more cognitively taxing the question, the more convoluted the errors.

The converse of this phenomenon is this: if teachers are consistently besieged with error-ridden writing, they are probably not seeing their students' best work, since all but category 1 students ought to be able to submit finished products with relatively few errors. The appropriate intervention for teachers across the curriculum, as the rest of this book tries to show, is to design better assignments, to build a process approach into the requirements, and to coach that process so that students submit thoroughly revised and edited work. It is more difficult to improve the quality of writing on essay exams (which in timed situations is necessarily first-draft writing), but Chapter Eleven suggests ways to build process components into an exam setting.

Traditional Procedures for Grading and Marking Student Papers May Exacerbate the Problem

Category 4 writers benefit from having teachers correct errors on their papers. These students usually produce few errors, and they can quickly learn the rules needed to correct them once they are pointed out. When there are more than a few errors in a paper, however, it can be demoralizing to have every one circled in red ink. More importantly, for category 3, 2, and 1 writers, marking errors on papers can be counterproductive because it deprives them of needed practice in finding and correcting their own errors.

We now turn in the final section of this chapter to considering more effective strategies for dealing with error than the traditional red-ink approach.

Responding to Error: Policies and Strategies for Teachers Across the Disciplines

With this brief review of research on error as background, we now face the pragmatic question of what instructors across the curriculum should do about error in their students' papers. The remaining pages of this chapter present my own answer to this question, based on what I believe the research recommends.

Help Students Appreciate That Unintentional Sentence-Level Errors Will Harm the Rhetorical Effectiveness of Their Writing

Faculty members across the disciplines might consider conveying to students a message something like this: "It is socially unacceptable to submit written work with an annoying level of error. You may damage yourself irrevocably in business and professional life if you do so. You might as well learn the habits of careful editing and proofreading now while you are in college."

Many students think that only English teachers care about sentence errors. Therefore, I like to make my students aware of the research of Hairston (1981), who conducted an attitudinal survey of business leaders and other professionals on their reaction to common sentence errors. She sent questionnaires to 101 professional people from occupations other than English, including business executives, attorneys, bank officers, real-estate agents, stockbrokers, small business owners, and engineers. Her questionnaire contained sixty-five sentences with different errors. She asked respondents to indicate their reaction to each error in one of three ways: "Does not bother me," "Bothers me a little," or "Bothers me a lot." Her respondents, she discovered, indeed recognize sentence errors and react strongly against many of them. She divided the errors into status-marking errors (errors that tend to indicate the writer's social, educational, or ethnic status, such as "them apples" or "he brung it") and non-status-marking errors of various levels of seriousness. Status-marking errors received the strongest negative reactions from her respondents, followed by non-status-marking errors in the categories she labeled "very serious" and "serious." I list these here.

Status-Marking Errors

Nonstandard verb forms in past or past participle: *brung* instead of *brought, had went* instead of *had gone*

Lack of subject-verb agreement: *we was* instead of *we were, he don't* instead of *he doesn't*

Double negatives

Objective pronoun as subject: *him and Richard were the last ones hired.*

Very Serious Errors

Sentence fragments

Run-on sentences

Noncapitalization of proper nouns

Non-status marking subject-verb agreement errors

Would of instead of *would have*

Insertion of comma between the verb and its complement

Nonparallelism

Faulty adverb forms

Use of transitive *set* for *sit*

Serious Errors

Verb form errors

Dangling modifiers

I as object pronoun

Lack of commas to set off interrupters such as *however*

Lack of commas in series

Tense switching

Use of a plural modifier with a singular noun: *these kind of errors*

Shift from "Editing-Oriented" Comments on Papers to "Revision-Oriented" Comments

In addition to explaining to students why professional writing requires careful proofreading and editing, teachers need to develop marking and commenting strategies that encourage those skills. To help instructors appreciate differences in teachers' commenting styles, I often give the following exercise to participants in writing-across-the-curriculum workshops. You might try spending five minutes or so doing the exercise yourself.

Exercise: Commenting on Student Papers

Background. Students in a lower-division philosophy course are assigned to evaluate opposing arguments by Peter Singer and Garrett Hardin on the issue of an affluent person's obligation to help the poor.

Task. Suppose that the following passage occurs in the middle of a student essay submitted about halfway through the term. How would you mark this passage? [The first part of the paper summarizes Hardin and Singer. This passage is the beginning of the evaluation section.]

> Garit Harden and Peter Singer have both writen essays that are thought provoking. Hardin has the strongest argument, on the other hand, Singer has some good things to say too but his arguements arent as strong as Hardins because he is to idealistic. Meaning he believes people will give up things like color TV and stereos to thrid world poor people even though they (the rich people) will have earned these things (TV and stereos) through their own hard work. This is what I don't like about Singer. Hardin believes in private property and I do too.
> Another weakness of Singer is . . .

In general, two different philosophies of commenting emerge from these workshops. The most common philosophy—which reflects an editing orientation—produces a marked paper like that shown in Exhibit 4.1. The teacher, in effect, identifies and circles errors, often with few comments (or none) about ideas or structure. The more numerous the errors, the less apt the teacher is to comment on anything else. A quite different philosophy—which is oriented toward revision—largely ignores sentence errors and concentrates on ideas and structure with the aim of evoking a revised draft exhibiting greater complexity and sophistication of thought (see Exhibit 4.2).

The editing-oriented philosophy sends the message that the student mainly needs to correct errors (even though the draft, if perfectly edited, would be weak in ideas and structure). The revision-oriented philosophy sends the message that the current draft needs to be dismantled and the ideas thought through again. Note, too, that the revision-oriented philosophy takes the writer's ideas seriously and finds something to praise. To the extent that the errors in this paper reflect haste, carelessness, and alienation, the revision-oriented comments may result in a new draft in which the writer's emerging pride in his work may lead to a marked decrease in the number of sentence errors. Chapter Fourteen deals at length with ways that faculty across the curriculum can adopt revision-oriented commentary in their own courses.

Exhibit 4.1. Editing-Oriented Commenting Strategy.

```
                Spell author's name correctly!

        Ga(it) Har(den) and Peter Singer have both
    wri(ten) essays that are thought provoking.
                              comma splice
    Hardin has the strongest argument, on the

    other hand, Singer has some good things to say

    too but his arg(uem)ents ar(ent) as strong as

    Hard(ins) because he is (to) idealistic. Meaning   Look up to,
                                                        too, two
    he believes people will give up things like

frag. color TV and stereos to thrid world poor

    people even though they (the rich people) will

    have earned these things (TV and stereos)          Don't put
                                                        antecedents
    through their own hard work. This is what I         of pronouns in
                                                        parentheses
    don't like about Singer. Hardin believes in         after the
                                                        pronoun.
    private property and I do too.

        Another weakness of Singer is . . .
```

Hold Students Responsible for Finding and Fixing Their Own Errors

The best way to make students responsible for finding and fixing their own errors is to adopt some version of Haswell's (1983) strategy of "minimal marking," explained in Chapter Fourteen. Using this system, teachers do not mark and correct errors; instead, they withhold or lower a grade until the student revises, reedits, and resubmits the paper for a new reading.

In not marking errors, the instructor hopes to create an environment that forces students to develop their own mental procedures for finding and correcting errors. Circling errors points out mistakes but does not teach students how to acquire new mental habits. Also, by not marking errors, instructors avoid sending the misleading message that a poorly written essay simply needs editing rather than revision. Time and again, the best advice to give students about a passage is not to edit it for errors but to rewrite it for clarity and coherence.

Exhibit 4.2. Revision-Oriented Commenting Strategy.

Garit Harden and Peter Singer have both writen essays that are thought provoking. Hardin has the strongest argument, on the other hand, Singer has some good things to say too but his arguements arent as strong as Hardins because he is to idealistic. Meaning he believes people will give up things like color TV and stereos to thrid world poor people even though they (the rich people) will have earned these things (TV and stereos) through their own hard work. This is what I don't like about Singer. Hardin believes in private property and I do too.

Another weakness of Singer is . . .

Handwritten margin notes:

Is this your first point about Singer —"A first weakness of Singer is that he is too idealistic" (?) Expand and explain

Excellent insight here—different attitudes about private property are at the heart of their differences — but you raise the point and then drop it without development

Good transition but implies that previous paragraph was about a "first weakness"— e.g., Singer's idealism?

In your next revision break the weaknesses of Singer into separate chunks and develop each. Also edit for sentence errors!

Conclusion: Keeping an Eye on Our Goals

The elimination of error from student writing is an enormously complex project. Teachers across the curriculum can best help with error by learning to live with it on essay exams but by not tolerating it on final products that have gone through multiple drafts. By emphasizing ideas and organization and by making students find and fix their own errors, instructors will be doing the best we can hope for in light of our current knowledge about language competence.

This approach may not be exactly what my colleague hoped for in calling for an "extended course in structure and grammar." But it will best lead, I think, to the goals that my colleague and I emphatically share together: the goal of helping students produce intelligent, graceful, well-argued, and largely error-free essays.

Designing Problem-Based Assignments

CHAPTER 5

Formal Writing Assignments

Part Two of this book focuses on the design of problem-based assignments to promote critical thinking and active engagement with course subject matter. The present chapter concerns the design of formal writing assignments, which calls for finished prose. Formal writing usually requires multiple drafts and is thus distinguished from equally important informal, exploratory writing aimed at generating, developing, and extending thinking on a subject. (How to use informal exploratory writing in your courses is the subject of Chapter Six.)

Formal writing can range from lengthy research papers to short (one- or two-paragraph) microthemes. The chapter's initial focus is on thesis-governed academic writing, but the concluding section surveys alternative kinds of assignments that let students write in a more personal voice in a variety of modes and styles.

The Traditional Method of Assigning Writing

In American universities, the traditional way to assign writing goes something like this: "There will be a term paper due at the end of the semester. The term paper can be on any aspect of the course that interests you, but I have to approve your topic in advance." About halfway through the term, students submit proposals for topics—usually stated as a topic area rather than as a research question or tentative thesis. The instructor either approves the topic or advises that it be narrowed, sometimes giving preliminary advice for bibliographic items. In many cases, no further contact between teacher and student occurs. At the end of the term, the teacher collects and grades the papers. Some teachers mark the papers copiously; others make only cryptic end comments. Much to teachers' disappointment, many students never pick up their papers from the teacher's office.

Alternative Approaches to Assigning Writing

As one of many alternative approaches, consider the method used by finance professor Dean Drenk (Drenk, 1986; Bean, Drenk, and Lee, 1986), who requires a series of short essays, each of which must support either the positive or the negative side of a thesis on a controversial question in finance. The theses, which Drenk sequences from easy to difficult, are constructed to cover various key issues in the field such as the following:

> The market is/is not efficient in strong-form, random-walk terms.
>
> Bonds are/are not more risky investments than stocks.
>
> Random diversification is/is not more reliable than selective diversification.

Each thesis support assignment requires students to understand and use key course concepts while simultaneously practicing the methods of inquiry, research, and argumentation in finance. Students must use library research skills to find relevant data on their assigned issues, analyze the data, develop reasoned positions, and produce empirically supported arguments. Drenk requires students to meet minimal standards on each thesis support essay before progressing to the next and encourages students to rewrite their essays for higher grades, thus stimulating revision. He provides feedback through an evaluative checksheet focusing on the quality of critical thinking, the clarity of writing, and the adequacy of empirical support.

Traditional and Alternative Methods Compared

The first of these methods—the traditional one—can be excellent for skilled upper-division students who have already learned the conventions of inquiry and argumentation in a discipline. At some point in their undergraduate careers, we want to turn students loose and say, "Okay, now talk and write like a new member of this discipline. Go find your own topic and do something interesting with it."

But for many college writers, such freedom is debilitating. Not yet at home with academic writing or with the discourse conventions of a new discipline, these students are apt to produce wandering "all about" papers rather than arguments or quasi-plagiarized data dumps with long, pointless quotations and thinly disguised paraphrases. Even worse, students may resort to outright plagiarism. Because the traditional term paper assignment does not guide students toward formulating a problem and developing a thesis, it often does not stimulate the complex thinking (and hence the need for multiple drafts) that teachers desire. In addition, traditional term papers often do little to enhance learning of course content. They supplement a course but do not focus students' mental energies on the most important or most difficult course concepts or issues.

In contrast, Drenk's thesis support assignments focus directly on course concepts and teach thesis-governed argumentation in the discipline. In investigating a series of issues in finance, students see that knowledge in this discipline is not a collection of inert principles and data but rather an arena for inquiry and argument. Moreover, because Drenk's thesis support essays are short (one to two pages), students can rework them through multiple revisions and transfer what they have learned from one essay to the next. Furthermore, Drenk's emphasis on standards, combined with his allowing of rewrites, often leads to a surprisingly high level of student work. "Although doubts always accompany teaching," Drenk says, "I know that I am successful as a teacher when students confess that they learned more through my writing assignments than through any other academic activity" (Drenk, 1986, p. 55).

The Effect of Slight Variations in Assignment Design

When designing formal writing assignments, instructors should consider carefully the kind of writing they hope for and the processes they want students to follow. Sometimes slight variations in the way an instructor designs a writing task can cause significant differences both in students' writing and thinking processes and in their final products. Consider my informal experiment with faculty in writing-across-the-curriculum workshops at three different institutions. Prior to each workshop, I wanted participants to read and react to an article on expressive writing by Randall Freisinger of Michigan Technological University (see

Freisinger, 1980). I asked faculty to write, as homework, an essay in response to any one of the following four options:

Option 1: Write a two- to three-page critical review of the Freisinger article. Here is your chance to write an essay illustrating what professors really want when they ask students to do an article or book review.

Option 2: Write a two- to three-page critical review of the Freisinger article, but structure it in the following way: part one should be a two-hundred-word abstract that simply summarizes Freisinger's essay without injecting any of your own ideas or opinions. Part two should answer the following question: "What do you consider to be the strengths and weaknesses of Freisinger's views?"

Option 3: One day you receive the following letter:

Dear Professor X:

I am in the process of collecting and reprinting major articles that have influenced the writing-across-the-curriculum movement in the past two decades. Your name has been recommended to me because of your participation in a recent writing-across-the-curriculum workshop.

One of the articles that has been nominated for my collection is Randall Freisinger's "Cross-Disciplinary Writing Workshops: Theory and Practice." Since you were asked to read this article for one of your workshops, I am very interested in your reaction to it. Did you think it was an important article? What impact did it have on you? Would you recommend that other people interested in writing across the curriculum read this article? Any information you could give me on your reactions to this article would be most appreciated.

Sincerely,
Snavely Snodgrass

Write a letter to Snavely responding to his questions.

Option 4: Write a mini-play in which two or more faculty members get in an argument over Freisinger's article. Choose any setting you would like for your play, such as a faculty lounge or a local tavern. If you want, you can have Freisinger himself make a cameo appearance in your play. Your goal here is to have at least one person who enthusiastically supports Freisinger's view of writing and language get in an argument with at least one person who thinks Freisinger is wrong. You can have as many other persons as you wish in the play.

What this experiment revealed is that the writing process reported by workshop participants differed significantly depending on which option they chose. Of the approximately sixty faculty who have responded to this assignment, only three chose option 1, whereas nearly half chose option 2. Perhaps surprisingly, the more prescriptive of the first two assignments was the more popular. Apparently a large proportion of faculty, as well as of students, prefer assignments with some guiding constraints.

The other frequently chosen option—about 40 percent of faculty—was option 3, the informal letter. But the difference in process between writers of option 2 and option 3 is revealing. Option 2 people reported spending two or three hours on the assignment and writing at least two drafts. They also reported a careful rereading of the Freisinger article in order to compose the abstract. Option 3 people, however, usually reported spending less than an hour on the assignment. (In fact, many say they chose option 3 because it seemed to require less work.) Most option 3 writers composed their letter in one sitting. Few reported revising their letters or rereading the Freisinger article prior to writing. Despite less time on task, however, the option 3 people often wrote more lively, provocative, and interesting pieces than the option 2 people.

What is the lesson here? I hypothesize that an option 2 assignment encourages careful planning (including, in this case, rereading of the article) and formal top-down organizing. An option 3 assignment encourages more personality, voice, energy, and spontaneity. In my own courses, I try to give students opportunities for both kinds of writing. My experiment with option 3 has led to the occasional "thought letters" I often require of my students as part of their exploratory writing for my courses (see Chapter Six). But I use assignments like option 2 to encourage thoughtful study of difficult material and to teach structured, analytical reading and response.

The last assignment—the mini-play—was chosen by only a handful of workshop participants, but their engagement with the assignment was intense. They "got into it," often reporting six or seven hours of work. In several instances, their plays evolved into humorous satires of their own institutions. Whereas the other writers wrote out of duty, the option 4 people wrote for their own pleasure. (In the jargon of composition specialists, the assignment became "self-sponsored.") The task become a creative project like writing the script for a banquet roast. Proud of their work, option 4 people wanted to go public, and at one institution they even insisted on performing their play as a workshop finale.

My point is that instructors can influence the thinking and writing processes of their students by varying such aspects of the assignment as the audience, the rhetorical context, the writer's assumed role, the purpose, or the format. When planning assignments, therefore, teachers need to consider not only the learning goals they have set for their courses but also the thinking and writing processes that they want to invoke in their students as learners.

The remaining sections of this chapter focus on issues of planning, designing, and giving formal writing assignments.

Review of Course Goals as Preparation for Designing Assignments

Designing critical thinking tasks works best if teachers focus their assignments on their main teaching goals for the course. Prior to designing assignments, teachers can inventory their course goals by considering answers to the following questions:

1. What are the main units or modules in my course? (For example, two weeks on X, four days on Y, and another two weeks on Z.)

2. What are my main learning objectives for each of these modules and for the whole course? What are the chief concepts and principles that I want students to learn in each unit or module?

3. What thinking skills am I trying to develop within each unit or module and throughout the whole course? (Such skills include ways of observing, habits of mind, questioning strategies, use of evidence—whatever thinking processes are important in your course or discipline. To put it another way, what ways of thinking characterize a historian, an accountant, a chemist, a nurse, and so forth?)

4. Based on previous students' experience, what are the most difficult aspects of my course for students?

5. If I could change my students' study habits, what would I most like to change?

6. What difference do I want my course to make in my students' lives—in their sense of self, their values, their ways of thinking? What is my unique stamp on this course? Ten years later, what do I want them to remember most about my course?

Of course, it is impossible to design assignments that have an impact on every facet of a course. But teachers can put together a combination of formal and informal writing assignments and other kinds of critical thinking tasks that will help students meet many of the teachers' course goals. (For a more detailed approach to articulating course goals, see "The Teaching Goals Inventory" in Angelo and Cross, 1993, pp. 13–23.) In designing formal assignments, teachers have numerous options. We turn first to short "write-to-learn" assignments focusing on specific course concepts or thinking skills.

Designing Short Write-to-Learn Assignments

Although writing to learn is often associated with informal, exploratory writing such as journals or learning logs (the subject of Chapter Six), teachers can also design formal assignments that help students learn important concepts in a course. In the following cases, consider how a physics professor and a psychology professor developed assignments focusing on key course concepts. The physics professor identified acceleration and velocity as difficult concepts for beginning physics students, while the psychology professor identified operant conditioning. Having identified these concepts, the professors then developed the following write-to-learn assignments (the physics assignment is drawn largely from Bean, Drenk, and Lee, 1986, p. 35).

You are Dr. Science, the question-and-answer person for a popular magazine called *Practical Science.* Readers of your magazine are invited to submit letters to Dr. Science, who answers them in "Dear Abby" style in a special section of the magazine. One day you receive the following letter:

Dear Dr. Science:

You've got to help me settle this argument I am having with my girlfriend. We were watching a baseball game several weeks ago when this guy hit a high pop-up straight over the catcher's head. When it finally came down, the catcher caught it standing on home plate. Well, my girlfriend told me that when the ball stopped in midair just before it started back down, its velocity was zero, but its acceleration was not zero. I said she was stupid. If something isn't moving at all, how could it have any acceleration? Ever since then, she has been making a big deal out of this and won't let me kiss her. I love her, but I don't think we can get back together until we settle this argument. We checked some physics books, but they weren't very clear. We agreed that I would write to you and let you settle the argument. But, Dr. Science, don't just tell us the answer. You've got to explain it so we both understand because my girlfriend is really dogmatic. She said she wouldn't even trust Einstein unless he could explain himself clearly.

Sincerely,
Baseball Blues

Can this relationship be saved? Your task is to write an answer to Baseball Blues. Because space in your magazine is limited, restrict your answer to what can be put on a single five- by eight-inch card. Don't confuse Baseball and his girlfriend by using any special physics terms unless you explain clearly what they mean.

Here's the psychology assignment.

Consider the following problem:

> In the morning, when Professor Catlove opens a new can of cat food, his cats run into the kitchen purring and meowing and rubbing their backs against his legs. What examples, if any, of classical conditioning, operant conditioning, and social learning are at work in this brief scene? Note that both the cats and the professor might be exhibiting conditioned behavior here.

You and some fellow classmates have been discussing this problem over coffee, and you are convinced that the other members of your group are confused about the concepts. Write a one- to two-page essay that sets them straight.

These assignments require students to apply the target concepts to new situations and to articulate their thinking processes clearly to a new learner. Assignments like these can prompt intense, purposeful rereading of textbooks and class notes while stimulating out-of-class discussions among students. Furthermore, students report that the act of writing often alerts them to gaps in their understanding. In the operant conditioning problem, for example, students reported in interviews with me that it was easier to explain how the professor conditioned the cats than how the cats conditioned the professor, yet it was in their contemplation of the latter case that the concept of a learned behavior became most clear.

From a teacher's perspective, these assignments—because they are short—have the additional benefit of being easy to grade. They use what we might call the principle of leverage: a small amount of writing preceded by a great amount of thinking. Such short assignments, or microthemes, can be very effective at maximizing learning while minimizing a teacher's grading time. (For a discussion of how to grade microthemes using "models feedback" rather than writing comments on the essays, see Chapter Thirteen, page 236.)

Using Short Write-to-Learn Assignments for Formative Assessment

In designing write-to-learn assignments, we obviously hope that they will help students learn the desired concepts. Often—to our disappointment and chagrin—this is not the case. What many students' reveal in their microthemes is the depressing variety of ways that they can misunderstand the very concepts we hoped they would learn.

Nevertheless, students' errors, mistakes, and misunderstandings can give us valuable insights into their thinking processes and provide clues about how to redesign and sequence instruction. As recent work in formative assessment has demonstrated (Angelo and Cross, 1993), teachers who regularly assess their students' understanding of concepts as a course progresses can adjust instruction to improve the quality of learning. For assessing students' learning, short write-to-learn assignments are particularly effective because they provide direct windows into students' thinking processes.

Consider three student responses to the physics microtheme on acceleration versus velocity. The teacher graded the microthemes on a 1 (lowest) through 6 (highest) scale using the grading rubric shown in Chapter Fifteen (page 263). The following microtheme received a top score of 6:

> Ask your girlfriend's forgiveness because she is absolutely right. An everyday definition of acceleration means speeding up. But the scientific meaning is more precise. It means the rate at which *speed* or *direction* changes over a certain period of time—two things really.
>
> Thus it is indeed possible for the ball to still be accelerating even when it has zero velocity. If the baseball had no acceleration when it stopped in mid air, it would float in the air where it stopped forever.
>
> A baseball can accelerate in either of two ways. It can change its speed or it can change its direction of travel. If it does either or both of these things over a period of time it has accelerated. As the baseball stopped in midair its speed—or velocity—became zero. Yet the acceleration was not zero because, like a stretched out spring, gravity was pulling at it. As you noticed, it soon turned around from going up and came thundering straight down toward the catcher's mitt. During any given interval of time, it was changing direction or speed (velocity). Because of this, its acceleration (a measurement taken over a period of time) was never zero.

In giving this microtheme a 6, the instructor felt that the student both understood the concept accurately and explained it well in his own words to a new learner.

In contrast, the following microthemes were rated in the 1 to 2 range because their writers failed to apply the concepts accurately. But the significantly different patterns of thinking in these low-success microthemes helped the teacher understand each writer's difficulty.

Student A's Microtheme

Acceleration is defined as the ratio of the change in velocity to the time over which this change occurs. When the pop-up left the hitter's bat it had a certain acceleration in the upward direction. This acceleration soon became deceleration (a decrease in speed with time) as the downward pull of the earth became strong enough to decrease upward acceleration to 0. This force is called gravity and by definition accelerates a free falling body at 32 ft./sec.^{2} in the downward direction. When the ball paused at the peak of its flight, before beginning its descent, the upward acceleration and the downward acceleration were equal, even though the ball was stationary.

Student B's Microtheme

It makes me sad to hear that you have lost your girlfriend over such a trivial problem. I have some good news for you, though. You are right. An object cannot have 0 velocity and have acceleration too. I hope that with the arguments I lay forth in the next few paragraphs you two can reconciliate.

First, velocity is defined as how far an object moves during a certain time. If an object is moving then, in any direction, it has velocity. An airplane is a good example of this. It flies at a certain velocity such as 160 miles per hour, which means it covers 160 miles every hour it is in the air. Next we need a definition of acceleration. This is simply the change in velocity over a certain period of time. If you have an object that is moving at a constant velocity, and covers the same amount of distance during each time period, then it cannot have any change in velocity and thus any acceleration. Going back to the airplane we see acceleration when it speeds up or slows down.

Now we can use these two above concepts to give an answer to your question. If you have an object having no velocity it can have no change in that velocity, thus it cannot be accelerating. If this is still not clear think of the airplane sitting in its hangar. It has no velocity just sitting there, right? Therefore it cannot be accelerating or it would run through the side of the building! The baseball is the same way. I hope that the explanation above will help your girlfriend to see the light.

Student A's microtheme reveals a problem-solving strategy commonly encountered among novices to any discipline—what one of my colleagues calls "text-parroting." Unsure of the answer, the student uses the textbook as a crutch, attempting to imitate its authority by creating a dense, academic-sounding style complete with impressive technical data ("This force is called gravity and by definition accelerates a free falling body at 32 ft./sec.^{2} in the downward direction"). To nonspecialist readers, this strategy is often successful—what students in my part of the country call a "snowjob." When shown student A's microtheme, beginning physics students (and many faculty members outside of science) often give it a top-ranking score of 5 or 6. When it is pointed out that student A never actually answers the question (is the girlfriend right or wrong?), the weakness of this microtheme starts to emerge. To help text-parroters make progress on their next microtheme assignment, the instructor can urge them to replace their current strategy ("When in doubt, sound like the textbook") with a more productive one in which they explain the answer in their own words. (To see how a history professor helps students overcome text-parroting, see Walvoord and McCarthy, 1990, pp. 97–143.)

In contrast, student B writes admirably in his own voice but is led astray by his inability to transfer his own private analogy (the airplane sitting in the hangar) to the problem of the baseball in midair. The microtheme's structure records the student's thinking process as he proceeds systematically from what he knows to what he is trying to learn. Despite his misunderstanding by the end (the middle paragraph shows a correct understanding of velocity and acceleration when applied to the simple example of the airplane in flight), the student may be only a few moments away from an "aha!" experience. A few probing questions from the instructor might make the concept snap into place for the student. By discussing microthemes such as this one, the instructor can review the concepts of acceleration and velocity while helping the class see where and how analogies can be helpful or break down.

My point here is that short write-to-learn assignments, though not guaranteeing student learning, nevertheless provide a window into students' thinking that allows the instructor to monitor student progress, to readjust instruction, and to develop teaching strategies that reach different kinds of learners. (For a detailed account of how a mathematics professor analyzes and responds to learning problems revealed in student writing, see Keith, 1989, pp. 141–146.)

The Process of Giving a Formal Writing Assignment

Whether you assign microthemes, two- to three-page essays, or long research papers, how you present the assignment to the class can affect your students' success.

Preparing a Student Handout for a Formal Writing Assignment

Students appreciate handouts explaining each writing assignment. Although some teachers give their writing assignments orally or place general explanations in their course syllabi, putting assignments on separate handouts has several advantages: (1) it meets the needs of sensing or concrete learners (as identified by personality inventories such as the Myers-Briggs), who comprise, according to Schroeder (1993, p. 22), perhaps 60 percent of our entering students and who seem paralyzed by vague assignments that do not specify what the teacher wants; (2) it gives all students something to refer to late at night when their class notes no longer seem so clear; (3) if your institution has a writing center, it helps writing consultants understand what the professor is looking for prior to a tutoring session; and (4) most importantly, it helps the professor identify potential problems with the assignment and thus clarify its purpose and focus. Explanations of assignments for formal essays—as worded for students—should usually include the following elements:

Task.   Explain what the student is supposed to write about. The instructor often presents the task as a problem or a question for the student to address, a thesis to support, or a rhetorical mode or form to follow.

Role and audience.   Generally, ask students to write from a position of power to audiences who know less about the topic than the writer or whose views on the topic differ from the writer's (for example, "Address your paper to students who missed last week's classes," or, "In your argument on old-growth forests, address your essay to the group that opposes your position—either the logging industry or Earth First," or, "Address your essay to peer-scholars in this discipline who are interested in your proposed question and will look forward to reading your findings and analysis"). Asking students to address the teacher, who typically knows more about the topic than the student, places the writer in an unnatural rhetorical position.

Format.   Specify expected length, manuscript form, and similar details. Sometimes an assignment also specifies a certain organizational pattern: "Place your thesis statement prominently near the end of your introduction," or, "Use the standard scientific report format."

Expectations about the process to be followed.   Specify a time schedule for completion of first drafts, peer review workshops, revisions, and so forth. Ask students to save all doodles, notes, outlines, and drafts and to submit these along with the final essay. (This requirement encourages students to follow the recommended process and effectively discourages plagiarism.)

Criteria for evaluation.   Explain how the final product will be graded. Will you grade essays holistically with a single letter grade? If so, what are the criteria for an A? Or will you grade analytically by weighing different features separately? If so, how much weight will be given to ideas? To organization and development? To sentence style and readability? To mechanics, appearance, and manuscript form? (See Chapter Fifteen for a discussion of grading.)

Here is an example of an effective assignment handout for an upper-division business course.

The Situation

You have recently been hired as a research assistant to business consultant Wilbur Jones, who has just taken on a new consulting project for Steamboat Beer, a growing regional firm that hopes to go national. One morning, Wilbur sends you the following memo:

> Before my meeting next week with the Steamboat people, I need information on beer companies that have recently lost market share. I want you to find out what went wrong with Pabst. Pabst Blue Ribbon was a major company when I was in college. Now you hardly even hear about it. Get back to me with an analysis ASAP. What happened at Pabst and why?

You have heard that Wilbur likes his reports succinct and to the point, with meanings highlighted up front. He is a "scan reader" who wants to get the gist of a report quickly.

Your Task

After reading, studying, and analyzing the assigned case materials on the Pabst Brewing Company, prepare your report for Wilbur. Make sure that it has two parts: (1) a brief chronological narrative showing what happened at Pabst, and (2) an analysis of what went wrong.

Process Stages for the Assignment

1. Read the case materials on Pabst.
2. Analyze case materials in small groups (we'll do this in class).
3. Write rough drafts; complete out-of-class peer reviews.
4. Submit "executive summaries" to instructor.
5. Rewrite drafts after peer review and comments on executive summaries by instructor.
6. Submit final product.

Grading Criteria

Quality of narrative (brief but clear picture of what happened at Pabst): 10 points

Quality of causal analysis (clearly stated causes, good support, plausible and convincing argument based on data): 30 points

Readability (top-down organization, good use of headings, clear sentences with no confusing passages): 20 points

Grammar and correctness: 10 points

Having a Colleague Critique Your Assignment Handout

A good way to fine-tune an assignment is to ask a colleague to read it and role-play a student, trying to predict how students would react. Then discuss with your colleague questions such as the following:

1. Is the assignment clear? Might a student misread the assignment and produce something not anticipated? Is its purpose clear? Will a student see how it fits into course goals?

2. Does the assignment seem interesting and challenging? From a student's perspective, how difficult is this assignment? How much time will it require?

3. What kinds of students would this assignment particularly appeal to? What kinds of students might not like this assignment?

4. Does the assignment specify or imply a suitable audience? Are the grading criteria clear?

5. Are the mechanics of the assignment clear (due dates, expected length, manuscript form, other particulars)?

6. Is the process I want students to follow as explicit as possible? Should I build checkpoints into the assignment (submission of a prospectus, abstract, peer review dates, and so forth)?

7. How easy or difficult will this assignment be to coach and grade?

Such discussions with colleagues may help you see ways to revise the assignment to make it both stronger and clearer.

Giving the Assignment in Class

When giving the assignment in class, allow plenty of time for student questions. No matter how clearly you think you have explained the assignment, students will ferret out ambiguities. If possible, show students an A paper from a previous class on a slightly different but related topic. Even better, if you can afford the class time, pass out a set of representative essays, strong and weak, and ask students to grade them for themselves in an in-class collaborative session. (See Chapter Nine, pp. 158–159, for a discussion of group scoring sessions.) You can then explain how you would grade the papers in order to clarify your expectations. Be prepared for a lively discussion!

Designing Assignments That Lead to Top-Down, Thesis-Governed Writing _____

Chapter Two and part of Chapter Three provide a rationale for top-down, thesis-governed writing—the prototypical structure of academic prose. Such writing begins with the presentation of a problem to be addressed; near the end of the introduction, after the writer has presented the problem, the writer states his or her thesis, often accompanied by a purpose statement or a blueprint statement that gives the reader an overview of the whole essay. The body of the paper then supports the thesis with appropriate arguments and evidence. Because thesis-governed writing does not come naturally to students, teachers need to encourage it. They can do so by structuring their assignments in one of three ways.

1. Present a Proposition (Thesis) That Students Are Supposed to Defend or Refute

Using this method, the teacher asks students to defend or attack a controversial proposition or to defend one of two opposing propositions. The teacher's task is to develop arguable propositions that cover major concepts in the course. When students are asked to support or attack an assigned thesis, their mental energies, from the start, are channeled toward analysis and argumentation and away from chronological or "all about" writing.

This proposed bridge design does/does not meet the criteria set forth by the city in its request for proposal. [Civil engineering]

"The path to holiness lies through questioning everything." Agree or disagree. [Religious studies]

Based on the attached case, the nurse supervisor should/should not honor the husband's request that his wife (a stroke victim) be assigned a new nurse. [Nursing]

Schizophrenia is a brain disease./Schizophrenia is learned behavior. [Psychology]

Mercury amalgam fillings are/are not safe. [Research project for a course in scientific argument]

Global warming is/is not a significant environmental threat at this time. [Environmental biology course]

An alternative is to present a controversial thesis but to ask students to take a position or approach that you specify.

Write a letter to the editor against the sales tax on the grounds of it being a regressive tax. Explicitly use ratio and proportion to explain to the uninformed reader the meaning of *regressive tax*. [Mathematics]

Upon arriving home for Christmas, you discover your father writing a letter to his representative in Congress urging the passage of legislation limiting beef imports from Argentina. He argues that such imports put ranchers out of business, cause U.S. packing houses to close, and generally make this country poorer. You, on the basis of your brilliant performance in Economics 105, engage your father in a spirited discussion (in other words, a heated argument). Write the argument that you use to convince him of the error of his position. Your father doesn't understand economic jargon, so any jargon you use must be explained. [Economics]

Thesis-support writing, as exemplified in these assignments, works best when students are urged to consider opposing views and to sift and weigh evidence on all sides. Teachers can help students consider opposing views by showing them how to add an "although clause" to a thesis statement along with appropriate qualifiers: "Although there is some evidence to suggest that schizophrenia is a learned behavior, the preponderance of current research favors the theory that schizophrenia is a brain disease." In addition, teachers can allow students to revise the provided thesis to represent their own arguments more accurately. (For further examples of thesis support assignments, see Chapter Seven, page 124; see also, in Chapter Nine, the "believing/doubting" strategy, pages 156–157; and the "evidence-finding" strategy, pages 157–158.)

2. Give Students a Problem or Question That Demands a Thesis Answer

A second way to encourage thesis-governed writing is to give students a question calling for a thesis statement answer. Often you will need to give background information and provide a context for the problem. The key to this kind of assignment is to sum up the problem in a one-sentence question, telling students that their thesis statements should be one-sentence answers to this question. Here are some examples (in each case, the instructor's focusing question is italicized):

Write an essay of no more than two double-spaced pages answering the following question: *Is a skilled trout fisherman on a variable interval or a variable ratio schedule of reinforcement?* Imagine that you are writing to a classmate who has missed the last week of lectures and finds the textbook explanations of "variable interval" and "variable ratio" confusing. [Psychology]

Gauss's law relates the field at the surface to the charge inside the surface. But surely the field at the surface is affected by the charges outside the surface. *How do you resolve this difficulty?* [Mullin, 1989, p. 207] [Physics]

Choose a question that Plato answers in one way and Aristotle answers in a different way (for example, "How do things change?"). Then, in the first part of your paper, explain to your reader the differences in these two theories. In the second part of your paper, evaluate the two positions, arguing that one position is stronger than the other. In this section, specifically answer the following question: What situation or thing does one theory explain well that the other cannot explain adequately? [Philosophy]

Note that some teachers, in an understandable effort to guide students' thinking, provide a whole series of interrelated questions instead of a single focusing question. My experience suggests that this practice confuses students more than it helps.

Confusing

In the graveyard scene of Hamlet, Shakespeare alters his sources by adding the clownish gravediggers. How does the presence of the gravediggers influence your interpretation of the scene? Do you think they are funny? Absurd? Blasphemous? How does Hamlet's attitude toward the gravediggers affect the scene? Do you think it is appropriate to sing while digging a grave? What about the jokes they tell? Do you think that Yorick was more like the gravediggers or more like Hamlet? Do you think it is appropriate to have a light-hearted moment like this in the middle of a tragedy? Is the scene really lighthearted?

Although the instructor probably thinks of these questions as helpful probes, students often feel overwhelmed by them. Because the questions seem parallel rather than hierarchical, students are apt to produce a series of short answers, addressing each question in turn, rather than a unified essay.

Better

In the graveyard scene of Hamlet, Shakespeare alters his sources by adding the clownish gravediggers. How does the presence of the gravediggers influence your interpretation of the scene?

Phrased as a single question, the assignment now forces the student to frame a single answer as a thesis statement for the essay.

3. Ask Students to Follow an Organizational Structure That Requires a Problem-Thesis Pattern

The most open-ended way of assigning thesis-governed writing is to give students complete choice of topic but to require that they follow a problem-thesis structure. Such a "generic" assignment guides students with surprising effectiveness toward thesis-governed writing.

Write an essay of X pages on any topic related to this course. Use the introduction of your essay to engage your reader's interest in a problem or question that you would like to address in your essay. Show your reader what makes the question both significant and problematic. The body of your essay should be your own response to this question made as persuasive as possible through appropriate analysis and argumentation, including effective use of evidence. Midway through the course, you will submit to the instructor a prospectus that describes the problem or question that you plan to address and shows why the question is (1) problematic and (2) significant.

Using the generic assignment has a number of advantages. First, for teachers who like to give students as much freedom as possible, the generic assignment permits free choice of topics while guiding students toward thesis-governed prose that addresses a real problem. By requiring that the introduction set forth a problem, the assignment implies both an audience and a purpose, thus helping inexperienced writers overcome their tendency toward "all about" papers, "and then" narratives, or unfocused data dumps. Second, in its focus on question asking, the assignment encourages teachers to discuss the process of inquiry in their disciplines. By teaching question asking in a discipline, teachers help students become active learners. Finally—and this is an advantage not to be taken lightly—the assignment is easy to coach. Well before the assignment due date, students can be asked to submit a prospectus explaining and focusing the question to be addressed (the prospectus later serves as a rough draft of the introduction). In responding to the prospectus, the instructor can guide the student toward an appropriately delineated question and thesis.

For shorter assignments, an even simpler method of screening is possible: teachers can ask students to submit two sentences— their introductory question and their thesis statement, which can be quickly checked for focus and direction. Conceptual problems noted at this stage can often be solved through individual or group conferences or through referral of the student to a teaching assistant or writing center consultant. (See Chapter Thirteen for further discussion of this screening technique.)

The Generic Assignment Adapted to Science and Engineering: The Scientific Report

The typical research report in the physical and social sciences or engineering follows the structure of the generic assignment in that the body of the report addresses a question or problem set forth in the introduction. But the body itself has a conventional structure that students need to learn. The following explanation of the scientific report serves as a generic assignment for the sciences.

The Formal Scientific Research Report

A formal scientific research report is a piece of professional writing addressed to other professionals who are interested in the investigation you conducted. They will want to know why you did the investigation, how you did it, what you found out, and whether your findings were significant and useful. Research reports usually follow a standard five-part format: (1) introduction, (2) methods, (3) results, (4) discussion of results, and (5) conclusions and recommendations.

Introduction. Here you explain briefly the purpose of your investigation. What problem did you address? Why did you address it? You will need to provide enough background to enable the reader to understand the problem being investigated. Sometimes the introduction also includes a "literature review" summarizing previous research addressing the same or a related problem. In many scientific disciplines, it is also conventional to present a hypothesis—a tentative "answer" to the question that your investigation will confirm or disconfirm.

Methods. This is a "cookbook" section detailing how you did your investigation. It provides enough details so that other researchers could replicate your investigation. Usually, this section includes the following subsections: (a) research design, (b) apparatus and materials, and (c) procedures followed.

Results. This section, sometimes headed "Findings," presents the empirical results of your investigation. Often, your findings are displayed in figures, tables, graphs, or charts that are referenced in the text. Even though the data are displayed in visuals, the text itself should also describe the most significant data. (Imagine that the figures are displayed on a view graph and that you are explaining them orally, using a pointer. Your written text should transcribe what you would say orally.) Your figures and tables must have sufficient information to stand alone, including accurate titles and clear labels for all meaning-carrying features.

Discussion of results. This is the main part of the report, the part that will be read with the most care by other professionals. Here you explain the significance of your findings by relating what you discovered to the problem you set out to investigate in your introduction. Did your investigation accomplish your purpose? Did it answer your questions? Did it confirm or disconfirm your hypothesis? Are your results useful? Why or why not? Did you discover information that you hadn't anticipated? Was your research design appropriate? Did your investigation raise new questions? Are there implications from your results that need to be explored? The key to success in this section is to link your findings to the questions and problems raised in the introduction.

Conclusions and recommendations. In this last section, you focus on the main things you learned from the investigation and, in some cases, on the practical applications of your investigation. If your investigation was a pure research project, this section can be a summary of your most important findings along with recommendations for further research. If your investigation was aimed at making a practical decision (for example, an engineering design decision), here you recommend appropriate actions. What you say in this section depends on the context of your investigation and the expectations of your readers.

More Personal Forms: Alternatives to the Top-Down, Thesis-Governed Essay

The foregoing discussion has emphasized top-down, thesis-governed writing, which typifies most academic discourse in most disciplines. In Chapters Two and Three, I discussed the benefits of assigning top-down, thesis-governed writing while also raising some theoretical and pedagogical objections to it (see especially pages 46–50).

For the kinds of reasons discussed in Chapter Three, a teacher may be wary of thesis-governed writing, or weary of it, or simply more attracted to more personal forms of writing that privilege the subjective, creative, personal voice of the writer. One alternative is a strong emphasis on journals and other kinds of informal, exploratory writing (the subject of Chapter Six). But there are also many ways to assign formal, finished-product writing that is not thesis governed: exploratory essays, reflection papers, personal narratives, myths, dialogues, letters, poems or short stories, magazine-style articles for popular audiences, advertisements, satires, parodies, and so forth. What follows are examples of alternative assignments.

Formal Exploratory Essays

An academically oriented alternative to thesis-based writing is an exploratory essay, which we might define as a *thesis-seeking* essay rather than a *thesis-supporting* essay (see Zeiger, 1985; Spellmeyer, 1989). The assignment typically asks students to propose a problem and then to write a narrative of their own thought processes in trying to think through the problem. Here is a sample assignment handout, easily adaptable to any discipline.

Write a first-person, chronologically organized account of your thinking process as you explore possible solutions to a question or problem related to this course. Begin by describing what the question is and how and why you became interested it. Then, as you contemplate the problem and do research, narrate the evolving process of your thinking. Your exploratory essay should include both external details (what you read, how you found it, who you talked to) and internal mental details (what you were thinking about, how your ideas were evolving). For this essay, it doesn't matter whether you reach a final position or solve the problem; your reader is interested in your process, not your final product. Show us, for example, your frustration when a promising source turned out to be useless. Show us how new ideas continually led you to reformulate your problem through expansion, narrowing, shifting of focus, or whatever. Make your exploratory essay an interesting intellectual detective story—something your readers will enjoy.

I often assign a formal exploratory essay as an intermediate stage in a research project leading ultimately to a thesis-governed term paper. To have content for the exploratory essay, students need to read widely, confronting the problem's complexity by wrestling with disagreements among the experts and so forth. Because the subject matter of the exploratory essay is *the student's thinking process,* the essay encourages and rewards critical thinking while giving teachers wonderful insights into the intellectual lives (and study habits) of their students.

Another version of the exploratory paper is used by Berlinghoff (1989) in teaching mathematics. Berlinghoff asks each student to write a paper focusing "on the *process of solving* a particular problem" (p. 89, emphasis in original). He begins the course by teaching students a number of problem-solving tactics such as "check the definitions," "restate the problem," "draw a diagram," "argue by analogy," "solve a similar problem," and "reason backward from the desired conclusion." He then gives each student a challenging mathematical problem to try to solve and asks the student to write a paper about his or her process. "The student is asked to describe," Berlinghoff explains, "how he or she used these problem-solving tactics to attack a particular question. Thus, there is always something to write about, regardless of whether or not the student can 'solve' the problem. Even a dead end is worthwhile, provided the path to it can be described. Moreover, by paying careful attention to the problem-solving tactics (because they provide a guaranteed source of material for their papers), students often succeed in doing a lot more mathematics than they think they can" (p. 90).

Reflection Papers

A popular assignment for many teachers is a "reflection paper," sometimes called a "reader-response paper" or a "personal reaction paper." Although this genre seems to vary considerably in its meaning from teacher to teacher, in most cases it evokes writing that is more exploratory, tentative, and personal than the standard top-down academic essay. Its essential nature is the exploration of the connections between course material and a person's individual life or psyche. Reflection papers are often assigned to elicit students' responses to complex, difficult, or troubling readings and invite the writer to "speak back" to the reading in a musing, questioning, and probing way. Here is how one philosophy professor assigns a reflection paper:

In a two- to three-page reflection essay, consider the following statement by Aristotle (*Ethics* II, 2) with respect to your own life:

> We are not studying in order to know what excellence is, but to become good, for otherwise there would be no profit in it. . . . [We must therefore] consider the question of how we ought to act.

Are you studying in order to become good? Explain what you think Aristotle is getting at and then explore your own response.

(For further discussion of ways to encourage responses to readings, see Chapter Eight, pages 143–146.)

A Potpourri of Other Kinds of Alternative Formal Assignments

Many other variations remain. What follows, in no particular order, is a potpourri of ten different kinds of alternative assignments.

1.   A psychology professor asks his students to write a poem from the perspective of a schizophrenic. The teacher claims that students learn a great deal about schizophrenia in their attempt to walk in a schizophrenic's shoes. The best poems are moving and memorable (Gorman, Gorman, and Young, 1986).

2.   A religious studies professor asks students to write a dialogue.

Write a dialogue between a believer (in God) and an unbeliever, in which the main issues that we have raised in class are debated. Each participant will be a spokesperson for a whole range of ideas and arguments, whatever serves to advance his or her basic position. As you write the dialogue, draw on the strongest ideas and arguments for each side that we have seen in this course. Wherever relevant, include your own responses or arguments. The point of this dialogue is not to have a clear victory for one side or the other; rather, the point is to engage the issues in an active and critical manner.

(For further examples of dialogue assignments, see Chapter Seven, pages 129–130)

3.   A literature teacher has students rewrite the ending to a short story or to retell a story from the perspective of a different narrator; a history teacher asks students to rewrite a historical narrative from a different point of view.

4.   A social psychologist requires students to interview someone who has a job, lifestyle, or worldview very different from the student's and then to write a "profile" of the person interviewed. The idea is for the student to encounter an "other" whose sphere of experience differs extensively from the student's.

5.   A women's studies professor asks students to create myths or parables to express their personal understanding or vision of the role of the feminine.

6.   A mathematics professor asks students to write their own "math autobiography" in which they reflect on their past math history and experiences. She reports getting very useful insights into the mathematical anxieties and learning problems of her students (as well as the causes of many of these problems).

7.   A history of religions professor asks students to write essays from the perspective of different persons—an exercise in decentering, seeing the world from a different context.

Write a brief letter back to Paul, as if you were a member of the Corinthian community, responding to his letter. You may choose any point of view you wish— arguing back from the point of view of a faction, repenting the error of your ways, or any other option you can think of.

(For further examples of role-playing assignments, see Chapter Seven, pages 127–128.)

8.   A history and sociology teacher (Bateman, 1990) asks students to do an ethnographic paper on another culture. The trick is to find a local subculture "where views and language and beliefs are just different enough to make their study fascinating" (p. 120). Bateman's solution? To have students explore subcultures right in their midst: the subcultures of paper carriers, kindergartners, Winnebago grandpas, root beer drive-in carhops, cheerleaders, formal wear distributors, and so on.

9.   A mathematics teacher has students write their own story problems relating mathematical concepts to real-world concerns. According to Rose (1989, p. 19), "When students write their own problems, they often choose situations from their own experience and thus see how mathematics applies to their own lives, giving them more confidence to read and solve word problems from the textbook. In addition, writing word problems demands clear, specific, and complete instructions, which requires good understanding of the mathematical concept underlying the problem. This activity also provides a break in the monotony of traditional mathematical tasks."

10.   A sociologist teaching an environment course asks students to write personal narrative essays about their encounters with the natural world, taking as their models such nature writers as Loren Eisely, David Quammen, Annie Dillard, and Lewis Thomas. In part, this course juxtaposes study of academic *articles* about nature and personal *essays* about nature. Students talk about what can and cannot be said in each genre.

Conclusion: Writing Assignments in the Context of the Whole Course

Developing high-quality writing assignments is one of the best ways for professors to improve student writing across the curriculum. A good writing assignment deepens students' engagement with course material, promotes critical thinking, and helps them learn the discipline's discourse—its characteristic methods of inquiry, analysis, and argumentation. This chapter has considered ways to design short assignments (microthemes) to promote the learning of key course concepts and to provide a useful means of formative assessment. It has also looked at three methods for assigning top-down, thesis-governed prose: giving students a thesis to defend, asking a question that demands a thesis answer, and requiring a problem-thesis structure. Finally, it has surveyed a variety of ways to assign alternatives to thesis-governed essays.

The next chapter focuses on informal, nongraded writing aimed at helping students generate and explore ideas, deepen their thinking, and make personal connections between their courses and their lives.

CHAPTER 6

Informal, Exploratory Writing Activities

Chapter Five focused on formal writing assignments calling for finished-product writing; this chapter focuses instead on unfinished, exploratory writing. Chapters Two and Three offer a justification for exploratory writing based on research into the writing processes of expert writers (where personal behind-the-scenes writing serves as a seedbed for ideas and as later-discarded scaffolding for finished products) and on studies showing its effectiveness for enhancing learning for students. Among composition scholars, its most commonly accepted name is *expressive writing*, the term used by Britton in his influential work summarized in Chapter Three (Britton and others, 1975). Many teachers across the curriculum, however, prefer terms such as *exploratory writing, unstructured writing, personal writing, freewriting, focused freewriting,* or simply *informal, nongraded writing.*

Whatever term we choose, what we mean is the kind of exploratory, thinking-on-paper writing we do to discover, develop, and clarify our own ideas. Exploratory writing is typically unorganized and tentative, moving off in unanticipated directions as new ideas, complications, and questions strike the writer in the process of thinking and creating. Examples of exploratory writing include journals, notebooks, marginal notes in books, nonstop freewrites, reading logs, diaries, daybooks, letters to colleagues, notes dashed off on napkins, early drafts of essays, and what physicist James Van Allen, author of more than 270 scientific papers, calls "memoranda to myself": "The mere process of writing," explains Van Allen, "is one of the most powerful tools we have for clarifying our own thinking. I seldom get to the level of a publishable manuscript without a great deal of self torture and at least three drafts. My desk is littered with rejected attempts as I proceed. But there is a reward. I am never so clear about a matter as when I have just finished writing about it. The writing process itself produces that clarity. Indeed, I often write memoranda to myself solely for the purpose of clearing up my own thinking" (Barry, 1989, p. 9). Van Allen's point is that the process of writing drives thinking. Sometimes exploratory writing gets transformed into a finished product. More frequently, as in Van Allen's "memoranda," exploratory writing is an end in itself. Typically, college students do not realize the value of exploratory writing and are not given nearly enough opportunities for doing it. Consequently, they do not get enough practice at the kind of thinking and learning that such writing can stimulate.

Common Objections to Exploratory Writing

Like meditation, exploratory writing takes practice, but once mastered, it is a powerful tool for focusing the mind on a problem and stimulating thought. Often teachers across the curriculum become believers in exploratory writing when they experience it firsthand in writing-across-the-curriculum workshops (see Abbott, Bartelt, Fishman, and Honda, 1992; Freisinger, 1980; Fulwiler and Young, 1982; Young and Fulwiler, 1986; Fulwiler, 1987a, 1987b; Belanoff, Elbow, and Fontaine, 1991).

Nevertheless, despite extensive empirical and testimonial evidence in support of exploratory writing, I have found that many of my colleagues remain unconvinced that assigning exploratory writing is worth the bother. Let's begin, then, by examining some of the objections that faculty raise against assigning exploratory writing in their classrooms.

If I Assign Exploratory Writing, I Have to Take Home Stacks of Journals

Many of my colleagues associate exploratory writing with wheelbarrow loads of student journals. As this chapter explains, there are plenty of ways other than journals to assign exploratory writing. There are also many ways of evaluating journals that will save you from carting them home in a wheelbarrow. Of course, requiring exploratory writing could mean taking home journals on occasion if requiring journals is your method of using exploratory writing and if you enjoy reading student journals (many teachers do—they are often more interesting than essay exams or formal essays, and they connect teachers deeply with their students as persons and learners). I often read the journals I assign in my own classes simply because they give me so many insights into the individuality of my students. But if reading journals is not for you, there are plenty of alternative ways to work exploratory writing into your courses.

Requiring Exploratory Writing Will Take Up Too Much of My Time

Another objection is that requiring exploratory writing takes up a lot of teacher time. This is so, however, only if the teacher feels compelled to read everything students write, which is equivalent, I would argue, to a piano teacher who listens to tapes of students' home practice sessions. Ideally, requiring exploratory writing should not take any teacher time because exploratory writing is writing for oneself with the intention of stimulating creativity or deepening and focusing thought. Students should do it for the same reasons professional writers do—its intrinsic satisfaction. In reality, though, most students need some teacher supervision to remain motivated, and teachers need to read some of their students' exploratory writing in order to coach their thinking processes. The trick is to read some of it, not all of it. This chapter gives hints for cutting down teacher time: some of the strategies in this chapter require almost no teacher time; other strategies allow plenty of flexibility in the teacher time required.

Students Regard Exploratory Writing as Busywork

A more compelling objection to exploratory writing is that students regard it as busywork. Although much of the published literature in writing across the curriculum features enthusiastic teachers proclaiming their students' satisfaction with exploratory writing, there will always be students who do not like it and will regard it as busywork. Whenever I assign journals, for example, I find that about 20 percent of my students never seem to warm up to them.

To some extent, enjoyment of exploratory writing may be related to learning styles (Jensen and Di Tiberio, 1989; see also my discussion of learning styles in Chapter Three, pages 39–41). Some students, either by disposition or by experience, are closure oriented and dislike the open-ended, seemingly goalless nature of writing for oneself. Another cause—if the journals are ungraded—may be students' grade orientation rather than learning orientation. Janzow and Eison (1990) report that 25 to 38 percent of students said that "written assignments (for example, homework and projects) that are not graded are a waste of time" (p. 96). Still another cause may be a teacher's failure to integrate exploratory writing effectively into the course so that it seems purposeful. But the most important cause, I would argue, is that many students have not yet learned to pose the kinds of self-sponsored questions or problems that drive true inquiry. Still viewing knowledge as "right answers" as opposed to arguments, students are not used to the kind of dialogic thinking that exploratory writing facilitates. In short, they see no need for exploratory writing because they see no need to explore.

From my perspective, then, the best response to this objection is not to abandon exploratory writing but to help students see its value. This chapter offers many suggestions for doing so. Let me offer here, though, two key strategies for getting students to become personally invested in exploratory writing.

First, try to incorporate students' exploratory writing directly into the texture of your course. Wherever possible, use their exploratory writing to stimulate class discussions or help them explore ideas for formal essays or exams. Many teachers open class with a question that students have explored the night before in a journal or thought letter. Some teachers have students share ideas from their exploratory writing in small groups. Others collect exploratory writing from a random selection of students each day as a way to check on students' learning and guide thinking. The point here is to help students appreciate exploratory writing as a purposeful part of the class.

Second, let them know that exploratory writing is something that expert writers do, that it is not simply an exercise for students. Students often get interested in exploratory writing when they see their teachers use it to think through ideas. Whenever possible, teachers should freewrite with their students during in-class writing sessions. Teachers can also model the process by bringing their own exploratory writing to class and sharing it with students.

Exploratory Writing Is Junk Writing That Promotes Bad Writing Habits

Because exploratory writing is generally done without concern for organization, sentence structure, spelling, or mechanics, some instructors feel that this kind of writing simply encourages students to practice all the bad habits they already have.

This objection—that you should not encourage sloppiness—appears reasonable enough on the surface. However, it seems based on a faulty analogy between writing and some sphere of human behavior where sloppiness is a moral error (housekeeping? auto mechanics?) rather than a developmental stage in a process. Exploratory writing is often inchoate because the writer has to sort through tangled strands of ideas that need to be written out and reflected on before they can be untangled and organized. Worrying about spelling and grammar when you are trying to discover and clarify ideas can shut down any writer's creative energy. Exploratory writing is messy because thought is messy.

Rather than junk writing, then, a better analogy for exploratory writing might be a musician's early practice sessions on a complex new piece or an architect's sketchbook of possible designs for a project.

Explaining Exploratory Writing to Students

Today, most students are familiar with exploratory writing as a way of learning, having been taught about freewriting or idea mapping in their high school or college writing classes. Many have kept journals or learning logs for courses outside of English. However, since teachers have a wide range of expectations about exploratory writing and have different goals for incorporating it into their courses, it is a good idea to explain to students what you expect when you assign exploratory writing. What follows is a student handout on "guided journals" that a psychology professor and I developed for an introductory psychology class. I include it here both as an example of one attempt to explain exploratory writing to students and as a further explanation to professors who may be fuzzy about the whole concept of expressive or exploratory writing. At the end of the handout, I have included several examples of guided-journal tasks that we developed for the course. (In this particular course, a student's course points for the journal depended on the number of journal entries completed each week.)

Many teachers have adapted this handout to their own courses, which have ranged from history to nursing to mechanical engineering. Generally, teachers provide their own course-related examples of freewriting and set up a grading scheme that fits their course plan.

Explanation of Exploratory Writing for Students

As part of the requirements for this course, you will keep a guided journal in which you will explore your responses to a daily question or problem that we will give you. The purpose of the journal is not to improve your writing skills (at least directly) but to stimulate thinking about issues, questions, and problems raised by your study of psychology. For the most part, you will be rewarded for the process of thinking, rather than for the end product you produce. The kind of writing you will be doing is called "exploratory" or "expressive" writing—that is, writing that lets you "think out loud on paper" without having to worry whether your writing is effective for readers. Therefore, such features of formal writing as organization, correct sentence structure, neatness, and spelling won't matter in your journal. This is writing primarily for yourself; it is not writing intended to be read by others.

Journal writing of this type can help many students become more productive and more focused thinkers. Research has shown that the regular habit of journal writing can deepen students' thinking about their course subjects by helping them see that an academic field is an arena for wonder, inquiry, and controversy rather than simply a new body of information. This way of looking at an academic field can make college more interesting, even exciting. The more you see yourself in this course asking questions and questioning answers, the more you will be thinking like a real psychologist.

How do I write a journal entry? We want you to employ a technique that composition teachers call *focused freewriting.* When you freewrite, you put your pen to paper and write nonstop for a set period of time. (If you compose at the computer and can touch-type, consider turning off the screen so that you can concentrate entirely on ideas without worrying about the appearance of the text.) Think aloud on paper without being concerned about spelling, organization, or grammar. Write as fast as you can. If your mind suddenly dries up, just write *relax* or a key word over and over again until a new thought springs into your mind. In regular freewriting, your mind can wander freely from topic to topic. In focused freewriting, however, you need to keep your entire entry focused on the assigned question or problem. Your purpose is to explore your responses to the question as fully as possible within the set time period.

Here is an example of a ten-minute focused freewrite on the question "Do you have any fears, phobias, or anxieties that might be explained by classical conditioning?"

> Let's see, do I have any fears or phobias? Maybe I should start out by just trying to see what fears and phobias I have. I am afraid of moths. I am a male and to be afraid of moths is to be laughed at. My girlfriend once laughed at me for about an hour it seems because a moth got into our car and I had to stop and get out because it flapped around in front of my face. I get kind of creepy right now just thinking about the flapping wings. It is the sound the moth makes that scares me. I wonder why I am afraid of moths. I haven't really thought about that before. Is that the result of classical conditioning? I can't remember a time when I first became afraid of moths. Let's see right now I just thought about how I am not really afraid of snakes but I used to be and that I can relate that to classical conditioning but I still want to think about moths. I'll come back. relax relax okay back to moths. Let's see, if this were caused by classical conditioning I would have to have had at one time a natural fear that wasn't a phobia—maybe like being afraid of being crushed by some giant flapping thing. Then I would have had to have had that natural fear be associated with something else (the moth). In Pavlov's dog the natural response was salivating and the natural stimulus was seeing the food—these were unconditioned responses and stimuli. Then the dog began associating the food with hearing the bell (conditioned response). I don't think that

applies to my fear of moths. At least I can't think of anytime I learned to associate moths with something that should have naturally aroused my fear. Maybe my fear of moths can be better explained by some other theory of neurosis like Freud's psychoanalytic theory. Maybe a moth stands for something deep in my dream life. Even as I write this, I feel my fear of moths growing. This is so stupid. How could I possibly be afraid of moths when . . . (time is up).

As you can see, this writer just followed the stream of his thought, which is a quite different technique from what you may be used to—that is, thinking first and then recording later what you thought.

How long is a journal entry? In general, we want each entry to be the result of fifteen minutes of concentrated thinking and writing. A skilled freewriter can easily write two or more pages of single-spaced prose (normal-sized handwriting, narrow rules, normal margins) in fifteen minutes. For this course, however, we believe that one full page of prose is a reasonable goal for fifteen minutes of freewriting. We thus consider one entry to be one page of prose, but we hope for somewhat more. When freewriting, set your watch for fifteen minutes and write nonstop (of course, you can stop long enough to uncramp your hand!). If you write a page or more of prose in that time, you have completed an entry.

Do I get automatic credit just for doing the entries? The syllabus specifies "quality" entries, yet this is a knotty problem to explain what we mean by "quality." You definitely will not be judged on things like spelling, organization, and grammar. But we will be looking for evidence that you are thinking seriously about psychology. Many of the entries will ask you to apply concepts explained in the text or in lectures. Your entries should show that you are wrestling with these concepts and have done your reading and studying before attempting your journal entries. Don't write about operant conditioning until you have studied that concept in your text. The student who wrote the freewrite on classical conditioning clearly has read the text and has tried to understand the concepts.

Unlike an essay examination, however, the journal gives you freedom to make mistakes. Writing in the journal helps you learn the concepts themselves, and if you get concepts mixed up, that is often okay. The journal should show evidence of trying, evidence that you are studying and thinking. The best journal entries will be interesting for someone else to read because they will show a mind truly struggling with ideas.

Procedures for keeping your journal. Every two weeks, you will be given a set of tasks, usually more than a dozen or so. Each entry will be a response to one task, and the more tasks you do, the more credit you get. Number your entries consecutively through your journal, and begin each entry on a new page. At the head of each entry, write the date and the number of the task you are responding to. It is important that you keep up with your journal every week.

Some Examples of Journal Tasks

Task 2. Suppose you are a parent who goes to a child psychologist for advice on how to get your ten-year-old child to practice the piano. The child rushes out of the room screaming every time you insist that he practice. What different advice would you get if the child psychologist were a behaviorist, a psychoanalyst, or a humanistic psychologist?

Task 10. Suppose you had a theory that laboratory rats fed a steady diet of beer and hot dogs could learn to find their way through a maze faster than rats fed a steady diet of squash, spinach, and broccoli. How would you design a scientific experiment to test this hypothesis? In your discussion, use the terms *experimental group, control group, independent variable*, and *dependent variable*. Before beginning this task, review pages 17–23.

Task 29. Read the mind-body problem on pages 114–115. Then explore your response to this question: "What is the difference between a human mind and a computer?"

Twenty-Five Ideas for Incorporating Exploratory Writing into a Course

The explanatory handout just presented describes what I call a guided journal. But there are many other ways to assign and use exploratory writing in a course. This section offers twenty-five suggestions for bringing the benefits of exploratory writing into the classroom. I use the expression "exploratory writing" in its broadest sense to mean any kind of informal writing done without revision primarily to help a writer generate, extend, deepen, and clarify thinking.

I invite readers to skim the following options, looking for those most apt to fit their course goals and teaching style. Options 1 through 4 focus on in-class exploratory writing; options 5 through 11 explain different kinds of journals; options 12 through 15 concern ways to deepen students' responses to course readings; options 16, 17, and 18 are change-of-pace ideas for stimulating creative thinking; and options 19 through 22 concern alternative ways to use exploratory writing such as thought letters, e-mail, and portfolios. Finally, options 23, 24, and 25 describe short nongraded exercises aimed at teaching thesis-based writing. (Of these last three, I especially recommend option 24 as one of my personal favorites.)

In-Class Writing

Perhaps the easiest way to use exploratory writing is to set aside five minutes or so during a class period for silent, uninterrupted writing in response to a thinking or learning task. Students can write at their desks while the teacher writes at the chalkboard, on an overhead transparency, or in a notebook. (Teachers who are willing to write with their students are powerful role models.) Here are four suggestions for using in-class writing.

1. Writing at the Beginning of Class to Probe a Subject. Give students a question that reviews previous material or stimulates interest in what's coming. Review tasks can be open-ended and exploratory ("What questions do you want to ask about last night's readings?") or precise and specific ("What does it mean when we say that a certain market is 'efficient'?"). Or use a question to prime the pump for the day's discussion ("How does Plato's allegory of the cave make you look at knowledge in a new way?"). In-class writing gives students a chance to gather and focus their thoughts and, when shared, gives the teacher an opportunity to see students' thinking processes. Teachers can ask one or two students to read their responses, or they can collect a random sampling of responses to read after class. Since students are always eager to hear what the teacher has written, you might occasionally share your own in-class writing.

2. Writing During Class to Refocus a Lagging Discussion or Cool Off a Heated One. When students run out of things to say or when the discussion gets so heated that everyone wants to talk at once, suspend the discussion and ask for several minutes of writing.

3. Writing During Class to Ask Questions or Express Confusion. When lecturing on tough material, stop for a few minutes and ask students to respond to a writing prompt like this: "If you have understood my lecture so far, summarize my main points in your own words. If you are currently confused about something, please explain to me what is puzzling you; ask me the questions you need answered." You will find it an illuminating check on your teaching to collect a representative sample of responses to see how well students are understanding your presentations.

4. Writing at the End of Class to Sum Up a Lecture or Discussion. Give students several minutes at the end of class to sum up the day's lecture or discussion and to prepare questions to ask at the beginning of the next class period. (Some teachers take roll by having students write out a question during the last two minutes of class and submit it on a signed slip of paper.) A popular version of this strategy is the "minute paper" as reported by Angelo and Cross (1993, pp. 148–153). At the end of class, the professor asks two questions: (1) "What is the most significant thing you learned today?" and (2) "What question is uppermost in your mind at the conclusion of this class session?" In another variation, the professor asks, "What is the muddiest point in the material I have just covered? (Tobias, 1989, pp. 53–54).

Journals

Journals can be assigned in a variety of ways, from totally open-ended ones to highly guided ones. Teachers need to find an approach to journals that best fits their own teaching style and their course goals. For an in-depth justification of journal writing as a way of learning and for detailed suggestions on the use of journals in a wide variety of disciplines, see the collection of articles in Fulwiler's *Journal Book* (1987a).

5. Open-Ended Journals. Here you ask students to write a certain number of pages per week or a certain length of time per week about any aspect of the course. Sometimes called "learning logs," such journals leave students free to write about the course in any number of ways. Students might choose to summarize lectures, to explain why a textbook is difficult to understand, to disagree with a point made by someone in class, to raise questions, to apply some aspect of the course to personal experience, to make connections between different strands of the course, to express excitement at seeing new ideas, or for any other purpose. The journal becomes a kind of record of the student's intellectual journey through the course. This is perhaps the most common way to assign journals and is widely reported in the writing-across-the-curriculum literature. An excellent description of the benefits of this kind of journal, from the perspective of a physics teacher, is provided by Grumbacher (1987):

> I began my research on what happens when students write in physics class not knowing what I would find. I discovered that:
>
> 1. the best problem solvers in physics are students who are able to relate the theories of physics to experiences in their lives;
> 2. [journal] writing helps students find the connections between experience and theory;
> 3. students will do more work than is required if they are seeking answers to questions they initiate;
> 4. keeping learning logs on a regular basis encourages students to initiate such questions;
> 5. students need many opportunities to play with the ideas of physics; they need time to work with a concept in a number of different contexts before rushing on to new information. . . .
>
> My students use writing and their logs the way real scientists have always used writing and journals: to clarify their thinking, to

explore the ideas of science, to search for connections between theory and practice, and to ask questions [p. 328].

6. Semistructured Journals. Although they give students nearly as much freedom as open-ended journals, semistructured journals provide guidance in helping writers think of things to say. For example, some teachers ask students to begin each entry by summarizing an important idea the student has learned since the previous entry, either from class or from reading, and then to respond to one or more additional questions such as these:

> What confused you in today's class or today's readings?
> How does your own personal experience relate to what you studied today?
> What effect is this course having on your personal life, your beliefs, your values, your previous understanding of things?
> How does what we have been studying recently relate to your other courses or to other parts of this course?

Many teachers develop their own sets of generic questions, appropriate to their disciplines, to guide students' journal entries. An example is a series of twenty-three "writing probes" developed by Kenyon (1989) to help mathematics students use journal writing to clarify their mathematical thinking. Here are some examples of these probes:

> What does that equation say in plain English?
> Why did you write that equation?
> Why are you stuck?
> What other information do you need to get unstuck?
> What makes this problem difficult?
> What were you thinking about when you did step X [p. 82]?

7. Guided Journals. In a guided journal, students respond to content-specific questions developed by the instructor. By designing tasks that require wrestling with important course material, the teacher guides students' out-of-class study time. Teachers usually ask students to write three or four times a week for fifteen minutes each time, but some give students only one or two questions per week and ask for more elaborated responses. Earlier in this chapter, I presented a student handout explaining a guided journal in a psychology course and including some sample tasks. Following are some additional examples of guided-journal tasks for a religious studies course and a physics course.

Identify a significant problem with respect to discipline within yourself, a friend, or a family member. How does the problem manifest itself? How would Peck diagnose the problem in terms of its various elements, and what would he say must occur in order to solve the problem?

> How have you seen religious beliefs function both to enhance and [to] restrict the spiritual growth of an individual?
>
> Choose a law or set of laws from Deuteronomy 12–17. Describe what effect you think such a law was meant to have on the Israelite society, and explain how this might have contributed to and/or detracted from making Moses' insights into God at Sinai a part of the fabric of everyday life.

Here are the physics tasks.

> Explain Newton's Third Law to your roommate, including examples from the real world.
>
> Describe the concept of momentum to your kid brother.
>
> Explain the differences and similarities between translational and rotational acceleration.
>
> Explain why deserts get hot while islands at the same latitude remain temperate [Jensen, 1987, p. 331].

8. Double-Entry Notebooks. The double-entry notebook, popularized by Berthoff (1987) and widely adopted across the curriculum, requires students first to reflect on course material and then later to reflect on their own reflections. It is thus also called a "dialectical notebook" or "dialogue journal." On right-hand pages of a standard spiral notebook, students are asked to make copious lecture and reading notes on the theory that putting course material into one's own words enhances learning. Then, on the left-hand pages, students are to create an interactive commentary on the material—posing questions, raising doubts, making connections, seeing opposing views, linking course material with personal experience, expressing confusion, and so forth. In a variation on the double-entry notebook, students use the right-hand pages to respond to course material in the manner of open-ended journals. Several days later, however, they are to reread their journals and on the left-hand pages comment on their previous comments. Students often find themselves in dialogue with their own ideas, amazed on a Friday how they could have felt a certain way the previous Monday.

There is some debate among composition researchers about the different effects of dialectic notebooks versus guided journals. The dialectic notebooks (as well as open-ended or semistructured journals) give students more freedom to ask their own questions, pursue their own issues, do their own pondering. However, guided journals may be more efficient at helping students achieve teacher-determined goals. For an empirically based comparison of the two modes, see MacDonald and Cooper (1992). (MacDonald and Cooper use the term *academic journal* rather than *guided journal*.)

9. "What I Observed/What I Thought" Laboratory Notebooks. A strategy for helping students see each step of a lab experiment as logical and purposeful rather than as a mere formula in a lab manual cookbook is a "what I observed/what I thought" lab notebook. Like a dialectic notebook, this kind of notebook uses two columns. The left-hand column contains empirical observations only ("The solution turned blue-green"). The right-hand column records the researcher's mental processes ("I therefore hypothesized that the solution contained copper. I then decided to run a confirmation test for copper"). The left-hand column could also contain mathematical calculations, in which case the right-hand column would explain why the researcher was making these calculations.

10. Contemporary Issues Journals. Here the teacher wants students to relate the course to contemporary issues and problems. The teacher asks students to read current newspapers and to write about how course material applies to current affairs. Especially useful for social science and ethics courses, as well as for all professional majors, this kind of journal usually generates considerable student interest by revealing the relevance of the course to life outside the academy.

11. Exam Preparation Journals. This method provides strong intrinsic motivation for exploratory writing and uses course exams to drive a maximum amount of learning. To use the method, the teacher, early in the course, gives out a list of essay questions from which midterm and final exam questions will be drawn. Students are instructed to devote a section of their journals to each question. Then students gradually work out answers to the questions as course material builds and develops. Some teachers allow students to use their preparation journals during the exams. While the exam is in progress, teachers can quickly look at each student's work and give course bonus points, if so desired, to students who have done a conscientious job of responding to each question.

Reading Journals or Reading Logs

Another use of exploratory writing is to focus specifically on course readings so that the writing helps students comprehend and respond to reading material. These strategies are all explained in Chapter Eight, "Helping Students Read Difficult Texts."

12. Marginal Notes or Focused Reading Notes. See Chapter Eight, pages 143–144.

13. Reading Logs or Summary/Response Notebooks. See Chapter Eight, pages 144–145.

14. Student Responses to Reading Guides. See Chapter Eight, page 145.

15. Imagined Interviews with Authors. See Chapter Eight, page 145.

Creativity Exercises

For a change of pace in their use of exploratory writing, teachers can assign creativity exercises and use them as the basis for class discussion or group sharing. These exercises, which are usually fun for students, stretch language and thinking skills in valuable ways.

16. Writing Dialogues. Ask students to write imaginary "meeting of the mind" dialogues between people with opposing views (B. F. Skinner, Dr. Spock, and your grandmother on child discipline; Jesus and the Grand Inquisitor on freedom; Copernicus and Ptolemy on the retrogression of the planets). Often these assignments make good out-of-class group projects for active learning wherein study teams of three or four students can write the dialogue together.

17. Writing Bio-Poems. A bio-poem uses a formulaic structure to create a poem expressing what the writer sees as significant or meaningful dimensions of a subject's life. In some settings, students might write bio-poems about themselves to help build community among classmates. But the method is particularly effective for helping students see the personal dimensions of important figures studied in a course. Thus, students could write bio-poems of Plato, Caesar, Copernicus, Frankenstein's monster, Rosa Parks, John Cage, or Eleanor Roosevelt. Or students could interview a homeless person, an elderly person in a nursing home, or an AIDS patient and create a bio-poem that lets us enter that person's life. The formula for a bio-poem is as follows (Gere, 1985, p. 222):

Line 1: First name
Line 2: Four traits that describe character
Line 3: Relative of (brother of, sister of, and so on) _____
Line 4: Lover of _____ (list three things or people)
Line 5: Who feels _____ (three items)
Line 6: Who needs _____ (three items)
Line 7: Who fears _____ (three items)

Line 8: Who gives _____ (three items)
Line 9: Who would like to _____ (three items)
Line 10: Resident of _____
Line 11: Last name

Here is a bio-poem written for a philosophy course (Yoshida, 1985, p. 124) on Dostoevski's Grand Inquisitor.

Inquisitor,
Cynical, bold, all knowing, and fearless.
Friend of no one, peer of few.
Lover of self, wisdom, and unconquerable knowledge.
Who feels neither pity nor compassion nor the love of God.
Who needs no man, save for himself.
Who fears the kiss that warms his heart.
And the coming tide which will not retreat.
Who radiates cold shafts of broken glass
And who fits all mankind with collar and chain.
Who would like to see the deceivers burned
And Christ to be humbled before him.
Resident of ages past,
The Grand Inquisitor.

18. Metaphor Games, Extended Analogies. Metaphoric or analogic thinking looks at X from the perspective of Y. It can make the familiar strange or the strange familiar. In my writing classes, I ask students to construct their own metaphors for the writing process, and afterward we compare the insights arising from each other's metaphors. "Writing an essay is like _____ (pulling teeth? having a baby? swimming? building a model airplane? baking a cake? growing a garden? enduring torture?)." This game can be extended to comparative analogies: "Journal writing is like _____, but formal essay writing is like _____."

Because analogic thinking is ubiquitous, it is an easy matter to create metaphoric or analogic games for courses in any discipline. Here are just a few examples: "Baroque music is like _____, but romantic music is like _____." "The difference between Aquinas's view of the human person and Kierkegaard's view is like the difference between _____ and _____." "Napoleon is to the French Revolution as _____ is to _____." More freewheeling teachers might push metaphor games to playful limits with metaphoric questions such as these: "How does the weather change as you go from Freud's view of the personality to B. F. Skinner's?" "If T. S. Eliot and Richard Brautigan were car designers, what would be the differences in their cars?"

Students almost always enjoy metaphor games, which open up complex questions about language, reality, and thought. Finding the apt metaphor can be a wonderful exercise in clarifying a concept. But as the fallacy of false analogy reminds us, metaphors also obscure and distort. Thus, analogy games can lead to interesting class discussions about the role of language in shaping what we know. (For further discussion of metaphoric games, see Elbow, 1981.)

Other Ideas for Using Exploratory Writing

Besides in-class freewrites, various kinds of journals, and occasional creativity games, there are many other ways to use exploratory writing. The following suggestions include ways to use exploratory writing that are more extensive than five-minute in-class freewrites and yet do not result in stacks of journals.

19. Occasional Thought Letters. A thought letter is a piece of exploratory writing longer and more focused than a journal entry but less structured and revised than a formal essay. Unlike a formal essay, which typically goes through numerous drafts, a thought letter is an early exploration aimed at a friendly audience. Its model is the kind of idea-exploring letter that a scholar might write to a trusted colleague when wrestling with a new problem. A student who ordinarily spends fifteen minutes on a journal entry might devote an hour or more of thinking and writing to a thought letter. A typical thought letter assignment calls for one to two pages of single-spaced typing, to be graded on depth and quality of exploration (as opposed to structure, spelling, and other mechanical aspects). A teacher might require one thought letter per week and later help students choose two of the best to be revised into formal graded essays. For teachers, the advantage of thought letters is that they are usually interesting to read and much less time consuming than formal essays because reading consists of observing the writer's thinking process, concentrating on emerging ideas with no need to comment on organization and style.

20. Electronic Mail. E-mail networks are becoming increasingly popular as a medium for exploratory writing. Davis (1993, p. 77) cites a biology teacher who poses a question through e-mail and asks students to respond and make comments. Other teachers have students send their exploratory writing to a class address, read each other's explorations, and then initiate conversations among themselves with copies sent to the instructor. Meacham (1994) reports use of an e-mail network in a large lecture class in developmental psychology and multiculturalism. One student evaluated the experience as follows: "I found the computer list to be a wonderful learning experience for me. I am not very good at speaking out in large groups of people. I found it comforting to be able to voice my opinions to others in the class via e-mail. . . . Many times, I feel lost in a class the size of ours. But the computer list seemed to keep my interest going on the issues discussed in class" (p. 38).

21. Exploration Tasks to Guide "Invention" for a Formal Writing Assignment. Hammond (1991), working with first-year law students and with literature students, describes a strategy for assigning exploratory tasks that helps students develop ideas for a formal essay. For each formal assignment, Hammond developed a sequence of focused freewriting exercises aimed at helping students explore the complexity of a problem or issue fully before they decided on their own thesis. Her goal, she explains, is to delay early closure. "My experience with college freshmen and first-year law students is that both of them tend to be so worried about getting to a 'right' answer that they abbreviate the process of invention: their need to arrive at a persuasive product makes them shortchange the analytical process" (pp. 71–72). To solve this problem, she designed a sequence of focused freewriting tasks that guide students through the required thinking processes. Representative questions for analyzing poetry are as follows:

> Freewrite on [poem's title] (5 minutes). Given this title, what do you think the poem may be about? What associations does it raise for you? What might draw you toward this poem or get in the way of your reading it?
> Putting the text aside, list all the images you remember. Circle three significant images you will write about. . . . Describe the first image (5 minutes). State what it means to you (3 minutes) [p. 78].

Her tasks continue, causing the student to consider carefully all the details of a poem before arriving at a thesis. She sums up the advantages of this approach as follows: "An advantage of focused freewriting over first-draft writing is that it prolongs and structures the exploratory stage, whereas draft writing tends to push for closure. Foreshortening the analytical process is one of the most fundamental problems of undergraduates and law students alike, and this procedure above all helps avert this premature closure" (p. 72).

Similar kinds of focused freewriting tasks can be designed for almost any kind of formal writing assignment. Here, for example, is a generic set of tasks for any kind of argumentative or persuasive essay addressing a controversial issue (adapted from Ramage and Bean, 1995, pp. 79–81).

Generic Exploration Tasks for an Argument Addressing an Issue

Write out the issue your argument will address. Try wording the issue in several different ways. (3 minutes)

Why is this a controversial issue? (For example, is there not enough evidence to resolve the issue? Is the current evidence ambiguous or contradictory? Are definitions in dispute? Do the parties disagree about basic values, assumptions, or beliefs? (15 minutes)

What personal interest do you have in this issue? What personal experiences do you have with it? How does the issue affect you? (10 minutes)

Pick one side of the issue, and come up with the best arguments you can in its favor. Freewrite everything that comes to mind that might help you support this side. (Three 10-minute sessions)

Now pick the other side of the issue and do the same thing. (Three 10-minute sessions)

As you found arguments in favor of both sides of the issue, what gaps in your knowledge did you discover? What additional research do you need to do? What further questions do you need to answer? (10 minutes)

Do the additional research.

Now that you have looked at all sides of the issue and done additional research, which side do you plan to argue for and why? (10 minutes)

You are now ready to write a rough draft of your argument.

22. Portfolio System. Another excellent means of using exploratory writing is to use a portfolio system in which students write rough drafts for five or six essays but select only one or two for revision into formal, finished products (Belanoff and Dickson, 1991). By creating a number of assignments on which students have to write drafts, the teacher can ensure representative coverage of main course concepts. Students' abandoned drafts constitute the exploratory writing for the course. The revised essays plus the drafts of the unrevised essays are submitted in a portfolio toward the end of the term.

Informal Tasks for Practicing Thesis Writing

For teachers who would rather have students practice thesis-governed, hierarchical writing instead of open-ended, exploratory writing but who still want the benefits of nongraded write-to-learn activities, an excellent option is to assign shaped writing exercises, including practice essay exams, thesis statement writing, and frame paragraphs.

23. Practice Essay Exams. Occasionally throughout the term, the teacher gives students an essay exam question due in class the next day (the student is instructed to set a watch and do the writing at home under simulated exam conditions). The teacher collects the practice exams, checks them off in a grade book, and then reads a random sampling (every student's practice exam gets chosen occasionally throughout the term). The teacher then makes duplicates of an A exam for class discussion or writes one under the same timed conditions set for students. Discussion of the exam constitutes review of course material as well as explanation of how to write essay exams.

Teachers who want to try this method might turn to Chapter Eleven, which explains how to teach students to begin their essays with a one-sentence thesis that summarizes the writer's answer to the whole question. The importance of this summarizing skill leads to the following exercise.

24. Thesis Statement Writing. One of my favorite exploratory assignments asks students to write just one sentence. The trick, however, is that the sentence must be a thesis statement, which I define for students as a one-sentence summary of an essay's argument. The advantage of thesis statement assignments is the amount of leverage it provides—a lot of thinking packed into one sentence of writing. Students are often amazed at the fullness of the ideas that can be concentrated into a good generalization through effective use of embedded clauses. For example:

> *Question.* "According to Robert Heilman, what is the difference between a tragedy and a disaster?"

> *Brief thesis.* According to Heilman, a disaster is caused by an accident or outside force, whereas a tragedy is caused by the hero's wrong choice.

> *Elaborated thesis.* For Robert Heilman, both disasters and tragedies bring about suffering or death; a disaster, however, is caused by an accident or outside force so that the hero's physical suffering is not accompanied by guilt, whereas a tragedy is caused by the hero's wrong choice leading to an agonizing discovery of personal responsibility, consequence, and spiritual suffering.

For instructors interested in teaching thesis-based academic writing, I know of no single exercise that does a better job of teaching students how thesis statements work or that gives better practice at creating the governing abstractions that are the key to academic writing.

25. Frame Paragraphs. Frame assignments give students an organizational pattern that guides their thinking about content. Students must come up with the needed generalizations and supporting data to flesh out the prescribed form. These are excellent assignments for teaching hierarchical structure. Here are some examples:

To figure out how fast a small steel marble will roll down an inclined plane, you need to have, at a minimum, the following pieces of information. First, you need to know . . . Second, you need to know . . . [Third, . . . Fourth, . . .]

Many people think that John Cage's music is . . . [generalization, then development]. However, I think it is . . . [generalization, then development].

The current tax structure is unfair to poor people for several reasons. First, . . . Second, . . . [Third, . . . Fourth, . . .]

As in practice exams, feedback for these assignments can come through discussion of A-worthy responses. (For further examples of frame assignments, see Chapter Seven, pages 126–127. For details on the use of frame assignments as small group problem-solving tasks, see Chapter Nine, pages 155–156.)

Evaluating Exploratory Writing

Throughout this chapter, I have referred to exploratory writing as informal and nongraded. Certainly exploratory writing should never be graded according to the criteria used for formal essays. However, if teachers prefer, they can weigh exploratory writing into a course grade on the basis of either students' time on task (quantity of writing produced) or students' engagement and complexity of thinking (quality of the thought content)—or both.

Using a Minus/Check/Plus System

In evaluating exploratory writing (if, for example, you required a journal or a series of thought letters), many teachers use a minus/check/plus system, with a minus indicating unsatisfactory performance, a check indicating work that meets teacher's expectations, and a plus indicating strongly engaged, high-quality thinking or exploration. What constitutes high-quality thinking varies from context to context. What I look for is evidence of dialogic thinking—seeing complexities, finding cruxes and puzzles, confronting inadequate explanations—so that I reward students for wading into the complexity of an issue. Teachers generally report that it is easy to distinguish insightful from superficial pieces of exploratory writing. The key question is not "How well written is this piece?" but "To what extent does this piece reveal engaged thinking about this topic?" I reward the process of thought rather than the product.

Most teachers translate the minus/check/plus system into a letter grade on the basis of some formula: a given number of checks equals a C; a certain combination of checks and pluses equals a B; a better combination of checks and pluses equals an A.

Weighing Exploratory Writing into the Course Grade

Once you have determined how you will translate minuses, checks, and pluses into a letter grade, your next decision is how much to weight the exploratory writing in computing the total course grade. There are numerous approaches here, ranging from negative penalties for failure to do assigned exploratory exercises to various kinds of positive incentives. Most teachers count the exploratory writing as some percentage of the course grade. The higher the percentage, the more time students will devote to it. My own experience suggests that basing a portion of the course grade (perhaps 10 to 15 percent) on exploratory writing greatly increases the systematic study time students devote to a course and results in more engaged learning.

Managing the Workload

Teachers who fear that requiring exploratory writing will increase their workloads inordinately should realize that many options are available, including some that take almost no instructor time. As the following list reveals, there are plenty of ways to use exploratory writing while still keeping your workload manageable.

Teacher Time Required for Exploratory Writing

No Out-of-Class Time

- Uncollected in-class freewriting (options 1–4)
- Exploratory tasks as "invention" for a formal essay (option 21)
- Exam preparation journals (option 11)
- Marginal notations in texts (option 12)

Minimal Time

- Thesis statement writing (option 24)
- Occasionally collected in-class freewriting (options 1–4)
- Pass/fail journals (quantity only—options 5–10)
- Exam preparation journals if teacher gives bonus grade for quality (option 11)
- Practice exams (option 23—time used mainly for writing model answers if students do not provide them; after first course, however, teacher has a portfolio of answers to reuse)
- Abandoned drafts in the portfolio method (option 22)

Moderate Time

- Journals graded minus/check/plus (ways to cut down on time: skim entries or read selected entries only, either chosen randomly by teacher or preselected by student)
- Weekly thought letters (option 19—usually enjoyable to read: often interesting and teacher does not red-pencil them)

Most Time

- Journals read and responded to thoroughly (many teachers report enough pleasure in reading journals that they compensate for their time by cutting down on other required writing, letting journals substitute for an essay exam or an additional formal paper)

Conclusion: Engaging Ideas Through Exploratory Writing

The evidence from both research and instructor testimony seems irrefutable: exploratory writing, focusing on the process rather than the product of thinking, deepens most students' engagement with course material while enhancing learning and developing critical thinking. Most teachers who try exploratory writing in their courses testify that they would never go back to their old way of teaching. The payoff of exploratory writing is students' enhanced preparation for class, richer class discussions, and better final-product writing. From in-class freewrites to reflective thought letters to systematic journals, exploratory writing can help most students become more active and engaged learners.

Coaching Students as Learners, Thinkers, and Writers

CHAPTER 7

Designing Tasks
for Active Thinking
and Learning

The chapters in Part Two suggest numerous ways to incorporate formal and informal writing assignments into a course. Part Three broadens the perspective to focus on the more general pedagogical goals of promoting active learning and critical thinking. Teaching strategies to achieve these goals include the use of writing assignments but are of course not limited to them. That is why Part Three contains chapters on designing critical thinking tasks (Chapter Seven), academic reading (Chapter Eight), small groups in the classroom (Chapter Nine), and other classroom strategies for active learning (Chapter Ten), as well as chapters on essay exams (Chapter Eleven) and teaching academic research (Chapter Twelve).

Throughout Part Three, I focus on the teacher's role as a coach (a metaphor for the critical thinking teacher used by Adler, 1984), or—if one prefers the metaphor used by the Johnson brothers in their many works on cooperative learning—as a "guide on the side" rather than a "sage on the stage" (see Johnson, Johnson, and Smith, 1991, p. 81). In adopting this role, the teacher presents students with critical thinking problems, gives students supervised practice at solving them, and coaches their performance through encouragement, modeling, helpful intervention and advice, and critiquing of their performance. As advocates of an inquiry-based pedagogy make clear (Hillocks, 1986; Kurfiss, 1988; Dillon, 1988; Bateman, 1990; Goodenough, 1991; Bonwell and Eison, 1991; Meyers and Jones, 1993), once professors focus on critical thinking, much of their classroom preparation time shifts from planning and preparing lectures to planning and preparing critical thinking problems for students to wrestle with. In Chapter One (page 4), I quoted Kurfiss's summary of the course features that characterized successful instruction in critical thinking. The purpose of the present chapter can be clarified by repeating three of those features:

2. Problems, questions, or issues are the point of entry into the subject and a source of motivation for sustained inquiry.
4. Courses are assignment centered rather than text and lecture centered. Goals, methods, and evaluation emphasize using content rather than simply acquiring it.
5. Students are required to formulate and justify their ideas in writing or other appropriate modes [Kurfiss, 1988, p. 88].

The teaching of critical thinking is thus rooted in the teacher's design of critical thinking tasks that make the course problem-centered instead of text- or assignment-centered.

The purpose of the present chapter is to provide a heuristic that can help professors create a wealth of critical thinking tasks for their courses. Once created, a critical thinking task can be used in a variety of ways:

- As an exploratory writing task (in-class freewrite, "question of the day" journal task, thought letter, and so forth—see Chapter Six)

- As a formal writing assignment (a microtheme or a longer formal paper—see Chapter Five)

- As an essay exam question (see Chapter Eleven) or a question for a practice exam (see Chapter Six)

- As a small group problem-solving task (see Chapter Nine)

- As an opening question for whole-class discussion or as a problem for an in-class debate, mock trial, simulation game, group presentation, or fishbowl exercise (see Chapter Ten)

The goal in designing critical thinking problems is to convert students from passive to active learners who use course concepts to confront problems, gather and analyze data, prepare hypotheses, and formulate arguments. The rest of this chapter offers practical suggestions for creating short, focused problems for students to think about.

Ten Strategies for Designing Critical Thinking Tasks

The design of critical thinking tasks gives professors great flexibility in incorporating critical thinking activities into their courses in that the tasks can be used either as homework assignments (exploratory writing, microthemes, study group projects) or as questions for in-class discussions or small group tasks. What follow are ten strategies for designing critical thinking tasks, each followed by one or more examples.

1. Tasks Linking Course Concepts to Students' Personal Experience or Previously Existing Knowledge

Tasks in this category are especially good for engaging students' interest in a problem or a concept before it is addressed formally in class or in readings. These tasks also help students assimilate new concepts by connecting the concepts to personal experiences. As cognitive research has shown (Norman, 1980), to assimilate a new concept, learners must link it back to a structure of known material, determining how a new concept is both similar to and different from what the learner already knows. The more that unfamiliar material can be linked to the familiar ground of personal experience and already existing knowledge, the easier it is to learn.

Think of examples out of your own personal experience to illustrate the uses of vector algebra. You might consider such experiences as swimming in a river with a steady current, walking across the deck of a moving boat, crossing the wake while water-skiing, cutting diagonally across a vacant lot while friends walk around the lot, or watching a car trying to beat a moving train to a railroad crossing. Use one or more of these experiences to explain to a friend what vector algebra is all about. Use both words and diagrams. [Mathematics]

Describe times in your own life when you have experienced role strain and role conflict. What are the key differences between these terms, and why is the distinction useful? [Sociology]

What are your current views toward what it means to live a full life? What specific things do you have to attain and work for in order to live as full a life as possible? [The instructor assigns this task near the beginning of the course; students reread their explorations at the end of the course to measure some of the changes in their thinking as a result of the course.] [Philosophy]

2. Explanation of Course Concepts to New Learners

One of the easiest ways to design critical thinking tasks is to ask students to explain course concepts to a new learner. This task gives students a teacher's role, making them search for ways to tie the course concept into the knowledge base of the hypothetical reader. It thus creates a purposeful rhetorical context wherein the writer writes to an audience for a reason. Because the stipulated audience knows less about the subject than the writer, the task helps students escape the student-to-examiner role that Britton finds debilitating for writers (Britton and others, 1975).

Explain to your mother why water stays in a pail when swung in a vertical circle around your head [Jensen, 1987, p. 331]. [Physics]

Write a procedure for finding the number *m* modulo *n* that a fifth grader could understand [Keith, 1989, p. 140]. [Mathematics]

Using layperson's language, explain to a new diabetic what is meant by the glycemic index of foods and why knowing about the glycemic index will help the diabetic maintain good blood sugar levels. [Nursing/nutrition science]

3. Thesis Support Assignments

As discussed in Chapter Five, one of the best ways to teach thesis-governed writing is to give students a controversial thesis to defend or attack. The assignment reinforces for students a view of knowledge as tentative and dialogic where divergent interpretations of reality compete for allegiance. In its concern for reasons and evidence, coupled with a demand that the writer or speaker attend to opposing views, the assignment requires a high level of critical thinking. Thesis support tasks make excellent microtheme, practice exam, or short essay assignments. They also make good "believing and doubting" exploratory tasks or collaborative learning exercises in which groups are asked to develop arguments for and against the thesis. (For additional examples, see Chapter Five, pages 87–88, and Chapter Nine, pages 156–157.)

People suffering from schizophrenia or manic-depressive disorder should/should not be forced to take their medication. [Nursing/medical ethics]

An electric dipole is placed above an infinitely conducting plane. The dipole does/does not feel a net force or a torque. Explain [Mullin, 1989, p. 208]. [Physics course in electricity and magnetism]

After all of Hamlet's shilly-shallying, Fortinbras is just what Denmark needs. Support or attack. [Literature]

Read the accompanying handout on how historians evaluate the credibility and reliability of primary documents. Based on the criteria set forth in the handout, determine whether Pericles's Funeral Oration is/is not reliable evidence. [History]

4. Problem-Posing Assignments

With this strategy, instead of giving students the thesis, as in strategy 3, you give students the question, which they have to try to answer through thesis-governed writing or to contemplate through exploratory writing or small group problem solving. Often the assignment specifies an audience also—a person other than the teacher who either poses the question or needs the answer. Most teachers can get a ready supply of these questions by sorting through old essay exams, which often make excellent small group tasks or write-to-learn tasks for journals, practice exams, or microthemes. Often the questions can be incorporated into humorous stories or problem situations that make the assignment more fun.

An hourglass is being weighed on a sensitive balance, first when sand is dropping in a steady stream from the upper to lower part and then again when the upper part is empty. Are the two weights the same or not? Write an explanation supporting your answer to this question. Write to a fellow student who is arguing for what you think is the wrong answer. [Physics]

Your thirteen-year-old sister mailed you a cartoon showing a picture of Frank and Ernest taking a number from the dispenser at an ice-cream parlor. The number they draw is $\sqrt{-1}$. Ernest has a puzzled look on his face. Your sister is taking a prealgebra class and is familiar with the idea of square roots such as $\sqrt{4} = 2$ and $\sqrt{81} = 9$. She also knows how to do arithmetic with positive and negative integers. However, she does not understand the cartoon and wants you to explain it to her. Prepare a written explanation for your sister that builds on her current mathematics background. [Mathematics]

You are an accountant in the tax department of Kubiak, Kartcher, and Elway, certified public accountants. Saturday morning, you are in Winchell's Donuts, as usual. Just as you finish reading the comics and start on your second apple fritter, a gentleman sits down beside you. He introduces himself as Fred O. McDonald, a farmer from up in the valley. He says he recognizes you as "that CPA who frequents the donut shop." Fred has a problem and asks tax advice from you. Here is Fred's problem:

> Last Tuesday, farmer McDonald planned to remove stumps from a pasture. So he drove out to the pasture, lit a stick of dynamite, and tossed it near the base of a stump. Fred's playful dog, Boomer, saw his master throw the "stick" and scampered to fetch it. Boomer picked up the stick. Fred yelled at the dog. Boomer, thinking he was going to be punished, ran under Fred's pickup truck. Boomer dropped the dynamite stick. The dog escaped harm just as the truck was totally destroyed by the blast. Fred wonders if he can deduct the loss of the truck for tax purposes.

Write a letter to Fred O. McDonald to answer his question. [Accounting] [Reprinted by permission from *Instructor's Manual with Lecture Notes to Accompany Concepts in Federal Taxation.* Copyright 1996 by West Publishing Company. All rights reserved.]

5. Data-Provided Assignments

In a sense, this strategy is the flip side of the thesis-provided assignment in strategy 3. In the earlier strategy, the teacher provides the thesis; students must discover reasons and evidence to support it or attack it. In this strategy, the teacher provides the data; students must determine what thesis or hypothesis the data might support. This strategy is particularly useful in the sciences for teaching students how to write the "findings" and "discussion" sections of scientific reports. The teacher can explain the research question and methodology for an experiment and then give students the researchers' experimental findings displayed in terms of graphs, tables, or charts. Students can then be asked, first, to write the "findings" section of the report and then the "discussion" section. The strategy can also be used in a variety of ways to teach students how to use statistical data in arguments.

Examine the attached unsorted data about Mary Smith, a stroke patient who is soon to be transferred from an acute-care facility to a convalescent center. [The accompanying data include admitting information, history and physical data, progress notes, nursing notes, and a social service report.] Based on these data, write a discharge summary for Mary Smith. Your audience is the nursing supervisor of the convalescent facility, and your purpose is to help the convalescent center provide the patient with optimal continuity of care [adapted from Pinkava and Haviland, 1984, p. 271]. [Nursing]

To what extent do the attached economic data support the hypothesis "Social service spending is inversely related to economic growth"? First, create a scattergram as a visual test of the hypothesis. Then formulate a verbal argument analyzing whether the data do or do not support the hypothesis. [Economics]

6. Frame Assignments

Frame assignments are analogous to those old dance lessons for which the instructor pasted footsteps on the floor. A frame assignment provides a topic sentence and an organizational frame that students have to flesh out with appropriate generalizations and supporting data. Students have to dance their way through the paragraph, but the assignment shows them where to put their feet. Often the frame is provided by an opening topic sentence, along with the major transition words in the paragraph. Students report that such assignments help them learn a lot about organizational strategies. More importantly, they see how structure can stimulate invention in that they must generate ideas and arguments to fill the open slots in the frame. (For use of frame assignments as exploratory writing tasks, see Chapter Six, pages 115–116; for their use as collaborative learning tasks, see Chapter Nine, pages 155–156.)

In the last act of *Hamlet*, Hamlet seems to have changed in several ways. First, Hamlet [development] . . . Second, Hamlet [development] . . . [Third, . . . Fourth, . . .] [Literature]

To solve the problem of homelessness in America, we must realize that not all homeless fit into the same category. In fact, we ought to specify X categories of homeless. First, [development] . . . Second, [development] . . . [Third, . . . Fourth, . . .] [Sociology]

Socrates and the Sophists differed in their beliefs about truth. On the one hand, Socrates argued that [development] . . . The Sophists, on the other hand, argued that [development] . . . [Philosophy]

7. Assignments Requiring Role-Playing of Unfamiliar Perspectives or Imagining "What If" Situations

Role-playing unfamiliar or disorienting perspectives or imagining "what if" situations makes an excellent critical thinking exercise. Piagetians have shown that a major block to critical thinking is egocentrism, that is, a person's inability to imagine alternative views. According to Flavell (1963), an egocentric thinker, in the Piagetian sense, "sees the world from a single point of view only—his own—but without knowledge of the existence of [other] viewpoints or perspectives and . . . without awareness that he is the prisoner of his own" (p. 60). Tasks requiring role-playing or "what if" thinking encourage what Piaget calls decentering—getting students outside of the assumptions of their own worldview. By asking students to adopt an unfamiliar perspective or a "what if" situation, we stretch their thinking in productive ways.

Look at this prehistoric cave painting [attached reproduction shows a speared deerlike animal]. Imagine that you are the Ice Age artist who created the animal painting on the cave wall. What could have motivated you to create such a painting? [Art history]

Hobbes said that we are obliged to obey the state only so long as it guarantees our security. How would he react to compulsory military service in time of war [Maimon and others, 1981, p. 201]? [History, philosophy]

Assume that space scientists, working with sports clothing manufacturers, have developed a superthin and superflexible space suit that allows athletes to run and jump freely on extraterrestrial soil. As an all-world sports promoter, your uncle, Squeebly Rickets, decides to schedule an exhibition baseball game on the moon. One of his first tasks is to provide instructions for laying out the baseball diamond and outfield fences. But then he begins to wonder, How will the lack of an atmosphere and the greatly reduced gravitational force affect the game? For help, he turns to you as an expert in physics. [Physics]

Suppose experiments showed that the Coulomb law for point charges q_1 and q_2 were actually

$$F = \frac{q_1 q_2}{4\pi\varepsilon_0 r^2}(1 + r/\lambda)\exp(-r/\lambda)$$

where λ is a new constant of nature that is extremely large. (It turns out that λ

depends on the mass of the photon m_γ with $\lambda = \infty$ for $m_\gamma = 0$.) Superposition still holds. Describe qualitatively how you would go about reformulating electrostatics. Quote results if you are able to, but mainly just indicate what procedures you would follow [Mullin, 1989, p. 207]. [Electricity and magnetism]

8. Summaries or Abstracts of Articles or Course Lectures

Writing summaries or précis of articles or lectures is a superb way to develop reading and listening skills, to practice decentering, and to develop the skills of precision, clarity, and succinctness (Bean, 1986). In composing a summary, the writer must determine the hierarchical structure of the original article, retaining without distortion the logical sequence of its general statements while eliminating its specific details. Summary writers must also suspend their own views on a subject to articulate fairly what is often an unfamiliar or even unsettling view in the article being summarized.

Teachers can assign summaries of various lengths. Perhaps the most common length is 200 to 250 words, but Angelo and Cross (1993) report successful use of one-sentence summaries in immunology, fundamentals of nursing, and physics for technicians (pp. 183–187). In another variation, Barry (1989, p. 24) reports good results assigning a "25-word précis"—a one-sentence abstract that must be exactly twenty-five words long. By requiring *exactly* twenty-five words, the assignment forces students through considerable revision, in which they must play with syntax and question the value of every word.

To promote careful listening and note-taking skills, some professors ask students to write summaries of their lectures. Chemistry professor Richard Steiner (1982) reported that having students write daily summaries of his lectures resulted in significantly improved test scores: "I decided that an effective way to utilize writing assignments as a way to promote understanding was to require written summaries of my organic chemistry lectures. Students were instructed to discuss briefly (one page) in writing the key points and relationships in each lecture. . . . [The collected data] indicate that the writing assignments directly contributed to student understanding" (p. 1044). Furthermore, by reading selected summaries after each day's lectures, Steiner was able to monitor places where students were having difficulty and adjust his lectures accordingly. (For further discussion of summary writing, see Chapter Eight, pages 145–146. See also Cohen and Spencer, 1993, who describe an advanced economics course in which the initial writing assignments—aimed at teaching economic argumentation—are a sequence of abstracts of significant professional articles in economics.)

Write a 200- to 250-word summary of Kenneth Galbraith's paper, "The Theory of Countervailing Power," which attempts to provide a theory that describes and accounts for the distribution of power. Your summary should accurately convey the content of the paper. It should be comprehensive and balanced with clear sentence structure and good transitions. [Political science]

Write a four-sentence summary of the attached scientific paper, followed by four questions. Your first four sentences make up a four-sentence summary of the scientific article—one sentence for each section of the paper. Recall that the *Introduction* states the question addressed in the study and explains why the question is important; *Methods* tells how the question was answered; *Results* shows the outcome of the experiment; and *Discussion* analyzes the results and suggests the impact of the new knowledge. Your second four sentences are four questions raised in your mind by the article. [Biology]

9. Dialogues or Argumentative Scripts

These assignments allow students to role-play opposing views without having to commit themselves to a final thesis. The freedom from traditional thesis-governed form, as well as the necessity to role-play each of the opposing views in the conversation, often stimulates more complex thinking than traditional argumentative papers, in which students often try to reach closure too quickly. By preventing closure, this format promotes in-depth exploration. The dialogue strategy is also recommended by Angelo and Cross (1993) as a useful strategy for formative assessment of critical thinking. According to Angelo and Cross, "Invented Dialogues provide rich information on students' ability to capture the essence of other people's personalities and styles of expression—as well as on their understanding of theories, controversies, and opinions of others. This technique provides a challenging way to assess—and to develop—students' skills at creatively synthesizing, adapting, and even extrapolating beyond the material they have studied" (p. 203).

Write a short dialogue (two to three pages) between a neo-elitist power theorist and a pluralist. First, take the role of the neo-elitist (be an intellectual son or daughter of Ganson) and explain to this poor, unenlightened pluralist the meaning and importance of the concepts of predecision politics and the mobilization of bias. Respond to this radical fluff in the role of a Yalie pluralist. Continue the dialogue by alternating roles; be sure to respond in the role of one theorist to the arguments raised by the other. [Political science]

For the design application we have been studying, your design team has proposed four alternative solutions: conventional steel roller bearings, ceramic bearings, air bearings, and magnetic bearings. As a team, write a dialogue in which each team member argues the case for one of the alternative solutions and shows weaknesses in the other solutions. [Mechanical engineering]

You fall suddenly into a weird time warp and find yourself in a tavern with Aristotle, Hegel, Arthur Miller, and literary critic Robert Heilman, all of whom have distinctive views on what constitutes a tragedy. They are arguing vociferously about Miller's *Death of a Salesman:* Is it a tragedy? Luckily, you have just studied Miller's play in your literature class and have strong feelings yourself on this matter. Write a mini-play in which you, Aristotle, Hegel, Miller, and Heilman express views on this question. [Literature]

10. Cases and Simulations

Case studies have long been a staple of instruction in law, medicine, and business (Di Gaetani, 1989; Boehrer and Linsky, 1990; Barnes, Christensen, and Hansen, 1994). In recent years, cases have also become increasingly popular in teaching writing (Tedlock, 1981; Shook, 1983). Cases often require the writing of elaborate scenarios and the assembly of extensive packets of data. For this reason, many instructors use cases already published in textbooks, either directly or adapted to their own needs. For example, Pinkava and Haviland (1984) report using nursing cases adapted from a composition textbook.

It is possible, however, to create your own short cases adapted from recent news stories, campus events, or developments in your professional field. Good cases generally tell a real or believable story, raise thought-provoking issues based on conflict, lack an obvious or clear-cut right answer, and demand a decision reached through critical thinking and analysis (Boehrer and Linsky, 1990; Davis, 1993). Cases can be used either for in-class simulations or for providing realistic contexts for writing assignments or small group tasks. (See also Chapter Ten, pages 179–180.)

Mr. X, a patient at City Hospital, suffers from kidney failure and requires periodic and fairly frequent dialysis, which is funded by the government. He is one of a number of patients who use the dialysis machine, and there are many other similarly afflicted individuals who are on a waiting list for the use of the machine. Mr. X finds dialysis quite painful and sometimes says that he would rather just forget the treatment and let the disease run its natural course. Lately he has begun to miss some of his treatments and has been failing to control his diet properly. He has even become abusive with the hospital staff who operate the dialysis machine. His wife is quite worried about him, especially since his behavior has changed toward her and their five children. Mr. X continues his erratic routine, sometimes taking his treatment quietly, sometimes taking it but abusing the staff, sometimes failing to take it at all. Suddenly, he begins to miss all his treatments. Two weeks later, he is rushed to the hospital in a coma.

He must have immediate dialysis if he is to survive. Should the hospital perform the dialysis, or should Mr. X. be allowed to die?

Initial roles. An ethicist taking a utilitarian position; an ethicist taking a deontological position; Mr. X's wife; a staff member; a representative of the people on the waiting list for the dialysis machine; a member of the Hemlock Society; members of the hospital board that will decide the case.

Conducting the simulation. Students discuss the case, taking their assigned roles.

Writing assignment. After hearing all the arguments presented by characters in the role-play, assume that you are a member of the hospital board that will decide the case, and write a three- to four-page argument supporting your position on the issue.

Conclusion: Strategies for Designing Critical Thinking Tasks _____

As a review of the ideas covered in this chapter, here is a checklist of strategies for designing critical thinking tasks for your courses. As suggested, these tasks can then be used in a variety of ways: in-class freewrites, at-home guided-journal tasks or thought letters, practice exams, microthemes, multidraft formal essays, small group collaborative tasks, or tasks for whole-class discussions or simulations.

1. Think of tasks that would let students link concepts in your course to their personal experiences or prior knowledge.

2. Ask students to teach difficult concepts in your course to a new learner.

3. Think of controversial theses in your field (for thesis support assignments or believer-versus-doubter exercises).

4. Think of problems, puzzles, or questions you could ask students to address.

5. Give students raw data (such as lists, graphs, or tables) and ask them to write an argument or analysis based on the data.

6. Think of opening "frame sentences" for the start of a paragraph or short essay; students have to complete the paragraph by fleshing out the frame with generalizations and supporting details.

7. Have students role-play unfamiliar points of view (imagine X from the perspective of Y) or "what if" situations.

8. Select important articles in your field, and ask students to write summaries or abstracts of them. (Or ask students to write summaries of your lectures.)

9. Think of a controversy in your field, and ask students to write a dialogue between characters with different points of view.

10. Develop cases by writing scenarios that place students in realistic situations relevant to your discipline, where they must reach a decision to resolve a conflict.

CHAPTER 8

Helping Students Read Difficult Texts

Whenever faculty get together to talk about student writing or critical thinking, they inevitably turn also to problems of student reading. Just as speaking and listening skills are intertwined, so too are writing and reading skills. Many of today's students are poor readers, overwhelmed by the density of their college textbooks and baffled by the strangeness and complexity of primary sources and by their unfamiliarity with academic discourse. Armed with a yellow highlighter but with no apparent strategy for using it and hampered by lack of knowledge of how skilled readers actually go about reading, our students are trying to catch marlin with the tools of a worm fisherman. We have to do more than take our students out to sea. We have to teach them to fish in the deep.

Fear of Deep Waters: Causes of Students' Reading Difficulties

Before we can help students improve their reading skills, we need to look more closely at the causes of their reading difficulties. Our students, of course, have learned to read in the sense of achieving basic literacy. Except for an occasional student with a reading disability, college students do not need to be taught reading in this ordinary sense. Rather, they need to learn how to fish academic texts, which constitute waters deeper than anything they have plumbed before. What factors send them home from the sea of academic reading frustrated by the expense of time and the emptiness of the catch? I can identify ten contributing causes.

1. Misunderstanding of the Reading Process

When experts read difficult texts, they read slowly and reread often. They struggle with the text to make it comprehensible. They hold confusing passages in mental suspension, having faith that later parts of the essay will clarify earlier parts. They "nut-shell" passages as they proceed, often writing gist statements in the margins. They read a difficult text a second and a third time, considering first readings as approximations or rough drafts. They interact with the text by asking questions, expressing dis-agreements, linking the text with other readings or with personal experience. The bigger the fish they go after, the greater the strug-gle in reeling it in.

In contrast, our students imagine that expert readers are "speed readers." Deceived by Evelyn Wood advertisements, stu-dents push themselves to read faster instead of slower. Conse-quently, they do not allot enough study time for reading and rereading. If they do not understand the text on first reading, they assume that it is the teacher's job to explain the text to them. Since teachers regularly do so, the students' reading difficulty initiates a vicious circle: the teacher's willingness to explain the text ("I have to lecture on this material because students are such poor readers") deprives students of the very practice and challenge they need to grow as readers ("I don't have to struggle with this text because the teacher will explain it in class"). Noting the fishermen's frustra-tion, we teachers buy fish for them.

2. Failure to Adjust Reading Strategies for Different Purposes

Besides understanding how skilled readers read difficult texts, stu-dents need to know that a good reader's reading process will vary extensively, depending on the reader's purpose. Sternberg (1987) argues that college students—facing enormous amounts of read-ing—must learn to distinguish among different reading purposes and adjust their reading speed accordingly. Some reading tasks require only skimming for gist, while others require the closest scrutiny of detail. Sternberg gave people a reading comprehension test comprising four passages, each of which were to be read for a different purpose—one for gist, one for main ideas, one for detail, and one for inference and application. He discovered that good readers varied their reading speed appropriately, spending the most time with passages they were to read for detail, inference, and application. Poor readers, in contrast, read all four passages at the same speed. As Sternberg puts it, poor readers "do not discriminate in their reading time as a function of reading purpose" (p. 186). The lesson here is that we need to help students learn when to read fast and when to read slowly.

3. Difficulty in Perceiving the Structure of an Argument as They Read

Unlike experts, inexperienced readers are less apt to chunk complex material into discrete parts with describable functions. They do not say to themselves, for example, "This part is giving evidence for a new reason," "This part maps out an upcoming section," or "This part summarizes an opposing view." Their often indiscriminate, almost random use of the yellow highlighter suggests that they are not representing the text in their minds as a hierarchical structure.

4. Difficulty in Assimilating the Unfamiliar

Developmental psychologists have long noted the "cognitive egocentrism" of new college students who have trouble walking in the shoes of persons with unfamiliar views and values (Flavell, 1963; Kroll, 1978; Norman, 1985; Bean, 1986; Kurfiss, 1988). No matter what the author really means, students translate those meanings into ideas that they are comfortable with. Thus, to many of our students, a philosophic Idealist is someone with impractical ideas, whereas a Realist is praiseworthy for being levelheaded. The more unfamiliar or more threatening a new idea is, the more students transform it into something from their own psychological neighborhoods. The deep harbors the strange and the terrifying. Better not to catch those ideas but rather to tame them into something familiar, to turn sea monsters into canned tuna. The insight of cognitive psychology here is that these problems are related neither to stupidity nor to intellectual laziness. They are as natural as crawling before walking, and we as teachers need to adopt appropriate strategies for dealing with them.

5. Difficulty in Appreciating a Text's Rhetorical Context

Students do not see what conversation a text belongs to. They do not understand what question is being addressed or why the writer was troubled by it. They have difficulty perceiving a real author writing for some important reason out of a real historical context. Particularly, they do not appreciate the political biases of different magazines and newspapers, the varying degrees of scholarly prestige of different journals and presses, and the significance that skilled readers often give to the reputation of the author. These problems are closely related to the following one.

6. Difficulty Seeing Themselves in Conversation with the Author

Possibly because they regard texts as sources of inert information rather than as arguments intended to change their view of something, inexperienced readers do not interact with the texts they read. Readers must will themselves to play two opposing roles: an open-minded believer who can succumb to the text's power and a skeptical doubter who can find weaknesses in the text. In playing these roles, an experienced reader carries on a silent conversation with the text's author.

7. Lack of the "Cultural Literacy" Assumed by the Text's Author

In the jargon of reading theorists, students do not have access to the cultural codes of the text—background information, allusions, common knowledge that the author assumed that the reading audience would know. Knowledge of cultural codes is often essential to making meaning of the text. So significant is this cause that Hirsch, Kett, and Trefil (1987) have made a national movement out of "cultural literacy," lack of which they claim is a prime source of students' reading difficulties in college.

8. Inadequate Vocabulary

Inadequate vocabulary hampers the reading comprehension of many students. Using a dictionary helps considerably, but often students do not appreciate how context affects word meanings, nor do they have a good ear for irony or humor. Moreover, the texts they read often contain technical terms, terms used in unusual ways, or terms that have undergone meaning changes over time.

9. Difficulty in Tracking Complex Syntax

Although students may be skilled enough reading today's college textbooks, which may be "dumbed down" through simplification of syntax, they often have trouble with the sentence structure of primary sources or scholarly articles. When they are asked to read a complex sentence aloud, their errors in inflection reveal their difficulty in chunking grammatical units; they have trouble isolating main clauses, distinguishing them from attached and embedded subordinate clauses and phrases.

10. Difficulty in Adjusting Reading Strategies to the Varieties of Academic Discourse

Students do not understand that prose styles, discourse structures, and argumentative strategies differ from discipline to discipline or from historical period to historical period. Just as they do not adjust their reading speed to differences in purpose, they do not adjustment their reading strategies to differences in genre. They do not understand, for example, that scientists often read the introduction and discussion section of scientific reports quite carefully but skip the methodology section and only skim the findings. To take another example, they do not understand that historians read primary sources quite differently from the way they read journal articles. They also do not understand why some writers labor to make themselves clear through highly mapped, thesis-up-front structures while others seem to seek obscurity through a difficult style and complex, organic organization. They have particular trouble with exploratory, digressive, process-oriented styles or with highly metaphorical or allusive styles. As anglers, they do not adjust their strategy to the kind of fish they seek.

Suggested Strategies for Helping Students Become Better Readers

Having examined these various causes, we recognize that reading skills, like writing skills, develop slowly over time as students move upward intellectually on Perry's developmental scale, as their vocabularies expand, as they grow in cultural literacy, as they increase their repertoire of reading strategies, and as they develop better study habits. Although we cannot teach reading directly, we can create learning environments that nurture reading growth. What follow are a number of suggestions for creating such an environment.

Explain to Students How Your Own Reading Process Varies with Your Purpose

Students appreciate learning how their professors read and study. You might take some class time to discuss with students your own reading processes. One approach is to create little research scenarios to help students see how and why your reading strategies vary. When you do your own research, for example, when do you skim texts? When do you read for gist but not for detail? When do you read carefully? Under what circumstances do you take notes on a text or write in the margins? When you read a scientific or technical article, when do you read the methodology and findings sections carefully and when do you skip directly to the discussion section? How much are you influenced by the credentials of an author? How much does the prestige level of a scholarly journal or the political bias of a magazine or newspaper affect the way you read a text?

The fifteen or twenty minutes it takes for such a discussion can sometimes have a powerful influence on students, especially if your course involves reading of primary and secondary sources.

Show Students Your Own Note-Taking and Responding Process When You Read

Just as it helps students to see a skilled writer's rough drafts, it helps them to see a skilled reader's marked-up text, marginal notations, and note card entries. Bring in a book or article full of your own marginal notes and underlinings, along with entries you make on note cards or responses you make in reading logs. Show them what sorts of things you write in the margins. Explain what you underline and why. If your reading is part of a scholarly project, show them how you take notes and how you distinguish between what the author is saying and your own reflections on the material.

Help Students Get the Dictionary Habit

Students should keep a dictionary in the room where they study and should perhaps carry a small pocket dictionary. They need to learn strategies that work for them when they encounter unfamiliar words. One strategy is to make small ticks in the margins next to words they are unsure of and to look them up later when they come to an appropriate resting place in the text. After they have looked up a word, they can review briefly the parts of the text in which it occurred before tackling the next portion.

Teach Students How to Write "What It Says" and "What It Does" Statements

A helpful way to teach students to understand structural function in a text is to show them how to write "what it says" and "what it does" statements for each paragraph (Ramage and Bean, 1995, pp. 32–34). A "what it says" statement is a summary of the paragraph's content—the paragraph's stated or implied topic sentence. A "what it does" statement describes the paragraph's purpose or function within the essay: for example, "Provides evidence for the author's first main reason," "Summarizes an opposing view," "Provides statistical data to support a point," or "Uses an analogy to clarify the idea in the previous paragraph." The "what is says" sentence for the paragraph you are now reading is "Teach students about structure by having them write 'what it says' and 'what it does' statements." The "what it does" statement is "This paragraph gives another strategy for improving reading." Asking students to write out "what it says" and "what it does" statements for each paragraph in a scholarly article in your field will ensure not only careful reading of the article but also increased awareness of structure.

Make Students Responsible for Texts Not Covered in Class

A good way to increase the amount of material covered in a course or to create space for active learning is to make students responsible for course readings not discussed in class. (For a justification of this approach from an economist, see Machlup, 1979.) This strategy signals to students that all learning in a course does not have to be mediated through the instructor. Not only does this strategy allow instructors to cover content material without feeling rushed to lecture over it, but it also breaks the vicious reading cycle discussed earlier (teachers explain readings in class because students are poor readers; students read poorly because teachers explain the readings in class). When students know they will be tested on material not covered in class, they are forced to a deeper level of struggle.

Develop Ways to Awaken Student Interest in Upcoming Readings

Students' reading comprehension increases when they are already engaged with the problem or issue that a reading addresses or are otherwise interested in the subject matter. The trick is to arouse students' interest in a text before they read it so that they are already participating in the conversation that the text belongs to. Perhaps they will thus be stimulated to read the text for their own reasons rather than for ours. Here are two strategies that might work.

Devise Interest-Arousing Pretests. One technique is to create an interesting nongraded pretest over the upcoming reading. Students will get a preview of the content of the reading, as well as an awareness of their own gaps in knowledge. If the test can make the content seem interesting or important, it may help awaken curiosity.

Assign an Exploratory Writing Task or a Collaborative Group Task on a Problem to Be Addressed in the Reading. Prior to assigning a reading, ask students to do their own thinking about a problem or question that the reading will address. For example, prior to assigning Plato's *Crito*, the teacher could present the following problem:

In the *Crito*, Socrates has been sentenced to death and waits for his execution. The state, perhaps embarrassed by its decision to kill Socrates, has made it easy for him to escape from prison. In this dialogue, Socrates's friend Crito urges Socrates to escape and go into exile. Socrates argues that his right action is to stay in prison and accept execution. Try to predict the arguments that both Crito and Socrates will make. Give at least three good reasons for escaping and three good reasons for staying and dying.

Having role-played the dialogue in advance (as either an at-home journal assignment or an in-class group task), students will be interested in comparing Plato's actual arguments to the ones they predicted.

Show That All Texts Reflect the Author's Frame of Reference and Thus Are Subject to Interrogation and Analysis

Students often become more interested in scholarly works, even textbooks, when they realize that every author necessarily distorts his or her subject. No textbook or scholarly work can give them the "whole truth" about subject X, only the author's version of the truth—a version necessarily distorted by the author's own selectivity, emphasis, and writing style. Teachers can awaken interest in these issues by photocopying the coverage of subject X from competing textbooks or other scholarly works and by having students explore the differences between them. An excellent example of this strategy is provided by Swartz (1987), who contrasts two anthropological analyses of the role of women in the !Kung society in the African Kalahari. One anthropologist implies that !Kung women live a life of second-class drudgery, while the second anthropologist, observing the same data, cast !Kung women as "a self-contained people with a high sense of self-esteem" (p. 114). Class discussion of the differences in two accounts of the same subject helps students better understand the concepts of point of view, frame of reference, and authorial bias. Once students realize that all texts filter reality by privileging some aspects of X while censoring others, they tend to read more actively, more alert to point of view and to the persuasive power (and distortion) of metaphor, style, and narrative arrangement.

Show Students the Importance of Knowing Cultural Codes for Comprehending a Text

Many students do not realize that a passage from a text can be baffling if the reader does not know its cultural codes. An author assumes that readers have a certain background knowledge. If that knowledge is absent, the reader can quickly get lost.

To illustrate the importance of cultural codes to students, I have developed the following strategy. I place on an overhead projector several cartoons and ask why persons new to U.S. culture might not see what's funny. One of my favorite is a "Far Side" cartoon showing a group of partying dogs hoisting drinks inside a doghouse. One dog is speaking to another; the caption says, "Oh, hey! Fantastic party, Tricksy! Fantastic! . . . Say, do you mind telling me which way to the yard?" Understanding this cartoon requires a surprising amount of cultural knowledge:

That dogs in middle-class America frequently live in doghouses

That at middle-class parties, people stand around holding drinks

That bathrooms are often hard to find in middle-class homes, so guests have to ask the host discretely where they are located

That middle-class homes have backyards

That dogs relieve themselves in the yard

Written texts require similar kinds of background knowledge. After discussing a few cartoons, I distribute a brief news article from the Cold War era, requiring reconstruction of cultural context. The article refers to NATO, to Reagan and Gorbachev, to ballistic and anti-ballistic missiles, to neo-isolationism, and to the way that America's nuclear arms threw the Marxist-Leninist engine of history off its tracks. Few of my students know what NATO is, understand the difference between ballistic and guided missiles, or appreciate the historical events and American attitudes that are packed into the term *neo-isolationism*. Fewer still can explain the "engine of history" metaphor. A discussion of this article quickly clarifies for students how knowledge of cultural codes facilitates comprehension of a reading.

One way to help students reconstruct a text's cultural codes is to create reading guides, the subject of the next strategy.

Create "Reading Guides" for Particularly Difficult Texts or for Texts with Unfamiliar Cultural Codes

Teachers can assist students greatly by preparing "reading guides" that steer them through difficult parts of assigned readings. Typically, these guides define key terms, fill in needed cultural knowledge, explain the rhetorical context of the reading, and ask critical questions for students to consider as they progress through the text. By requiring students to freewrite their responses to several of the guide questions, teachers can use exploratory writing to encourage reflection.

Help Students See That All Texts Are Trying to Change Their View of Something

This strategy relates closely to the preceding one. Students tend to see texts as conveyers of inert information rather than as rhetorically purposeful messages aimed at effecting some change in the reader's view of the subject at hand. If students become more aware that texts are trying to change their views in some way, they can become more active in their desire to interrogate the text by deciding what to accept and what to doubt. A useful exercise to help students appreciate the rhetorical nature of a text is to ask them to freewrite responses to the following trigger questions:

1. Before I read this text, the author assumed that I believed . . . [fill in].
2. After I finished reading this text, the author wanted me to believe . . . [fill in].
3. The author was/was not successful in changing my view. How so? Why or why not?

Teach Students to Play the "Believing and Doubting Game"

The "believing and doubting game" (Elbow, 1973, 1986) teaches students the reader's double role of being simultaneously open to texts and skeptical of them. When playing the believing game, students try to listen empathically by walking in the author's shoes, mentally joining the author's culture, seeing the world through the author's eyes. By stretching students toward new ways of seeing, the believing game helps students overcome their natural resistance to ideas and views different from their own. In contrast, the doubting game asks readers to play devil's advocate, raising objections to the writer's argument, looking for its weaknesses, refusing to be taken in by the text's rhetorical force. To help students practice believing and doubting, the instructor can design exploratory writing tasks, in-class debates, or small group tasks that can encourage students to see both strengths and weaknesses in any author's stance.

Elbow's believing and doubting game is similar to what Paul (1987) calls "dialogical thinking" or "strong sense critical thinking." For Paul, the crucial habit that strong sense critical thinkers must develop is the active disposition to seek out views different from their own: "If we do not have informed proponents of opposing points of view available, we have to reconstruct the arguments ourselves. We must enter into the opposing points of view on our own and frame the dialogical exchange ourselves" (p. 129). Thus, according to Paul, students must be taught "to argue for and against each and every important point of view and each basic belief or conclusion that they are to take seriously" (p. 140). (For an application of methodological belief and doubt to a political science course, see Freie, 1987; see also "Pro and Con Grid" in Angelo and Cross, 1993, pp. 168–171.)

To apply this strategy to the teaching of reading, instructors need to emphasize that scholarly articles and other assigned readings are voices in a conversation that students need to join. For students, writing in the margins or otherwise responding to texts will begin to make sense when they see their responsibility to imagine and consider alternative points of view and thus to evaluate an author's thesis, reasons, and evidence.

Developing Assignments That Require Students to Interact with Texts

To conclude this chapter, let's consider ways that teachers can use exploratory or formal writing assignments to help students become more active and thoughtful readers. When assigned as homework, brief write-to-learn tasks can have a powerful effect on the quality of students' reading. Some of the following strategies are cross-referenced in Chapter Six as widely used methods of assigning exploratory writing.

Marginal Notes Approach

Many teachers report success simply from forbidding students the use of underlining or yellow highlighters. Instead, they insist on copious marginal notations on the borders of the text itself. (If students plan to resell their texts or are reading library books, they can take marginal notes on separate pages keyed to the book page.) "Every time you feel the urge to highlight or underline something," the teacher can advise, "write out why you wanted to underline it in the margins. Why is that passage important? Is it a major new point in the argument? A significant piece of support? A summary of the opposition? A particularly strong or particularly weak point?" The teacher can then exhort the students: "Use the margins to summarize the text, ask questions, give assent, protest vehemently—don't just color the pages." The goal here is to get students to carry on lively dialogue with the author in the margins. The instructor can occasionally start class discussions by asking a student to read his or her marginal notations next to a certain passage.

Focused Reading Notes

Another strategy is to have students take reading notes on sheets of paper divided into four or five columns. For a heading at the top of each column, give students a key word or phrase identifying a theme or concept that you want them to be aware of as they read. For example, in assigning *Crito,* the instructor might give students headings such as "Crito's Values," "Socrates's Values," "Use of Analogies," "City or Family Versus the Individual," and "Your Own Questions or Responses." Students then enter reading notes in the appropriate columns. Students find that even minimal guidance such as this gives them a focusing strategy for their reading. Once students learn this system, teachers can provide new "note headings" for each course reading. As students become skilled at discovering key issues and values in a reading, they can begin developing their own headings.

Reading Logs

Like an open-ended journal, a reading log requires that students write regularly about what they are reading but gives them freedom in choosing what to say. Students can summarize the text, connect it to personal experience, argue with it, imitate it, analyze it, or evaluate it. Often teachers are interested in how a reading affects students on the personal level. They therefore encourage personal response in the reading log. Readers can describe their emotional, intellectual, or philosophical responses to the text and call into consciousness the hidden memories and associations the text triggers. The reader answers questions such as "What does this text mean to me?" and "What effect does this text have on my values, my beliefs, my way of looking at the world?" You can ask students to make these responses regularly in their reading log or occasionally in a more formal reflection paper.

Summary/Response Notebooks

A summary/response notebook is a slightly more structured version of a reading log. It requires students to make two opposing responses to a text: first to represent the text to themselves in their own words and then to respond to it. The following instructions are typical:

For each of the readings marked with an asterisk on the syllabus, you will write at least two pages in your notebooks. The first page will be a restatement of the text's argument in your own words. You can write a summary, make an outline, draw a flowchart or a diagram of the reading, or simply take careful notes. The purpose of this page is to help you understand as fully as possible the structure and details of the author's argument. This page should help you recall the article in some detail several weeks later. Your next page is to be your own personal reflections on or reactions to the article. Analyze it, illustrate it through your own experience, refute it, get mad at it, question it, believe it, doubt it, go beyond it. I will skim your notebooks looking for evidence of serious effort and engaged thought.

Responses to Reading Guides or Guided-Journal Questions Keyed to Readings

Another effective technique is to devise critical thinking questions that require students to respond thoughtfully to a text and then to build these into the course as part of a reading guide or a guided journal. (The guided journal is explained in Chapter Six, pages 107–108.) By providing questions for students to respond to, you can get students to focus on points in the readings you find particularly important. You can often begin class discussions by having one or two students read their responses to one of your questions.

Imagined Interviews with the Author

A change-of-pace strategy is to ask students to write dialogues in which they interview the author or otherwise engage the author in arguments with several antagonists (Francoz, 1979). Often the instructor asks the student, as interviewer, to play devil's advocate, arguing against the author's views and then inventing the author's response. Students generally enjoy the creativity afforded by this assignment, as well as the mind-stretching task of role-playing different views. Some teachers ask groups to conduct mock panel discussions in which one group member plays the author of the article and others play people with different views.

Summary Writing

If one prefers to assign formal writing, an excellent way to promote reading skills is to ask students to write summaries or abstracts of articles (Bean, Drenk, and Lee, 1986; Bean, 1986). Summary writing requires that the reader separate main ideas from supporting details, thereby providing practice at finding the hierarchical structure of an article. Moreover, it requires that readers suspend their own egocentrism, leaving out their own ideas in order to listen carefully to the author. An added bonus for the teacher is that summaries—submitted as microthemes—are easy to grade quickly. (For an example of how an economics professor uses a series of summary assignments to teach argumentation in economics, see Cohen and Spencer, 1993. See also the discussion of summary writing in Chapter Seven, pages 128–129.)

Multiple-Choice Quiz Questions Developed by Students

A useful technique for some courses is to have students write their own multiple-choice quiz questions for each textbook chapter they read in a course. Students might be required to turn in their questions each week. Teachers can provide guidelines for the kinds of questions they want students to write and incorporate student questions into objective quizzes. According to my colleagues who use this strategy, students read texts more perceptively when they write their own test questions. They begin distinguishing between main and subordinate material, between points and data, and between concepts and illustrations.

Writing "Translations"

A final strategy is to ask students to "translate" a difficult passage into their own words (Gottschalk, 1984). According to Gottschalk, "Creating the translation can help the reader see why a passage is important, or troublesome, and come to terms with its difficulties or significance" (p. 401). This is a particularly useful way for students to practice deciphering syntactically complex prose. The act of close paraphrasing also focuses students' attention on precise meanings of words.

Conclusion: Strategies Teachers Can Use to Help Students Become Better Readers

The following list summarizes teaching strategies that address the reading problems discussed in this chapter.

Students' Problem	Helping Strategy
Poor reading process	• Give tests or writing assignments on readings that you don't cover in class. • Require students to write expressively in response to texts (reading logs, summary/response notebooks). • Require marginal notes. • Show students your own reading process.
Failure to reconstruct arguments as they read	• Assign summary writing. • Have students make outlines, flowcharts, or diagrams of articles. • Help students write "gist statements" in margins summarizing main points as reading progresses. • Go through a sample text with students, writing "what it says" and "what it does" statements for each paragraph.
Failure to assimilate the unfamiliar; resistance to uncomfortable or disorienting views	• Explain this phenomenon to students so that they can watch out for it; point out instances in class when students resist an unfamiliar or uncomfortable idea; draw analogies to other times when students have had to assimilate unfamiliar views. • In lectures or discussions, draw contrasts between ordinary ways of looking at the subject and the author's surprising way. • Emphasize the "believing" side of Elbow's "believing and doubting game."
Limited understanding of rhetorical context	• Create reading guides that include information about the author and the rhetorical context of the reading. • Through lectures or reading guides, set the stage for readings, especially primary materials. • Train students to ask these questions: Who is this author? Whom is he or she writing to? What occasion prompted this writing? What is the author's purpose?
Failure to interact with the text	• Use any of the response strategies recommended in this chapter—reading logs, summary/response notebooks, guided journals, marginal notations, reading guides.
Unfamiliarity with cultural codes	• Create reading guides explaining cultural codes, allusions, historical events, and so forth.

- Show students the function of cultural codes by discussing the background knowledge needed to understand cartoons or jokes.

Unfamiliar vocabulary

- Urge students to acquire the habit of using the dictionary.
- Create reading guides defining technical terms or words used in unusual ways.

Difficulty with complex syntax

- Have faith that practice helps.
- Refer severe problems to a learning assistance center.
- Have students "translate" complex passages into their own words; also have students practice rewriting particularly long sentences into several shorter ones.

Failure to adapt to different kinds of discourse

- Explain your own reading process: when you skim, when you read carefully, when you study a text in detail, and so forth.
- Explain how your own reading process varies when you encounter different genres of text: how to read a textbook versus a primary source; how to read a scientific paper; how to read a poem; and so forth.

CHAPTER 9

Coaching Thinking Through the Use of Small Groups

This chapter proposes that one of the best ways to coach critical thinking—and to promote the kind of productive talk that leads to thoughtful and elaborated writing—is a goal-directed use of small groups. The suggestions in this chapter represent only one of many ways to use small groups in the classroom. To use MacGregor's (1990) metaphor for the collaborative learning movement—an "arbor of vines growing in parallel, crossing and intertwining" (p. 29)—the approach taken in this chapter is only one of many vines that comprise the collaborative learning movement. In tracing the origins of these vines, MacGregor identifies and describes at least six different root systems: the experiential learning practices of Dewey, Piaget, and Vygotsky; the "cooperative learning" movement associated with David Johnson and Roger Johnson at the University of Minnesota and Robert Slavin of Johns Hopkins University; the learning community movement, in which teachers, often working together in interdisciplinary teams, become colearners with students in pursuing a complex, many-faceted, multidisciplinary problem; the various disciplinary approaches to small groups, such as Kenneth Bruffee's work in rhetoric and composition or Uri Treisman's work with study groups in mathematics; such problem-centered approaches as Harvard's case method; and the influence of various grant-funded networks of individuals and institutions interested in collaborative approaches to education.

The particular approach to collaborative learning taken in this chapter represents an integration of Hillocks's "environmental mode" of teaching (1986, pp. 113–131), Bruffee's methods of collaborative learning using "consensus groups" (1983, 1984, 1993), and various studies of small group interaction (including D. W. Johnson and F. P. Johnson, 1991). Teachers who already use small groups will have undoubtedly developed methods and approaches somewhat different from those I describe here. However, other teachers may not have tried small groups, preferring to use class time for lecturing, leading whole-class discussions, or conducting other activities that involve the whole class rather than autonomous small groups. My goal in this chapter is to suggest small groups as another strategy for these teachers to consider. The method I describe here might best be characterized as a goal-oriented use of small groups aimed at giving students supervised practice in disciplinary thinking under the tutelage of the teacher as coach. This method has a consistent rhythm: the teacher presents a disciplinary problem requiring critical thinking; students work together in small groups to seek a consensus solution to the problem; and the teacher coaches students' performance by observing their process and critiquing their solutions.

According to Bruffee (1993, pp. 24–25), the pedagogical effectiveness of this method was demonstrated in the late 1950s by Abercrombie's research in educating medical students at University Hospital in London. Abercrombie (1960) found that her students learned diagnostic skills more powerfully if they were placed in independent groups to address a diagnostic problem. The use of small groups did not lead simply to a pooling of knowledge, as if each student held one piece of the solution. Rather, collaborative learning promoted argumentation and consensus building: each student had to support a hypothesis with reasons and evidence in an attempt to sway the others. The improved thinking grew out of the practice of formulating hypotheses, arguing for their adequacy, and seeking a reasoned consensus that all group members could support.

The methods used by Abercrombie in medical training can be extended to classrooms in any discipline. By presenting small groups with critical thinking problems to wrestle with, teachers can create an environment of productive talk that leads to greatly enriched inquiry, analysis, and argument. The goal of each task is not to have small groups come up with the "right answer" but to come up with reasonable, supported answers that they will be asked to defend later in front of the whole class. On occasion, these answers will surprise the teacher with their sophistication and cogency; in my own field of literature, I often find my view of a novel or a poem reshaped by the arguments of my students. Truly, the purported expert can become a colearner in such a setting.

There are several advantages of this goal-directed way of using small groups. First, this approach is particularly effective at helping students learn teacher-specified thinking strategies. Hillocks (1986) and Hillocks, Kahn, and Johannessen (1983) have shown that having students work independently in small groups on purposefully designed and sequenced tasks (what these researchers call the "environmental mode" of teaching) produces significantly higher levels of thinking—as measured by the degree of precision and elaboration in written arguments—than the lecture method, whole-class discussion methods, or nondirective group work.

A second advantage is that the method described here can be adapted to large classes, even in lecture halls where students have to turn around in their seats to form groups. Whereas it is nearly impossible to lead a whole-class discussion in a room of two hundred students, it is entirely possible in a large class to give students a critical thinking task, have students work with their neighbors for ten minutes or so, and then ask representative groups to present and justify their solutions. I have personally made extensive use of small groups in classes of seventy-five students (students sat in five-person groups in a large open room), and I have observed group work conducted in large lecture halls.

Finally, this method can be easily integrated with other teaching strategies. A teacher might lecture for several days, then switch to a day or so of using small group sessions, and then switch again to whole-class discussions or other activities. Or any given day might include a variety of strategies, one of which is a small group session.

Sequence of Activities for Using Small Groups During a Class Period

To work a small group activity smoothly into a class period, teachers might consider the following approach, which combines a small group session with a subsequent plenary session.

Designing the Task

A good small group task, like a good writing assignment, needs to be carefully designed. Good tasks present open-ended critical thinking problems that require solutions justified with supporting arguments. Typical tasks ask students to reach consensus on a solution to a disciplinary problem; when consensus is impossible, students can also "agree to disagree," in which case final group reports will include majority and minority views with clarifying explanations of the causes of disagreement.

Many disciplinary problems can be used interchangeably either as small group tasks or as formal or informal writing assignments (for a heuristic for designing tasks, see Chapter Seven). Small group tasks can also be used in conjunction with a formal writing assignment to help students brainstorm ideas for an upcoming essay, discover and rehearse arguments, or critique rough drafts. In these cases, the small group tasks promote exploration of ideas needed for the essay. In all cases, a good small group task promotes controversy, has a product, can be accomplished in the specified time limit, and is directed toward a learning goal for the course. Further discussion of the design of small group tasks occurs later in this chapter.

Assigning the Task

If possible, the task should be given to students in a handout or on an overhead projector. The task should specify the question or problem to be addressed, the time limit, and the final product. Times specified can be anywhere from a few minutes to a full class hour; however, if teachers want to integrate a complete cycle of activities into a fifty-minute class, they typically limit the small group activity to fifteen to twenty minutes, thereby allowing time for group reporting and critiquing in a plenary session. To keep conversations focused and on task, groups should always be responsible for creating a product—usually a written product such as a thesis statement, list of pros and cons, idea map, outline of an argument, or group-composed paragraph but sometimes an alternative project such as a drawing or a group presentation. The point here is that conversations are generally more focused, elaborated, and sustained when each group has to "go public" with a product. For example, "As a group, discuss your reaction to Plato's *Crito*" is not as effective a task assignment as this:

As a group, propose a list of significant questions you would like to have the teacher address or the class discuss regarding Plato's *Crito*. Your initial list (which you will hand in to the instructor) should include a dozen or so questions. Then reach consensus on what you consider your three best questions. Your recorder will write these questions on the board and will explain to the class why your group considers them pertinent, interesting, and significant questions raised by *Crito*. Time: 15 minutes.

Teachers might consider collecting and critiquing the written products during the first weeks of class as a way of signaling the importance they attach to group work.

Completing the Task

Once students understand the task, the teacher lets the students work on the problem independently. Some teachers believe it is best to leave the room entirely and not to return until it is time for the plenary session. This strategy signals to students their autonomy from the instructor and their responsibility for forming their own knowledge communities. Other teachers like to wander from group to group as a resource person or eavesdrop from a corner of the room. What often surprises teachers is the amount of noise generated by the groups. My own experience suggests that despite the noise, it is best to keep all groups in the classroom rather than to allow some to go into the hall or into separate rooms. The loud hum in the room actually stimulates participation and draws groups close together into tight circles.

Group Reporting

When the allotted time is up, recorders from each group report their group's solution to the class as a whole. (In large classes, the teacher usually asks only a representative sample of groups to report.) Although teachers vary in how they ask students to report, what works best for me is to insist on formal reports from groups: the recorder has to stand and present the group's consensus in an impromptu speech, thus practicing the kind of speaking skills that will be demanded on the job after college. The reports are not supposed to be "summaries of what the group talked about"—like minutes of a meeting—but actual persuasive presentations of each group's consensus solution. By putting pressure on recorders to make effective public speeches, I know the recorders will put pressure on groups to stay on task.

Group Critiquing and Plenary Discussion

As groups report, the teacher begins to move back into the discussion, challenged now by the need to respond productively to group solutions, which are often confounding in their assortment of strong and weak ideas. Disagreement among the groups generally stimulates further discussion of the problem as the class, guided by the instructor, struggles toward a larger consensus. The instructor must help the class synthesize group reports by pointing out strengths and weaknesses while often praising and legitimizing views that are different from his or her own. The students are especially eager to hear the teacher's solution to the collaborative task. In giving it, the teacher not only represents the expert views of the disciplinary community (or one of the expert views) but becomes a powerful role model for the kind of arguing strategies that the discipline uses and values. But the teacher is now more vulnerable, more at risk, than in a lecture setting. After working independently, students are more confident in their own views. They become less passive, more active in raising questions, more challenging as audiences. For me, the class discussions that follow small group work are among the most stimulating, challenging, and satisfying of my all teaching experiences.

Relating the Task to the Learning Sequence

The best small group tasks are clearly related to some ongoing purpose that the teacher should make plain to students. Perhaps the task prepares students for a lecture that follows or focuses attention on key points or controversies in material just covered. Or perhaps the task requires students to sum up and synthesize readings and lectures or to become engaged in a new problem about to be explored in the course. Frequently, also, the task may be integrated with an upcoming formal writing assignment and allows students to talk through their ideas prior to writing. Since many students expect teachers to lecture, they will better accept collaborative work as "serious learning" if the teacher explains how the task relates to course goals. (For an extended example of a history teacher who successfully integrates small group tasks, writing assignments, and lectures into a semester-long course design, see "Arguing and Debating: Breihan's History Course" in Walvoord and McCarthy, 1990).

Typical Small Group Tasks

In my own approach to collaborative learning, I like to identify both a disciplinary content goal and a thinking or arguing goal for each task. Thus, for the *Crito* task described earlier, the teacher's content goal is to stimulate careful reading of *Crito*, to engage students in independent discussion of the text, and to see if students raise the same kinds of questions that have intrigued generations of commentators. (They often do.) The thinking skills goal is to increase students' ability to pose self-sponsored questions about a text.

I find that in designing collaborative tasks, I rely extensively on the following strategies.

1. The Problem-Posing Strategy

In this approach, the instructor gives students a disciplinary problem framed as an open-ended question to which students must propose and justify an answer. To keep students on task, I often ask groups to summarize their answers in one-sentence "thesis statements," which they write on the chalkboard. Recorders then present justifying arguments supporting the thesis when they make their reports. If groups cannot reach consensus, I ask for a majority thesis and at least one minority thesis.

We have examined four alternative approaches to the design of a digital data-recording device for Company X's portable heart defibrillator. Which solution should be chosen and why?

In what way, if any, is Jackson Pollack's *Autumn Rhythm* different from the results of a monkey throwing paint at a canvas?

According to Fullinwider, three theories are frequently used to defend preferential hiring for both African Americans and women: compensatory justice, social utility, and distributive justice. Using one or more of these theories, address this question: Is the legislature's proposed veterans preference law just?

Your author has quoted Peter Berger, an important American sociologist, to the effect that we are in "bondage" to society. Elsewhere that same author says, "In sum, society is the wall of our imprisonment in history." Your friend, I. M. Punker, rubs his hand through his orange hair, touches his nose ring, and says, "Nonsense. I am my own person, free to do whatever I want." Which of these two views does your group most agree with? Defend your choice with arguments.

2. The Frame Strategy

Using this strategy, the instructor gives students a mapping sentence that predicts the shape of a short essay but not the content. Students have to create content topic sentences to head each predicted section and develop a supporting argument for each one. Often the instructor can include in the task a blank tree diagram or an outline indicating the slots that students' ideas must fit. This task requires not only that students generate ideas but also that they place these ideas within a clear structure. (For further examples of frame questions, see Chapter Six, pages 115–116, and Chapter Seven, pages 126–127.)

Based on the data about the Pabst Brewing Company that you studied last night, what do you now think are the causes for this company's precipitous loss of market share? Place your solution into a frame that begins with the following sentence:

> "There are X main causes for Pabst's loss of market share. First, [state the cause and support it] . . . Second, . . . Third, . . ." Continue with as many causes as your group determines.

Although Krauthammer's argument for rebuilding state mental institutions is persuasive in a number of ways, our group finds potential problems with his plan. First, . . . Second, . . . [Third, . . . Fourth, . . .]

3. The Question-Generating Strategy

This strategy is particularly effective for teaching the art of question asking in a discipline. After instruction in the kinds of questions asked by a particular discipline, the teacher breaks students into groups and has them brainstorm possible questions related to topics that he or she provides. After this phase, groups must then refine their lists into the two or three best questions and explain why each question is a particularly good one. (This is the strategy used in the earlier *Crito* example.)

Carefully observe this [poem, graph, statistical table, painting, advertisement]. What aspects of it puzzle you or intrigue you? As a group, pose three good questions that emerge from your observation of the item.

Now that you have studied the six levels of questions in Bloom's taxonomy, use the taxonomy to develop test questions about Chapter Six in your text. Ask at least two questions at each level of the taxonomy. Recorders should be prepared to explain why you think each question fits its respective level.

Scientists often pose research questions that have the following generic structure: "What is the effect of X on Y?" For example, "What is the effect of varying amounts of light on the growth of *Escherichia coli*?" or "What is the effect of an improved freshman advising system on students' retention rate between the freshman and sophomore years?" Using these examples as models, develop three good research questions that you could ask about each of the following topics: steroids, day-care centers, the human immunodeficiency virus, gangs.

4. The Believing and Doubting Strategy

The "believing and doubting game," coined by Elbow (1973, 1986), asks students first to enter imaginatively into the possible truth of any statement, arguing in its favor (the believing game) and then to stand back from it, adopting a healthy skepticism (the doubting game). To use this strategy with small groups, the instructor gives students a controversial thesis and asks them to generate reasons and supporting arguments for and against the thesis. Angelo and Cross (1993, pp. 168–171) discuss a similar strategy using pro and con grids. (For further discussion of the believing and doubting game, see Chapter Seven, page 124, and Chapter Eight, pages 142–143.)

The overriding religious view expressed in *Hamlet* is an existential atheism similar to Sartre's.

Baccalaureate engineering programs should be extended to five years.

The eighty-three-year-old stroke victim described in the case study should be informed of her daughter's terminal cancer.

5. The Evidence-Finding Strategy

The instructor's goal here is to have students find facts, figures, and other data or evidence to support a premise. In my own discipline of literature, this task often means finding textual detail from a poem, novel, or play that might be used to support an argument. In other disciplines, it might mean using data from library, laboratory, or field research. Such tasks teach students how experts in a field use discipline-appropriate evidence to support assertions. (Note that this strategy is ineffective if it leads simply to students' thumbing through their books or lab notes during a collaborative session. I usually assign data-finding tasks several days in advance so that students can find the evidence as homework. Collaborative groups then work to sort, classify, and evaluate the evidence gathered in advance by participants.)

"Our design group recommends the choice of air bearings over conventional steel bearings for this application because air bearings will give better performance at a lower cost." Support this claim with the evidence needed to make it persuasive to both engineers and managers.

"Although Hamlet claims to be putting on an antic disposition, at several places in the play he goes over the line and seems to lapse into genuine madness." What places in the text could be used to support this assertion?

Your textbook describes typical kinds of problematic behaviors that children exhibit in kindergarten. You believe that a particularly unruly child—we'll call him Martin—would benefit emotionally from repeating kindergarten next year rather than entering first grade. Martin's parents are adamantly opposed to holding Martin back. What evidence might you use to help Martin's parents appreciate your side of this issue?

Note that in working on an evidence-finding task, students usually discover what teachers already know: that the evidence is ambiguous and that a strong evidential case can often be made against the thesis as well as for it. Such ambiguity generally unsettles beginning college students, who expect the "experts" to know the right answer and who have not yet realized the extent to which arguers select and shape data to support a point. (See the discussion of Perry's developmental theory in Chapter Two.) Teachers need to help students confront and endure such ambiguity, confident that doing so helps them move higher on Perry's scale of intellectual growth.

6. The Case Strategy

Among the most popular ways to use small groups is to devise cases that require decision-making and justification. If a case involves different roles, each group can initially be assigned one or two of the roles and asked to devise the best arguments it can from the assigned perspectives. (For further discussion of cases and for an example, see Chapter Seven, pages 130–131.)

7. The Norming Session Strategy

This strategy, which is also discussed in Chapters Thirteen and Fifteen, helps students internalize the criteria by which the instructor will judge their formal essays. The instructor passes out three or four student essays from previous classes (with names removed) and lets students, in groups, rank the essays and develop arguments justifying their rankings. Later, in the plenary session, the instructor reveals his or her own rankings and initiates a general discussion of grading criteria for essays. Often teachers discover that students have erroneous notions about what teachers look for in a formal essay, particularly when they are learning the thinking processes and stylistic conventions of new disciplines. (See also Chapter Thirteen, page 219, and Chapter Fifteen, pages 259–262.) For an excellent illustration of how a sociology professor conducts a collaborative norming session (complete with examples of student essays on the topic of ethnocentrism), see Bateman (1990), pp. 110–116. For examples of norming sessions based on freshmen placement essays, see White (1973–1981, 1992).

8. The "Rough Draft Workshop" Strategy

Perhaps the most common use of small groups in writing courses is the "rough draft workshop," in which students read and respond to each other's work in progress. The goal of these workshops is to use peer review to stimulate global revision of drafts to improve ideas, organization, development, and sentence structure. (Chapter Thirteen, pages 222–225, gives detailed suggestions for using small groups for peer review.)

9. The Metacognitive Strategy

Another effective use of small groups, discussed in detail by Bruffee (1993, p. 47), is to ask students to consider their own thinking and negotiating processes metacognitively. This strategy is especially useful when small groups produce solutions that strike you as off-base or just plain wrong. Our authoritarian impulse is to tell the groups that their answers are wrong and show them the right answer. Another approach, however, is to say instead that the class's solutions differ considerably from those of most experts in this field. A subsequent metacognitive task is to send students back into small groups to analyze the differences in reasoning processes between themselves and the experts. According to Bruffee, "The task is to examine the process of consensus making itself. How did the class arrive at its consensus? How do the students suppose that the larger community arrived at a consensus so different from their own? In what ways do those two processes differ?" (p. 47). The effect of this approach, in my experience, is to deepen students' understanding of how knowledge is created: instead of accepting (and perhaps just memorizing) the "right answer" based on the teacher's authority, students struggle to understand the principles of inquiry, analysis, and problem solving used by the experts to arrive at their views. They consider an answer not only a product but also the result of a process of disciplinary conversation.

Making Small Groups Work

The substantial body of research on small group interaction and strategies for team building is too vast to be summarized here, but I can provide a few tips that may prove helpful in making small groups work.

What Is the Best Size for Groups?

Bruffee's review (1993, p. 32) of the research on small group dynamics indicates that the best size for classroom consensus groups is five students; six work almost as well. Groups larger than six are unwieldy and "dilute the experience" for participants. Groups of four tend to divide into pairs, and groups of three tend toward a pair and an outsider. In contrast to in-class consensus groups, long-range "working groups" (collaborating, say, to write a research report together) seem to function best when they are smaller—groups of three seem optimum. Smaller groups also work better for peer review sessions, in which dyads are often appropriate.

How Do You Form a Class into Groups?

If you use groups only occasionally, the standard method is to divide the number of persons in the class by the size of the groups you want and have students count off by that number. Then all the ones go to one part of the room, the twos to another part, and so on. An alternative, of course, is simply to have students form their own groups by moving their chairs from rows into small group circles. I rarely use this method, however, because group sizes tend to vary and because friends end up sitting together, leading to too much "insider" chit-chat. (When you have the class count off by numbers, friends usually get split up.) Although letting friends sit together may be helpful in a large class or on the first day of class, a formal method for establishing groups leads to more businesslike behavior.

When you use groups extensively, it is often a good idea to form permanent or semipermanent groups that can establish bonds among their members. You then need to consider the next question.

Should You Form Groups at Random or According to Some Distributive Scheme?

When forming permanent or semipermanent groups, some teachers like to ensure diversity—different learning styles, different aptitude or skill levels, different majors, different backgrounds, and so forth—so they wait to form permanent groups until they have gathered the appropriate data about their students. Others find that randomly formed groups work adequately. I personally tend toward randomly formed groups, except that I try to make them heterogenous by gender in order to avoid all-male or all-female groups. I also mix non–native speakers in with the rest of the class so that they get as much practice as possible speaking English with native speakers.

What Roles Should Members Play?

Opinion is divided here, for there are numerous ways to organize small groups and assign roles (see D. W. Johnson and F. P. Johnson, 1991). My own preference is to have decentralized leadership by asking groups to select a recorder and a checker for each task, rotating the roles regularly. The recorder's job is to make the report to the plenary session; therefore, the recorder has to keep the group on task, directing the discussion toward the ideas he or she will need to make a good report. In essence, the recorder is both leader and secretary. A dominant person placed in that role has to be quiet in order to get the group's help and take notes; a shy, quiet person in that role has to give a formal presentation at the plenary session and so must practice speaking up during the discussion. The checker has only one role: to make sure that everyone contributes. If someone is not participating, the checker intervenes to urge that the person join the discussion.

How Do You Teach Groups to Work Well Together?

Students need some initial instruction on why you think group work is valuable, what benefits they can expect to get from group activity, and how they can best learn to work together. Much research has been done on ways to teach groups to work together (see Spear, 1988; Golub, 1988; Slavin, 1990; D. W. Johnson and F. P. Johnson, 1991; D. W. Johnson and R. T. Johnson, 1991; Johnson, Johnson, and Smith, 1991; Bruffee, 1993).

One approach is to give students tips on group interaction. I start by explaining Carl Rogers's theory of empathic listening (1961), which forbids person A from expressing disagreement with person B unless person A can accurately summarize person B's argument. I give students an exercise requiring careful listening, giving them practice in walking in someone else's shoes (Bean, 1986).

A teacher can also help students see how differences in learning style, gender, or ethnicity can explain some of the ways that various people behave in groups. For example, extroverts on the Myers-Briggs Type Indicator (MBTI) like to think through an issue by talking out their ideas with others and are therefore apt to be vocal and engaged in group discussions (Jensen and Di Tiberio,

1989). Introverts, in contrast, like to think privately about an issue before talking about it and are often uncomfortable arguing in groups, although they listen carefully and take in what everyone is saying. Teachers can thus point out that quiet people in groups are often listening more carefully and thinking more deeply than their body language might indicate. Such persons, the instructor could explain, often have much to say but will be reluctant to say it until they are ready or until the group gently encourages them to contribute. To take another example, Myers-Briggs "judgers" reach decisions rapidly and are often impatient with an indecisive group that talks a problem to death. In contrast, MBTI "perceivers" resist early closure and want to talk through all possible points of view on an issue before reaching a decision. When students understand such differences in learning styles, they become more tolerant of classmates' behaviors that would otherwise annoy them. (For further discussion of learning styles, see Chapter Three, pages 39–41.)

Other differences worth discussing involve gender and culture. The class might discuss how the socialization of males in American culture tends toward decision making based on abstract rigorously applied principles, whereas females tend to be more concerned with the interpersonal dimension of decision making (Belenky, Clinchy, Goldberger, and Tarule, 1986; Gilligan, 1982). At the cultural level, the teacher might explain that Americans often state their desires bluntly and assertively in ways that would seem rude in many Asian cultures, where the expression of desire would be masked in roundabout conversation.

Another approach for helping groups work well together is to explain to students the positive value of conflict. I explain that the creative dialectic of thesis-antithesis-synthesis works well only in an atmosphere of conflicting views. By showing students how conflict generates creative thinking, the teacher can help students welcome disagreements and see how a watered-down compromise that no one really likes is less valuable than a true synthesis that seems better than either of the original views.

To promote healthy conflict, the teacher can discuss "egothink" and "clonethink." One kind of group dysfunction (egothink) occurs when members simply express vociferously their own opinions without trying to reach a higher level of understanding. The converse phenomenon (clonethink) occurs when the group quickly agrees with the first expressed view and decides that its task is over. Effective groups need to monitor their discussions, trying to steer a middle road between egothink and clonethink.

In addition to giving tips about group interaction, teachers can help students work in groups by providing regular opportunities for self-monitoring. At fairly regular intervals, groups need to shift their focus from the task at hand to an evaluation of their own group process (Morton, 1988). At the conclusion of a group task, for example, the instructor could ask students to freewrite their responses to a question such as this: "How well did your group work together on this task?" Then students could be asked to share their responses with the group. Students need opportunities to get problems and frustrations out on the table and talk through them.

Another self-monitoring strategy is to give students questionnaires that ask them to rate their own group skills in such areas as active listening, making contributions, encouraging others to speak, and keeping the conversation on task. D. W. Johnson and F. P. Johnson (1991) provide numerous examples of self-monitoring questionnaires for groups.

The Controversy over Using Small Groups: Objections and Responses

Of course, not all teachers are as enthusiastic about small group work as I am. Many teachers choose not to use small groups in the classroom for pragmatic, pedagogical, or philosophical reasons. Before closing out this chapter, I would like to respond briefly to some of the objections that my colleagues have raised against using small groups. My purpose is not to be polemical but simply to clarify some of the issues in ways that might help professors decide what role, if any, the use of small groups might play in their own teaching.

Using Small Groups Takes Minimal Teacher Preparation or Skill

Perhaps the most frequent objection made by my own colleagues is that using small groups seems like a lazy way of teaching requiring little out-of-class effort or in-class teaching skill. Compared with the time and scholarship needed to prepare a good lecture, the preparation time for small group work seems minimal: put the students in groups, ask them a question, leave the room, and *voilà*, you're an innovative teacher.

In response, I must acknowledge that small group teaching looks easy—in fact, its practitioners can sometimes be observed wandering the halls while their students are working in groups. However, as with other modes of instruction, there are well-prepared and ill-prepared users of small groups. The well-prepared teacher is hardly lazy: the use of small groups described here is a goal-directed form of teaching that places heavy emphasis on task sequencing and overall course design. Planning a good small group task demands articulation of course goals, identification of a particular goal to be addressed in the task, design of the task, and placement of the task within a sequence of learning activities, many of which include lectures and other kinds of class discussions. Thus, the preparation time for using small groups can be extensive. In-class teaching skills come into play during group reports and plenary sessions, where the teacher integrates class discussion with short lectures that present the teacher's (or the discipline's) expert perspectives on the problem the groups have just addressed. For me, the whole-class discussions that follow a collaborative learning task are among my most intense, most productive, and most challenging experiences as a teacher and a learner. (For a discussion of how a peer observer should evaluate a course taught through collaborative learning, see Wiener, 1986.)

Small Group Work Reduces the Amount of Time Students Spend with the Teacher

Another objection to small groups is that it reduces classroom contact between student and professor. Students pay tuition to learn from professors, not sit in groups with the professor absent. At one workshop I shall never forget, a professor excoriated me: "Collaborative learning is unethical. I would be abdicating my professional responsibilities if I deprived students of time spent with me as teacher, especially when they are yet untrained to work independently." Behind this objection is the obvious fear that small groups leave the blind leading the blind.

In defense of small groups, however, I would argue that small group sessions are not really time away from the teacher (who has constructed the task and is observing behavior) any more than a scrimmage game at basketball practice is time away from the coach. Nor does collaborative learning let the blind lead the blind. A better metaphor might be novices practicing with novices under the tutelage of the teacher as coach. In any discipline, the progress of new learners ought to be measured, at least partly, by what they can do independently of the teacher when face to face with a new disciplinary problem requiring critical thinking. What we aim for is their ability, when confronting a new problem, to think and write like members of our discipline. What goal-directed small group work provides is supervised practice at these skills.

What distinguishes this process from the blind leading the blind is the teacher's systematic intervention. An essential feature of this approach to collaborative learning is the teacher's critique of the students' performances at the conclusion of a task. These critiques start as conversations between the teacher and group recorders, who must present a sustained argument in response to the problem posed in the collaborative task. Soon the conversation expands to include the whole class. Disagreements between teacher and students promote genuine discourse because the students, emboldened by group support, are not simply passive note takers. The teacher must become a true rhetor, representing the discipline by bringing the best reasons to bear on the teacher's claims. In hearing the teacher's response, students have access not only to the teacher's thinking and knowledge but also to the way arguments are structured and elaborated in the discipline. And in arguing back, in differing from the teacher's views, students move toward becoming autonomous thinkers who can join the conversation of the discipline.

Collaborative Learning Is Based on Social Constructivist Theories of Knowledge

Objectors on these grounds cite Kenneth Bruffee's argument (1983, 1984, 1993) that collaborative learning reflects a nonfoundational, social constructivist view of knowledge. Based on an epistemology derived from Richard Rorty, Thomas Kuhn, Clifford Geertz, Erving Goffman, and others, collaborative learning promotes, according to some of my colleagues, a dismaying philosophical relativism. Thus, Bruffee accepts as nonproblematic what he calls a nonfoundational view of knowledge, which "assumes that we construct and maintain knowledge not by examining the world but by negotiating with one another in communities of knowledgeable peers" (1993, p. 9). However, many of my own colleagues object to this view from a variety of empirical, idealist, and phenomenological perspectives.

My response here is that the philosophical relativism of collaborative learning depends on the way that teachers themselves regard their own knowledge. Certainly no practitioner of collaborative learning believes that the solutions generated by student groups are all equally valid. The purpose of the plenary sessions is to critique the novices' solutions according to the rules of argument in the discipline. The question is, does the teacher believe that the profession's solutions are also socially constructed? Bruffee apparently does, whereas many of my colleagues do not.

My own personal bent is to finesse this controversy by turning from the philosophical issues toward the pragmatic concern of what works in the classroom to teach critical thinking, and for me a goal-directed use of small groups works whether the teacher has a foundational or a nonfoundational view of knowledge. As a pedagogical tool for teaching thinking, what is central to this approach to small groups is its consistent rhythm: the presentation of a teacher-designed problem, student practice at conducting an inquiry to solve the problem, and teacher critique of the students' performance. Such a teaching method does not depend on the teacher's endorsement of a Rortian view of knowledge.

It seems impossible, however, to avoid the political implications of collaborative learning, which does, I think, decenter the teacher. In a collaborative classroom, the teacher's arguments compete with arguments coming from various student groups. These arguments cannot simply be dismissed by an appeal to authority. The teacher must defend his or her views through the rules of reason. As a teaching method, collaborative learning is thus powerfully symbolic in conveying to students a view of academic life as rational dialogue rather than right answers dispensed by an authority.

Small Group Work Devalues Eccentricity and Teaches Social Conformity

According to these objections, the ideal of group consensus stifles creativity by forcing a leveling of talents. These objectors say that group work devalues the individuality of our potential artists, rebels, eccentrics, loners, and geniuses. From a Marxist perspective, collaborative learning is simply the latest example of how the colleges serve the needs of capitalists (Myers, 1986a). Today's business world no longer wants colleges to produce free-thinking individualists; it wants genial, cooperative team players. Thus, collaborative learning becomes the new fad among educators at the same time that the fiercely independent, cigar-chewing boss is being replaced by the committee and the team.

These objectors are right in asserting that some students work better individually than in groups. But unless we reject completely the goal of preparing students for careers after college, it would be unfortunate indeed if these individualistic students had no experience whatever working in groups. Given that teamwork and committee work are essential parts of professional life in America, even our most eccentric geniuses can benefit from collaborative learning, which can serve as a learning laboratory for problems students will face throughout their lives.

The other branch of this objection—that collaborative learning values consensus over difference—seems grounded in a false premise equating consensus with conformity. There is a qualitative difference between conformity—an easy and quick acquiescence to the first thesis produced by a group member—and a synthesis reached through dialectic conversation. In my own experience, group work does not suppress eccentric and individualistic ideas but in fact gives them a chance to be aired and tested in group conversation. Often creative insights come from shy persons who would never venture their ideas in front of the teacher and the whole class. What I observe in small groups is a lot of genuine exploration, elaboration, and shifting of ideas. Collaborative learning, far from promoting conformity, gives students opportunities to flex their own muscles, to push against the teacher, to try out their own wings.

Conclusion: Some Additional Advantages of Small Groups _____

I have argued in this chapter that using small groups in the classroom can be a powerful form of active learning, giving students the opportunity to practice disciplinary inquiry and argumentation under the tutelage of a teacher as coach. Hillocks (1986) and others have demonstrated the effectiveness of the method in producing measurable advances in the quality of thinking reflected in student writing. In addition, it gives students space to pursue their own lines of thought and test them against the thinking of their professors.

In closing, I would like to mention the social advantages of collaborative learning—advantages that should not be lightly dismissed. These are the ways that collaborative learning promotes student interaction and friendships, develops leadership skills, and celebrates diversity. Students in a collaborative learning class get to know each other well. Groups meet outside of class for coffee or meals. They exchange phone numbers. They sign up together for classes in later terms. The significance of this interpersonal dimension became especially apparent to me when I opened a letter from a former student:

> Of course, I've never forgotten the small-group work we students did in your . . . class two years ago, but now I can understand more clearly the value of that small-group work. Especially after spending a couple years in Japan and experiencing a certain "culture shock" upon my return to this country, I realized that there is a great lack of interpersonal trust in American society. . . . What strikes me now about the small-group work we did in your class is that it reinforces interpersonal trust, cooperation, sharing. . . . That kind of small-group work encourages people to be social beings and does much more than simply teach people how to revise a term paper. . . . I think that this trust-building dimension of small-group work should be its greatest selling point to school administrators, etc.

Another advantage of collaborative learning is the practice it gives in leadership, group interaction, and public speaking. Collaborative learning is particularly effective at increasing the leadership skills of female students and for getting male students used to turning to women for help in pressure situations.

Finally, collaborative learning takes advantage of the rich diversity of students at many of today's colleges and universities. In almost all of the collaborative groups I have established at my own university, traditionally aged American students have been integrated with international students and older students, many of whom bring fascinating, troubling life experiences to bear on issues related to the course. The opportunity to stimulate conversations of consequence among such diverse groups of people and to promote friendships among them is one of the joys of teaching through small groups.

CHAPTER 10

Alternative Approaches to Active Learning in the Classroom

Chapter Nine focused on the use of small groups to promote critical thinking and active learning. This chapter turns to other classroom teaching strategies that promote active exploration of ideas through talking and writing. In most of these strategies, the instructor encourages inquiry by presenting students with disciplinary problems that stimulate critical thinking and by making students responsible for formulating their solutions in language, either spoken or written. (For more comprehensive treatments of active learning, see Bonwell and Eison, 1991; Meyers and Jones, 1993; and Davis, 1993.)

Increasing Active Learning in Lecture Classes

Lecture courses, by nature, place students in a passive role and imply a transmission theory of knowledge in which students "receive" the ideas and information "sent" by the instructor. Johnson, Johnson, and Smith (1991) provide a helpful summary of the problems with lecture teaching based on research into such matters as listener attention span, learning styles, retention patterns, and levels of reasoning stimulated by different modes of instruction. They conclude that although lectures are appropriate in many circumstances, they tend to reach only those students who "learn auditorily, have high working memory capacity, have all the required prior knowledge, have good note-taking

skills, and are not susceptible to information-processing overload" (p. 89).

Fortunately, there are many ways to make lecturing more
effective for a wider range of learners. Johnson, Johnson, and
Smith suggest a variety of cooperative education techniques for
getting students more involved in listening to and processing a
lecture. Their approach is similar to many of the teaching strategies recommended by Davis (1993), who cites research noting that
students have, on average, attention spans of approximately ten
to twenty minutes (p. 99). Consequently, Davis shows, the most
successful lecturers change the pace several times during a class
session by breaking the lecture into parts punctuated by student-
centered activities in which the instructor gives students a problem to solve at their seats, switches to discussion for a few
moments, assigns an in-class freewrite, and so forth. As we have
seen elsewhere in this book, astute use of formal or informal writing assignments—integrated into the overall course design—can
also make students more active learners in lecture courses. This
section reviews several active learning strategies specifically
adapted to lecture courses.

Use Cooperative Learning Groups to Help Students Listen to Lectures

Johnson, Johnson, and Smith (1991, pp. 91–92) recommend that
instructors design their lectures so that the cooperative learning
groups can help one another absorb the lecture content. The
groups can be simply pairs (if students are seated in a large lecture
hall) or groups of three to five (if movable chairs are available). The
class time proceeds according to the following rhythm.

1. Opening discussion (five or six minutes) in learning groups
   in response to a question presented by the instructor or to an
   "advance organizer" that outlines the upcoming lecture.

2. First lecture segment, lasting ten to fifteen minutes, "about the
   length of time an adult can concentrate on a lecture" (p. 91).

3. Learning group discussion based on a question presented
   by the lecturer (four or five minutes). Each person answers
   the question individually and then compares answers with
   group members. Before proceeding with the lecture, the
   instructor asks one or two groups to summarize their
   answers as a check on learning.

4. Second lecture segment, followed by discussion period.
   Continue this alternation as time allows.

5. Final discussion aimed at summarizing the whole lecture and integrating it into students' previous knowledge.

An alternative way of handling the discussion between lecture segments is to use what Johnson, Johnson, and Smith (1991) call "cooperative notetaking" (pp. 97–98). With this strategy, the instructor asks student pairs to compare their lecture notes and help each other flesh them out.

Require Lecture Summaries

Another strategy for promoting better listening is to have students write one-page summaries of your lectures. At the beginning of each class, collect the previous day's lecture summaries; later, read a random selection as a check on student understanding. Chemistry professor Richard Steiner (1982) reports two benefits from this process: students learned more from the lectures, and the instructor was able to make adjustments in his lectures based on his new awareness of problem areas. (For further discussion of summaries, see Chapter Seven, pages 128–129, and Chapter Eight, pages 145–146.)

Develop Guided-Journal Tasks Keyed to Your Lectures

In this approach, the instructor designs guided-journal tasks that require students to use concepts or information from the lectures. For example, tasks can ask students to link lecture material to their own experiences, to apply lecture material in new contexts, to argue for or against certain propositions in the lectures, or to raise new questions. The key here is to design tasks that cannot be completed unless the student pays close attention to the lectures.

Another use of guided-journal tasks (or in-class freewrites) is to engage students with a problem that the day's lecture will address or to activate prior learning and personal experience that will facilitate learning of new material. The teacher's goal here is to till the soil prior to planting the seeds in lecture. (See Chapter Six, pages 107–108, for an explanation of guided journals; see Chapter Seven for suggestions on the design of tasks.)

Conduct Feedback Lectures

In a feedback lecture, the instructor stops at an appropriate point in a lecture and asks students to write for several minutes on what is currently puzzling them or gives students a thought problem keyed to the current point in the lecture. The instructor then asks a student or two to read what they have written or collects a random sampling for reading after class. These freewrites serve as a means of intellectual communication between students and teacher and provide a window into students' thinking processes. Besides providing valuable feedback for the lecturer, the freewrites serve as a kind of seventh-inning stretch for students, refocusing their attention and increasing listening during the last part of the class period. Angelo and Cross (1993, pp. 148–153) call this approach the "minute paper."

Deliver Narrative Lectures That Model the Thinking Process

Another way to promote critical thinking is to model it. Occasionally give a lecture that takes students through your own thinking process in addressing a problem or that summarizes the history of scholarship on a classic disciplinary problem. At the beginning of the lecture, pose the problem that puzzled you or your disciplinary community. Then, in detective story fashion, re-create for students the process of your thinking (or your discipline's collective thinking), complete with false starts, hunches that did not work out, frustrations, and excitement. (In effect, this is your own "lecture version" of the exploratory essay explained in Chapter Five, pages 92–93.) Used to regarding their professors as repositories of received knowledge, students enjoy seeing them occasionally as active critical thinkers wrestling with a problem.

Ask Students to Question Your Lectures

If appropriate to your discipline, at the beginning of a lecture or a series of lectures, introduce a major question or issue that your lectures will address, telling students that not all scholars in your discipline will agree with your views. Then give students a writing assignment in which they have to summarize your "answer" to the question and respond to it through analysis and further questioning. Perhaps they will even be persuaded to argue against your position. The point is to help students see your lectures as arguments rather than as mere information.

Design a Formal Writing Assignment in Which Students Must Integrate Lecture Material

Another good strategy is to develop a writing assignment that cannot be accomplished unless students have thoroughly understood lecture material. One suggestion is to create an assignment that compares a point of view you have taken in a series of lectures with an alternative point of view they learn about through assigned readings or library research.

Increasing Active Learning in Discussion Classes

Whereas lecturing is often regarded as a passive form of instruction for students, most teachers think of discussion classes as active. However, discussion classes often fail to produce the kind of active learning desired. Particularly problematic are discussions in which the teacher simply tries to elicit correct answers, bull sessions where the discussion wanders aimlessly, and guessing-game discussions where the students are not asked genuine questions but are led to guess "what the instructor is thinking." Another problem with discussion classes, paradoxically, is that the teacher frequently monopolizes the talking. Brown and Atkins (1988) summarize research studies of discussion classes showing how often teachers, without realizing it, dominate the talk time; one study showed that teachers talked about 86 percent of the time, even though these teachers saw themselves as leading a discussion (p. 59). A related problem is that in many cases, the discussion is carried on by only a few students, while the majority (usually many more than the teacher realizes) listen passively. Davis (1993) cites studies reporting that in classes of fewer than forty students, "four or five students accounted for 75 percent of the total interactions per session" (p. 79). And even in discussions where there is lively give-and-take throughout the whole class, there often is not enough "space" for any one student to develop a point at length. A student is often cut off in midargument by the next person who wants to contribute. Indeed, as we all know from personal experience, participants in discussions often spend their time planning out the next point they want to contribute rather than listening actively to fellow participants.

The following suggestions address some of these problems.

Increase Wait Time

A simple strategy for improving class discussion is to increase your "wait time" after asking a question. Studies (including Rowe, 1987) have shown that many teachers, after asking a question, rarely wait more than a few seconds before initiating discussion (if hands go up) or giving prompts (if hands do not go up). Instead, try waiting fifteen or thirty seconds (or even a full minute) before calling on the first person. As hands start going up, acknowledge students with eye contact, but say quietly, "Let's wait for a few moments until everyone has formulated an answer." This approach gives all class members time to engage the question. Even better, let students free-write for several minutes following your opening question of the day. You can then begin discussion by asking one or more students to read their opening freewrites. Shy students can often be drawn into the discussion if they are asked to read a freewrite.

Use Discussion Strategies Derived from Inquiry Teaching

An extensive body of literature focuses on whole-class discussion techniques for promoting inquiry and critical thinking. The literature addresses the kinds of questions to ask, strategies for responding to student contributions, and techniques for keeping discussion on track and moving forward. Although the literature is too extensive to summarize here, it reveals, in general, that inquiry teachers pose the same kinds of open-ended critical thinking problems used by collaborative learning teachers. However, they prefer to guide whole-class discussions themselves rather than to relinquish the time to independent small groups. Of course, many teachers move back and forth easily between whole-class discussions and use of small groups. (For instructors interested in whole-class inquiry techniques, I especially recommend Welty, 1989; Bateman, 1990; Gulette, 1992; Davis, 1993, pp. 63–95; and the collections of essays in Wilen, 1987, and Christensen, Garvin, and Sweet, 1991.)

Use Out-of-Class Exploratory Writing to Prime the Pump

The use of learning logs, dialectic journals, reading logs, thought letters, or guided-journal tasks can prime the pump for class discussions. By designing your course so that out-of-class exploratory writing is keyed to in-class discussion topics, you can greatly increase your class's readiness to engage in lively discussion. See Chapter Six for advice on how to use exploratory writing.

Use Interest-Generating Questionnaires to Stimulate Discussions

Davis (1993) sometimes begins class discussions by distributing a brief questionnaire eliciting students' initial positions on issues or problems relevant to the day's discussion material. She collects the signed questionnaires and then uses them to stimulate discussion: "Ellen, I see you answered the first question in the negative. Daniele, I note that you disagree with Ellen," or, "Amber, your answer to question four is intriguing. Can you tell us more?" (p. 68).

Have Students Generate the Questions to Be Discussed

Steffens (1989) reports a technique for increasing engagement with readings and for making students more active learners in class. He has students in his history seminars generate the questions to be addressed in class discussion. When students have completed a new assigned reading for the course, he puts them in small groups to generate lists of questions raised by the readings. He reports that these initial discussions about questions are themselves lively and profitable. Each group has to reach consensus on one or two key questions group members would like the class to discuss. Once groups have reported their questions, the whole class works together to rank them. From then on, the format switches from small group discussion to whole-class discussion, with the teacher now participating in addressing the questions raised by the students. Steffens summarizes the process and the benefits this way: "As the semester continued, students came to class with their favorite questions already in mind. As soon as they arrived, they sat with their groups and began working out the questions for the day. . . . The wealth of questions helped to reinforce the intended impression that learning about the seventeenth century, or any other historical topic, can never be finished and over with. There is always more of interest to investigate" (p. 128).

Early in the Course, Hold a Discussion About Discussions

Davis (1993, pp. 76–77) suggests a valuable strategy for use early in a course. Make two columns on the chalkboard, one headed "characteristics of good classroom discussions" and the other headed "characteristics of poor classroom discussions." Let students, calling on their own experiences, brainstorm the features of effective and ineffective discussions. Based on ideas emerging from the class, develop criteria for good discussions, focusing on both student and teacher behaviors. This approach gives teachers an idea of what students expect from their instructors in leading a discussion, while also highlighting the responsibilities of students.

Consider Time-Outs to Write the Discussion

Sometimes discussions get so heated that more hands are in the air than you can call on. One way to promote thoughtful learning in such a situation is to stop for five minutes and have everyone freewrite the contribution he or she wants to make to the group. This method gives students the "space" to articulate their arguments without fear of being interrupted before they can get their own ideas clarified. Once the freewrites are completed, the instructor can resume the class discussion, perhaps by inviting several students to summarize their freewrites.

Using Alternative Classroom Activities _____

The suggestions so far have been aimed at increasing active learning in the traditional classroom settings of lectures or whole-class discussions. The teacher's goal in these settings is to increase the number of students actively engaged in critical thinking, either by involving more students in classroom discussions or by extending and deepening the classroom discussions through the use of writing. The rest of this chapter is devoted to alternative classroom formats or settings that can promote critical thinking and active learning.

Classroom Debates

The classroom debate, focusing on a controversial proposition related to a key course issue, can generate considerable class enthusiasm. The following suggestions for holding classroom debates can be adopted to most classroom settings.

Suggestions for Holding an In-Class Debate

I. Choose a debatable issue.
   A. Be sure the issue is pertinent to the learning goals of the course, is of interest to the students, and includes plausible arguments on both sides.
   B. If the issue requires research, be sure the material is readily accessible through course texts, previous lectures, library reserve, and so forth.
II. Formulate the issue in a clear, positive proposition.
   A. Avoid lengthy, ambiguously worded propositions.
   B. Make sure key terms are stated so that a simple "definition of terms" can be made.
   C. Avoid negatives in the proposition.
III. Carefully prepare the class for the debate.
   A. Through lecture, reading, and discussion, prime the students for the debate by covering needed background and context, but do not exhaust the arguments on both sides or show favoritism to one side.
   B. Determine the *time allotments* of each speaker. Hold them to this exactly in order to keep the debate within one class period. For a fifty-minute class, try the following allotments:
      Affirmative (5 minutes)
      Negative (5 minutes)
      Affirmative (5 minutes)

Negative (5 minutes)

(Break: 5 minutes)

Negative rebuttal of affirmative (3 minutes)

Affirmative rebuttal of negative (3 minutes)

Negative's response (3 minutes)

Affirmative's response (3 minutes)

Total time: 37 minutes (This allows about ten minutes at the end for judges' reports.)

C. Explain the responsibilities of each speaker:

First affirmative: define the main terms and outline of the affirmative case.

First negative: contest any badly defined terms and outline the negative case.

Second affirmative and second negative: complete the case, especially with evidence.

Rebuttals: show weaknesses in the most important arguments of the opposing case.

D. If you have time, you can add a two-minute "cross-question" period after each of the four speeches. The opposing side can ask any questions of the speaker but must give time for answers and not turn the cross-question period into a speech.

IV. Set up teams.

A. Teams can consist of two, four, or five persons (for cross-question debate).

B. Students not debating are judges and must keep a record of the arguments and a verdict.

C. Allow teams adequate time to prepare the case, at least a weekend or a full week.

D. Sometimes it is helpful to allow a class period or half-period for teams to meet, especially the day before the debate. In two-hour classes, the first hour can be used.

V. Hold the debate.

A. Keep time exactly, and insist on a close following of the format.

B. End with a report from each judge: verdict with reasons (based on notes).

VI. Follow up: It can be very helpful to have each student write up a two- or three-page summary of either the affirmative or the negative side of the debate in a speech or essay format. Insist that these summaries be coherent and not merely journalistic accounts of who said what. Include thesis, reasons, and evidence.

"Meeting of the Minds" Panel

An alternative to the classroom debate is a Steve Allen–style "meeting of the minds" panel discussion in which students are assigned to role-play different figures who bring alternative points of view to the discussion topic. For example, in a psychology course, Sigmund Freud, B. F. Skinner, and Carl Rogers could discuss the causes of teenage pregnancy. Prior to the panel, one group of students would prepare to role-play Freud, another Skinner, and a third Rogers. Each group would select its "actor" for the actual panel.

Fishbowls

In the fishbowl strategy, a small number of students are selected to sit in "hot seats" in the center of class, where they respond to critical thinking questions about subject matter that have been passed out several days in advance. The rest of the class, seated around the students in the fishbowl, gets to critique the performance of the fishbowl students after the session. Pressure to perform well in the fishbowl motivates at-home study.

Paper Presentations

In this strategy, which adapts to a large class some of the strategies of seminar teaching, the professor staggers due dates of short formal papers rather than having them due all at the same time. The strategy works best if the formal papers are short enough to fit on one single spaced page. At each class meeting, one or two papers are due, depending on the size of the class, the length of the term, and the number of required essays. Through prior course design, the instructor gives different assignment topics to each student so that the papers due on any given day coincide with that day's discussion topic. Students come to class with enough photocopies of their essay for all their classmates, and each day's discussion is initiated by the arguments in the papers due that day. Some teachers then give students several additional days to revise their papers in light of the classroom critique and ensuing discussion. Teachers report that the pressure to "go public" forces students to do their best work and that the quality of the papers initiates excellent classroom discussion of the material. The paper load is easy for the instructor to handle because it involves grading only one or two papers each day—all of which have been critiqued in class at the draft stage several days earlier.

Paper Chase–Style Cold-Calling

In the classic 1973 movie *The Paper Chase,* Professor Kingsfield presents a powerful, chilling image of the rigorous professor. His style is to pose a thinking problem and to call on students at random, grilling them mercilessly, each question followed by a more complicated one. Sheer terror motivates his students. His goal, in the jargon of social construction, is to induct them into the discourse community of lawyers. He never asks questions that elicit "correct answers"; rather, each question forces students to formulate an argument supported by chains of reasons and evidence.

Although Kingsfield the man is few persons' model of the ideal teacher, his pedagogical goals are like those of other teachers of critical thinking. Whereas the collaborative learning instructor gives critical thinking problems to small groups or the discussion teacher to the whole class, the "cold-calling" professor gives them to one student at a time in front of the whole class. Though one can hardly recommend Kingsfield's style (he drives one poor student toward suicide), many of my colleagues use similar techniques with great effectiveness (including extremely positive student evaluations). Because the method has the frightening potential to devastate many students—especially beginning students—teachers who use it successfully with undergraduates seem to combine Kingsfield's commitment to the discipline with a nurturing concern for students. Their positive regard of students is revealed through in-class humor, patient explanation of how this strategy teaches the "thinking on your feet" skills students will need in their careers, and the teachers' ability to encourage students who perform poorly. They soften the Kingsfield image by learning students' names, smiling, speaking to students before and after class, encouraging them to come to office hours, writing notes to students, greeting them in the halls, and the like. Thus, cold-calling, if wedded in some way to warmth and care, can be a powerful means of stimulating critical thinking.

Case Studies and Simulation Games

Case studies and simulation games can be useful across a wide range of disciplines. A case study usually presents a fictional scenario leading up to one or more dilemmas requiring problem solving or decision making. When class time is used to act out the case, with different students being assigned different roles to play, the case study becomes a simulation game. Common simulations include mock trials, mock city council or legislative meetings, and mock meetings of corporation stockholders or school boards.

Usually, the simulation assignment includes background information on the problem, biographical synopses for each role in the simulation, and packets of data bearing on the problem. Simulation games can be combined with writing assignments in which participants do the kind of writing appropriate to their role (legal briefs, letters to the editor, proposals, and so forth). (For further discussion of cases, see Chapter Seven, pages 130–131.)

Group Papers

Another fairly common practice is the group or collaborative paper in which teams of students work together to write one paper. This method is an attractive way of reducing the teacher's paper-grading load while giving students extensive practice at the kinds of group interactions common in professional life. Team writing or joint authorship is common in business and the sciences, so these disciplines are particularly well suited for group papers, but many humanities professors use the strategy also. Here, for example, is a group assignment for a course in business ethics, from philosophy professor Kenneth Stikkers.

Instructions for Group Project

You will be assigned to a group to argue, using empirical evidence, for or against one of the following statements:

   a. Capitalism provides fertile ground for the cultivation of virtue.
   b. Equality, justice, and a respect for rights are characteristics of the American economic system.
   c. A concern for ethics significantly undermines one's chances for success in a competitive market economy.

   1. Consider material from Chapters Three and Four of your text as you begin to develop strategies for your argument. Also, be sure to define key terms in the proposition you are defending or refuting.
   2. There will be no regular class on Thursday, [date]. You will have this time to use in whatever way your group judges best—for example, brainstorming, strategizing, or preliminary library research. Additional group meetings will have to be arranged by the groups themselves.
   3. Each group will submit on Tuesday, [date], a formal essay presenting the best argument it can make for the position it has been assigned to argue. Who will be responsible for what tasks and how the essay will be written—for example, who will be responsible for its typing—are matters to be decided by the group.
   4. Supporting arguments and evidence in the essays must be adequately and properly documented by means of footnotes or endnotes. Each essay must have a substantial bibliography—at least three good entries for each group member.

5. Each essay must run to at least five pages. The instructor is more interested in the quality of arguments than in the quantity of information.
6. The instructor will evaluate each group essay, and each person will evaluate the contribution of his or her group's members to the group effort. Individual grades will be based on both evaluations. (The instructor has each student fill out an evaluation sheet ranking the contributions each group member made to the group. The instructor then determines a grade for each individual using a formula based on the group grade for the paper and the individual rankings provided by the groups.)

(For further examples of collaborative writing assignments, including a sample peer evaluation sheet, see Lunsford and Ede, 1990, pp. 251–258.)

In-Class Games and Nonverbal Activities

Many teachers have reported success in developing activities that involve ways of knowing other than the strictly verbal. Mathematicians have developed classroom games that teach mathematical reasoning. Literature professors regularly have students stage dramatic scenes in their literature classes or produce drawings or group tableaux that represent their interpretation of important moments in a literary work. In a religious studies course on liturgy, students have to invent a new ritual and invest it with religious significance or create their own myths and convert them into paintings, sculpture, dance, or music. A common assignment in counseling classes is to have the person being counseled create a typical family scene and assign other students in the class to act out typical family roles. In both communications classes and foreign-language classes, students are being taught how to "read" body language and to be better attuned to the politics of space in different cultures. All these are examples of classroom activities that engage a wide variety of learning styles.

Conclusion: Engaging Ideas Through Active Learning

Through strategies that promote active learning, teachers hope to make students more engaged and inquisitive learners, more powerful thinkers, and better arguers. Outside the classroom, a good way to stimulate active learning is to assign exploratory or formal writing that presents students with critical thinking problems keyed to the reading and learning objectives of the course. In the classroom, active learning can be promoted through small group work as detailed in Chapter Nine or through other kinds of teaching methods and learning activities, as suggested in this chapter. Through a mixture of such methods, instructors hope to maximize students' intellectual growth.

CHAPTER 11

Enhancing Learning and Critical Thinking in Essay Exams

Essay exams play an important yet problematic role in any writing-across-the-curriculum program. This chapter examines the pedagogical and theoretical problems posed by essay exams and then suggests ways that some of them may be overcome. It also describes strategies for helping students improve their ability to write essay exams.

The Importance of Essay Exams

Professors who value writing in their courses often take special pride in their use of essay exams rather than objective tests. These professors feel that essay exams, by requiring students to analyze and argue, can reveal students' mastery of subject matter in a way that objective tests cannot match. (Many specialists in measurement and assessment dispute this claim, as we shall see.) In addition, essay exam questions, unlike most out-of-class writing assignments, ask students to synthesize concepts and draw together various strands of course material. As a result, essay exams—more than out-of-class writing assignments—help students see the whole course in perspective and thus can be powerful tools for learning. Finally, essay exams help students learn to think and compose rapidly, providing apt preparation for professions that require working with documents under deadline conditions.

Why Essay Exams Are Problematic _____

Nevertheless, essay examinations pose problems for many educators, specifically for specialists in testing and measurement, who compare essay exams to objective tests, and for specialists in writing across the curriculum, who compare them to other kinds of formal and exploratory writing assignments. Let's look at the problems with essay exams from each of these perspectives.

The Measurement and Testing Perspective

For the most part, specialists in educational testing and measurement prefer objective tests over essay exams even when the instructor wishes to test at the upper levels of Bloom's taxonomy (1956) of education objectives. Jacobs and Chase (1992), cautiously endorse essay exams for testing higher cognitive skills but prefer a series of short ten-minute essays rather than one or two in-depth ones. The literature in this field generally takes a foundationalist, perhaps even positivist, view of knowledge, regarding a course's content as a body of objective testable material that students can learn at various levels of depth and subtlety. Based on this assumption (which many faculty who support essay exams will not grant—especially those with postmodern doubt about the objectivity of knowledge), assessment specialists believe that the extent of any individual student's learning can be measured by skillfully constructed objective items ranging from simple recall questions to questions measuring Bloom's upper levels of analysis, synthesis, and evaluation.

Although proponents of essay exams often claim that essays are more effective than objective tests at measuring a student's critical thinking about course material, assessment specialists claim that expertly designed multiple-choice items can do the same thing (Clegg and Cashin, 1986). Cashin (1987) identifies six limitations of essay exams, four of which are particularly relevant to this discussion. I summarize these as follows:

1. They can sample only limited content. Because essay exams involve so much writing time, they can "only sample a very small portion of the domain of content and skills to be learned." Consequently, students' scores reflect "the luck of the draw" rather than their "command of the entire domain" of what was taught (Cashin, 1987, p. 2).

2. They are not reliable. Research reveals that scores assigned to a given essay vary from scorer to scorer. Perhaps more disturbing, the same scorer will assign different grades to the same essay at different times.

3. Scores may be influenced by the scorer's impression of the student. Unlike scores on objective tests, the scores on essay exams often reflect the teacher's previous impressions of the student—the "halo effect."

4. Scores reflect factors not related to content knowledge. Scores on essay exams are influenced by the students' handwriting, grammatical and spelling skills, and other writing skills not directly related to course content.

As a consequence of these limitations, "especially with respect to reliability," Cashin recommends limiting the use of essay exams only to "learning outcomes that cannot be satisfactorily measured by 'objective' items" (p. 2). For Cashin, these situations may occur if the instructor specifically wants to emphasize writing or wants "to encourage students to explore attitudes more than testing for cognitive achievement" (p. 2). Even then he warns teachers to use essay exams only "when the instructor has more confidence in his or her ability as a critical reader than as an 'objective' test constructor" (p. 2).

The Writing-Across-the-Curriculum Perspective

Specialists in writing across the curriculum tend to bring to this issue different assumptions and concerns, focusing more on learning than on testing. Skeptical of the positivist metaphor of a course subject as a "body" or "domain" of material, the mastery of which can be measured empirically, these persons tend to locate knowledge in the ability to join a discourse—to use course materials to make arguments. From this perspective, essay exams are preferable to objective tests. The objection to essay exams from the writing-across-the-curriculum perspective is that they tend to replace other more effective kinds of writing assignments. Teachers have only so much time to devote to student writing. Teachers who grade lots of essay exams tend to reduce their requirements for other formal or exploratory writing assignments, which are generally more effective than essay exams both at teaching writing skills and at promoting learning and critical thinking. The effect is that writing as testing drives out writing as learning.

The reduced learning from essay exams results largely from the minimal time on task they require. A midterm exam typically keeps students actively writing and thinking for fifty minutes or so, a final exam for two to four hours. In contrast, a guided journal or a series of thought letters could involve fifteen to twenty hours of active thinking during a term, and a short formal essay assignment, by itself, could involve a dozen hours or more. Thus, the power of essay exam questions to stimulate synthetic thinking is diminished by the small amount of time students actually spend on the task.

A related problem is that essay exams send the wrong message about process. In-class essay exams, when submitted to teachers, are almost always unedited, unrevised first drafts. During the entire life cycle of an exam answer, its only reader is the teacher. (Students themselves almost never read their own exam answers—either before turning them in or after getting them back.) Therein lies the problem. As we saw in Chapter Two, the teaching of writing is largely the teaching of revision. In learning to revise, students learn first to become better readers of their early drafts—a process that leads to deepening and complicating of thought through discovery of weaknesses and gaps, attention to alternative views, subsequent reformulation of the logic and structure of the argument, and so forth. These powerful thinking activities associated with revision are lost in a timed exam setting.

Another problem—related to the reliability issue raised by specialists in testing and measurement—is that teachers are not consistent in what they look for on essay exams. (For an interesting survey of the literature on reliability in the scoring of essay exams, see Jacobs and Chase, 1992, pp. 106–109.) As students go from teacher to teacher, the criteria for exam answers shift mysteriously. Some teachers look for thesis-governed arguments, in which case much of what a student has learned in the course has to be omitted or reshaped to keep the essay focused on the proposition at hand. Other teachers reward "all about" exams in which students need to unload everything they know about topic X. Some teachers demand well-organized essays; others are willing to sift through confusing strings of material looking for required points that they check off in the margins. Some teachers want straight feedback of material from readings and lectures; other teachers want fresh insights that go beyond what was covered in class. My sense is that few students know what any one teacher really wants in an exam and that teachers vary so much in what they want that weaker students never get the hang of writing exams.

Finally, students are seldom taught how to write essay exams. This problem could be addressed if teachers shifted their emphasis from testing to learning. In such cases, students could be required to rewrite weak exams until they had achieved at least the B level. Teachers could work as coaches by showing students the kinds of "thinking moves" needed to write A-worthy answers. The payoff for this coaching would be students' rethinking of course material and learning the strategies of effective exam writing. In practice, however, students are rarely given much feedback on their exams; even more rarely are they allowed to rewrite an exam for a better grade.

How We Can Improve Our Use of Essay Exams

Despite these problems with essay exams, my own view—coming from the writing-across-the-curriculum perspective—is that essay exams are preferable to objective tests when examining students' ability to think critically about course material. Essay exams send the important pedagogical message that mastering a field means joining its discourse, that is, demonstrating one's ability to mount effective arguments in response to disciplinary problems. My own view, then, is that we should not eliminate essay exams but rather improve their effectiveness without letting them replace other kinds of writing assignments. Our goal would be twofold: to increase the amount of learning derived from essay exams and to increase students' ability to write serviceable prose under pressure. I believe we could improve our use of exams by taking four basic actions: (1) teaching students how to write essay exams, (2) building more opportunities for process into the exam setting, (3) improving the focus and clarity of our exam questions, and (4) establishing more consistent grading criteria and improving grading methods to improve reliability. Let's look at each in turn.

Teaching Students How to Write Exams

Particularly in lower-division courses, where students are still learning academic discourse, instructors need to teach students how to write essay exams. Exhortations such as "be clear" or "plan before you write" do not do much good. Fortunately, several genuinely helpful techniques can be implemented in most classrooms.

In-Class Norming Sessions. The teacher collects from a previous class four to six exams graded from A to C- or D. (It's best to have the exams typed to facilitate photocopying and to avoid the variable of difficult handwriting.) Students read the exams and, in small groups, rank them from best to worst, trying to predict what grades the teacher gave. After the groups have reported their consensus on grades, the teacher explains the grading of the essays and leads a discussion. Internalizing the criteria for A exams is a good start toward learning how to write them. Norming sessions are also salutary experiences for instructors, who are forced to articulate their criteria for good exam answers. Because the exams focus on course content, the norming session also serves as a review of course material. (See Chapter Nine, pages 158–159, and Chapter Thirteen, page 219, for further discussion of norming sessions.)

Practice Exams. Many teachers have had good results giving students practice exams. Some teachers have their students write a twenty-minute essay in class under exam conditions and then ask selected students to read their exams aloud. Through class discussion, teachers can help students see what constitutes a strong exam. Another technique is to use practice exams as homework. You can reuse all your old exam questions by having students respond to one or two per week as homework under self-timed conditions. The teacher can treat these as exploratory writing and provide coaching through models feedback (see Chapter Thirteen, page 236). Not only does this technique improve exam writing, but it also promotes learning in a premium way. (For further discussion of practice exams, see Chapter Six, pages 114–115.)

Teaching Students to Begin an Exam with a Thesis Statement. Another good way to teach exam writing is to show students how to begin their answers with a thesis statement opener, which can be defined as a one-sentence summary answer to the overall question. By opening with a thesis, students are forced to plan their answers in terms of both content and organization. The one-sentence thesis statement thus serves as both a summary and a map of the whole essay. Here are some examples:

> *Question:* How does Darwin's theory of evolution threaten the Elizabethan notion of a great chain of being?
>
> *Opening sentence:* Darwin's theory of evolution threatens the Elizabethan notion of a great chain of being by challenging the idea that creatures are linked in an ascending order of hierarchies that reflect a divine purpose and intelligence at work in the universe. [Humanities]
>
> *Question:* When the tablecloth was pulled from underneath the dishes, the dishes stayed on the table. Why?
>
> *Opening sentence:* The dishes remained on the table because the rapidly moving tablecloth did not give them much momentum, which is a product of both force and time [Kirkpatrick and Pittendrigh, 1984, p. 161]. [Physics]

(For additional discussion of thesis statement writing, see Chapter Six.)

Group Thesis Statement Writing. As the examples just given suggest, teaching students to open with a thesis statement forces them to plan ahead and to conceptualize their whole response at once.

This skill is so valuable, in fact, that teachers can have students practice writing thesis statements in collaborative groups. An excellent way to review course material while teaching exam-writing skills is to give students practice exam questions in class and ask them in small groups to compose effective opening sentences for the answer. (See Chapter Nine, page 155, for further discussion of this method.)

Showing Examples of A-Worthy Exams. After each exam, place copies of representative A-graded answers in the library or read several A answers aloud in class. Seeing what an A essay looks like is often better feedback for students than putting comments on the exams themselves.

Letting Students Revise an Exam. Occasionally, a student can benefit greatly from the opportunity to rewrite a weak exam, particularly if the weakness stems from an unsuccessful strategy or approach as opposed to a lack of preparation or study. Often students improve remarkably following a bit of coaching in what constitutes a strong answer. Students are gratified by the experience of succeeding and may learn skills that can be transferred to other exams in other courses.

Building Opportunities for Process into the Exam Setting

A second major strategy for improving essay exams is to build opportunities for process into the exam setting. Although time normally cannot be provided for multiple drafts during an in-class exam, instructors can develop strategies for focusing students' studying prior to the exam so that they do considerable prewriting or invention ahead of time. What follows are several strategies that generally result in better exams and more focused learning.

Revealing Potential Exam Questions in Advance. One of the easiest techniques, employed by many professors, is to hand out a list of potential exam questions a week or so ahead of the exam. Diligent students are apt to prepare answers for all the questions, especially if they have been trained to begin an answer with a one-sentence summarizing thesis. On a review day, groups could be asked to create thesis statements for each of the answers. These thesis statements could then be compared and discussed in a plenary session. (It should be noted that many assessment specialists recommend against handing out questions in advance on the grounds that one may simply be testing "the students' ability to memorize someone else's thinking" [Cashin, 1987, p. 3]. Here again, the assessment community's emphasis is on testing rather than cooperative learning.)

Exam Preparation Notebook. A more formal elaboration of the strategy just described is to require exam preparation notebooks. In this approach, teachers give out a list of fifteen or so possible final exam questions at the beginning of the term and ask students to dedicate a separate section of their notebooks to each question. Throughout the term, students enter ideas from readings, lectures, and discussions relevant to each of the questions and explore their thinking through expressive writing. (See Chapter Six, page 109, for further discussion of this very effective technique.)

Crib Sheets. Another variation on the strategy of handing out potential questions in advance is allowing or even requiring a crib sheet for each question. Instead of simply hoping that students will prepare for the exam, you require that they bring to the examination session a three- by five-inch crib sheet for each question. Writing as minutely as they wish, students can cram whatever information they want onto the note cards. Some students will put a thesis statement and an outline on the cards; others will put lists of supporting data. Students can use the crib sheets during the examination, and they must turn all of them in with their exams—including those for questions not asked.

In lieu of requiring the crib sheets, teachers can simply allow their use. Most students will prepare them voluntarily in order to remain competitive on the exam. Although this method may seem to diminish the testing nature of an exam, it greatly enhances the power of exam questions to promote learning and critical thinking. It is an especially valuable strategy for problem-focused exam questions that do not have a single right answer but require extensive argument and support on the student's part.

Take-Home Exams. Among the most popular ways to allow process is to switch from in-class to take-home exams. However, the rules for take-home exams differ widely from instructor to instructor. Some teachers treat them like formal essays. They urge students to revise extensively and encourage use of peer review and even help from writing centers. These teachers envision their students' spending as much time on the take-home as they would on a formal essay. Other teachers treat take-home exams as less pressured and more convenient versions of in-class examinations, to be done under the honor system fairly quickly and without help. These teachers expect minimally edited one-draft writing done in perhaps three or four hours instead of two. According to conversations

I have had with students, the main objection they have to take-home exams is not knowing what the competition is doing or what the teacher expects. A part-time student who has cleared the decks for finals week might spend ten to fifteen hours on the exam. The harried full-time student with a job might have only three or four hours at maximum. The latter student might be justified in wondering if the exam is fair. Teachers should be aware of these concerns and try to help students resolve them in advance. Each teacher should be particularly clear on the following issues:

1. Are multiple drafts expected? That is, will this be graded like a formal essay?

2. Is the exam open-book and open-notes, or is it closed-book on the honor system?

3. May the student get help from a writing center or learning center consultant or from fellow classmates?

4. How much time does the teacher intend students to spend?

5. How long should the exam be?

Jacobs and Chase (1992, pp. 126–127) recommend setting a page limit for a take-home exam and penalizing students for exceeding it.

Improving the Focus and Clarity of Exam Questions

A third broad strategy is for teachers to improve the focus and clarity of their exam questions. In Chapter Five, I argued that good writing on the student's part begins with good assignments on the teacher's part. Nowhere is this connection clearer than in an exam setting, where a student needs to start moving in the right direction within the first five minutes.

In recent years, composition researchers, attempting to develop effective assessment examinations of writing proficiency, have studied the connection between the kinds of writing tasks students are given and the quality of writing they produce fifty minutes later (Brossell, 1983). Most of the findings are predictable, but some findings seem counterintuitive, even surprising. I list several of them here because I believe they can be translated from a writing proficiency setting to an essay exam setting in a content area.

Limit Choice. Although teachers often believe they are doing students a favor by giving many options among questions, when given too many choices, students waste time getting started and then become hampered by doubts about their choice. In fact, weaker students sometimes conflate the questions so that in answering question 3, say, they begin bringing in material more relevant to questions 1 and 2. The current practice for proficiency exams in composition is to give only one question but to make sure that it is an excellent one. Cashin (1987) agrees with this view, but from a measurement perspective. He advises teachers to "avoid optional questions" because "it is almost impossible to write several essay questions which are of equal difficulty. . . . The result is that different students are taking tests of varying difficulty but you will grade these the same. This may penalize the 'better' students because they may choose the more difficult (challenging) questions and so will not score as well as students who choose the easier questions" (p. 3). (See also Jacobs and Chase, 1992, p. 113.)

Keep Each Question Short and Avoid Subquestions or Hints. In an attempt to stimulate ideas or guide thinking, teachers sometimes add a series of subquestions under the main question or otherwise provide hints about possible directions to take in the exam essay. But this extra "help" may be counterproductive. Students feel constrained to answer each of the subquestions in turn or slavishly to follow the suggested direction. It is better to ask your question and stop. (See Chapter Five, pages 88–89, for further discussion of the negative value of subquestions.)

Call for Thesis-Governed Writing and Avoid Tasks Phrased as Imperatives. Perhaps most surprising, students seem to do best when the task is stated either as a thesis that must be supported, modified, or refuted or as a single question the answer to which will be the writer's thesis statement. What students do not do as well on are tasks stated as imperatives using such verbs as *discuss, analyze, evaluate,* and *compare and contrast.* Imperative tasks result in a far greater number of aimless answers than tasks stated as a thesis or a focusing question. The use of imperatives is acceptable, however, if the imperative verb is sufficiently contextualized to avoid ambiguity and if the implied problem is clear. The following list gives some example questions.

Less Effective Questions	Improved Questions
Pick one of the following, and write an essay about it: (a) Gothic cathedrals; (b) Charlemagne; (c) the Black Death.	"There is a connection between the worldview of a culture and the kind of architecture it produces." To what extent does this quotation explain the differences between Romanesque and Gothic churches?
Discuss the use of pesticides in controlling mosquitoes.	What are the pros and cons of using pesticides to control mosquitoes?

Analyze the influence of Platonic thought on Christianity.

"The otherworldly focus of twentieth-century fundamentalist Christianity owes more to Plato than to Jesus." Agree or disagree with this proposition.

Establishing More Consistent Grading Criteria and Improving Grading Methods

A final broad strategy is to develop grading criteria and explain them to students and then to establish grading methods that apply those criteria reliably.

If we want students to become savvy exam writers, we need to be up front about the criteria we use in grading essay exams. How much do we reward intelligent generalizations even if the supporting data are fuzzy as opposed to regurgitation of data without much argument? Do we want the essay to read like finished writing, or do we scan it for the points we are looking for, checking them off with ticks in the margin? Do we penalize grammatical and spelling errors, or do we read past them? Chapter Fifteen shows teachers how to articulate their grading criteria and gives advice on developing scoring guides using holistic, analytic, or primary trait scales. These can be developed for essay exam questions as well as for formal out-of-class essays.

One of the stickiest issues an instructor faces is what to do about exam answers that are riddled with sentence errors. Although I cannot presume to answer this question for others, I will offer my own recommendations (no doubt controversial) for dealing with sentence-level errors in an exam setting.

As explained in Chapters Two and Four, first-draft writing, even by highly skilled writers, often contains awkward sentence structures and mistakes in grammar and punctuation. The more difficult the subject matter, the more frequent the tangled sentences. My own belief is that in an exam setting, we must learn to live with these problems. Since students haven't time to revise, they are unable to find and correct the numerous errors that show up naturally in drafts. I therefore recommend reading demandingly at the macro level (thesis, organization, use of evidence) and forgivingly at the micro level (sentence structure, punctuation errors). We would all be happier, of course, if students could write error-free first drafts, but since this skill is not being tested in a content area exam, I recommend reading primarily for content.

I take the same position on spelling errors. In formal out-of-class essays, poor spelling needs to be severely penalized. Poor spellers have to understand the negative message their prose sends to readers; they must discover their own strategies for getting misspellings out of their final drafts (reading their drafts backward, hiring a proofreader, using computer spell-checkers, whatever works). But a writer cannot worry about spelling during the act of composing itself. Teachers who insist on accurate spelling during timed writing—or even worse, teachers who tell students to bring dictionaries to the exam—are doing a disservice to struggling writers. While other writers are getting their ideas in order, the poor speller is thumbing through a dictionary. We do not know the neurological or environmental causes of poor spelling. We do know that it is not easily remedied. I treat poor spelling in a written exam the way I would treat the problems of a stutterer in an oral examination: with sympathy, patience, and forgiveness.

Finally, what about the nonidiomatic English of our second-language students? Like the problems of poor spellers, the problems of non–native speakers of English are exacerbated in test situations. As long as an institution is willing to accept students who have not yet acquired fluency in English, we have to overlook idiomatic problems in exam settings. (Even in formal out-of-class writing, we must recognize that fluency cannot be attained quickly and that we should help our foreign students make progress rather than penalizing them for what they cannot yet do.) When language problems are so severe that the teacher cannot follow the writer's argument, then a failing grade is justified. But if the writer's argument can be followed, I recommend overlooking idiomatic and syntactic errors resulting from second-language interference.

Once professors have established grading criteria for exam answers and have made their own separate peace with the sentence error dilemma, their final responsibility is to establish grading practices that increase reliability by minimizing the halo effect and other factors leading to overly impressionistic grading. Davis (1993, pp. 277–279) provides an excellent summary of the literature on this issue. Based on my own experiences, I recommend the following:

- Do not look at students' names when you read the exams. Have students write their names on the back of the exams, or even better, ask students to identify their exams with a random four-digit number they choose on the spot. After you have graded all the exams, ask students to identify their numbers.

- Grade the exam one question at a time. Rather than read the whole exam of each student, grade all the responses to question 1, then all the responses to question 2, and so forth.

- Shuffle the exams after you complete each question so that you read them in a different order. Record scores in such a way that you do not know what a student received on question 1 when you grade question 2.

- If possible, read a random sample of exams rapidly before you make initial decisions about grades. Your goal here is to establish "anchor papers" that represent prototype A, B, and C grades. Then, when you come to a difficult essay, you can ask yourself, "Is this better or worse than my prototype B? How about my prototype C?"

The foregoing methods, all of which grew out of research in the evaluation of writing (White, 1994), help eliminate the halo effect and provide psychological assistance in eliminating extraneous factors.

Conclusion: Getting the Most from Essay Exams

Essay examinations are valuable writing assignments if the exams do not replace even more valuable formal or exploratory writing assignments. From a writing-across-the-curriculum perspective, problems with essay examinations arise primarily when teachers regard them as sufficient components of writing in a course. Once we recognize the problems posed by the exam setting—time constraints that prevent writing as process—we can take steps to improve our examination procedures so that students learn more course content from our exams while improving their skills at writing under pressure.

CHAPTER 12

Encouraging Engagement and Inquiry in Research Papers

The traditional "term paper"—by which most instructors mean a major research paper—can be one of the most valuable assignments we give students, especially in upper-division courses where students are learning to pose research problems in their majors. To make term papers fully effective, however, we need to change the way some of our students perceive them. Despite our admonitions that students should do their own thinking and analysis in term papers, many students regard a research project as an encyclopedic "all about" report on a topic area rather than as a thesis-governed response to a significant and interesting problem or question. We all know students' tendency to manufacture a term paper by patching together passages closely paraphrased (or even copied) from their sources. There is something mechanistic about the way many of our students produce research papers, something disturbingly unlike the motivated inquiry and analysis that we value.

And yet many undergraduates pursue research with gusto. In March 1994, I had the opportunity to attend the National Conference on Undergraduate Research at Western Michigan University in Kalamazoo. For two days, I attended conference presentations on topics ranging from chemistry to linguistics. I was impressed by the fascinating range of problems that undergraduates posed and by the quality that can be achieved once a student understands how the conversation of a discipline works. Here are some examples of research problems posed by these undergraduates (National Conference on Undergraduate Research, 1994):

What is the effect of watching violence in films on heart and brain activity in ten adult subjects?

What differences in gender and ethnic status, wealth, age, political involvement, and American Bar Association rating are there among the federal judges appointed by President Clinton and those appointed by Presidents Bush and Reagan?

What are the effects of hippocampal lesioning and ipsilateral monocular occlusion on spatial memory in rats?

What is the relationship between the cycle structure of a permutation that is an involution and the shape of the tableaux associated with it by Schensted's algorithm?

What was the cultural role of the prostitute in ancient and medieval India, and what subsequent historical forces have caused that role to change?

The question before us, then, is how to transform students from uninspired pseudo-plagiarists into engaged undergraduate researchers. What goes wrong when students regurgitate sources in a term paper? What goes right when they become invested in real inquiry, like those several thousand undergraduates at Kalamazoo? The purpose of this chapter is to explore the many obstacles that block students from becoming engaged researchers and to offer suggestions for improving the way we teach research writing. The chapter begins with a discussion of student alienation and of its opposite, curiosity and wonder, the spirits that drive inquiry. The middle section examines the complexities of term paper writing, my goal being to help teachers appreciate how baffling research writing is to newcomers to academic discourse. The concluding section offers suggestions for the successful teaching of research writing to undergraduates.

Term Papers and Alienation

Students' traditional conception of the term paper, as discussed in Chapter Two, is rooted in school reports often paraphrased from encyclopedias. The traditional assignment for school reports (for example, "Write a report on North Dakota") calls for "all about" writing that is entirely informational rather than analytical or argumentative. Its college-level equivalent is a cut-and-paste assemblage of passages paraphrased from a couple of sources supplemented with a padded bibliography (see Larson, 1982).

The term paper often creates a vicious cycle of cynicism among teachers and students. This cynicism is humorously captured by

William McKeachie in his influential *Teaching Tips: A Guidebook for the Beginning College Teacher* (1986, p. 125):

> When undergraduates are required to turn in a term paper they seem to face three alternatives.
>
> 1. Buy one, or borrow one from a friend or fraternity or sorority file. The student may have this retyped or, if there are no marks on it, simply retype the title page inserting his or her own name for that of the author.
> 2. Find a book in the library that covers the needed material. Copy it with varying degrees of paraphrasing and turn it in. Whether or not to list this book in the bibliography is a problem not yet adequately covered by student mores, although it is agreed that if it is listed in the bibliography it should be well hidden between two references with Russian (first choice) or German (second choice) authors.
> 3. Review relevant resources and, using powers of analysis and integration, develop a paper that reveals understanding and original thinking.
>
> Most teachers prefer that their students adopt the third alternative. Few of us, however, have evolved techniques for eliminating the first two.

Many teachers report similar discouragement. Cohen and Spencer (1993), writing about upper-division term papers in economics, complained that student papers were "mediocre, regurgitative, and uninspired." And at the end of the term, these authors report, "over half of the students never picked up their papers. That pile of uncollected papers was a sure sign of student alienation from their writing. . . . When students were asked about the lack of coherent arguments in their writing, typical responses were: 'How can you expect an undergraduate to say anything original?' or 'How can I [the novice student] tell you [the expert instructor] anything you don't already know?'" (p. 222).

Reinvoking a Sense of Wonder: What We Can Learn About Research Writing from Elementary Teachers

The student comments just given provide some insight into students' alienation—their sense of powerlessness, of having nothing original to say. Their writing has no personal connection to their own sense of wonder. Meyers (1986), in his discussion of critical thinking, argues persuasively that humans are by nature curious and wondering creatures with an innate drive to pose questions and make sense of their surroundings. But how do you connect research writing with wondering and pondering?

Consider the revolution going on in many elementary schools where inquiry-based teaching strategies are changing the environment in which writing occurs. An influential figure in this revolution is Lucy McCormick Calkins, a professor of English education at Teachers College, Columbia University, and a veteran second-grade teacher, who argues that research writing should begin in the early grades—not as a concern for footnote form but as a celebration of curiosity and a child's natural joy at sharing discoveries. What are some of the research problems posed by McCormick's students? "How do you care for a teddy bear?" "Why do people need tongues?" "What's the difference between a butterfly and a moth?" (Calkins, 1986, pp. 271–293).

Or consider the teaching strategies of a social science teacher in a local elementary school. She gathers her third graders into a circle and tells them the story of a Makah whaling expedition three hundred years ago off Cape Flattery. Asking her children to imagine themselves living in the Makah village, she begins weaving her magic of question asking. What would you be wearing? What would your clothes be made out of? Who made the clothes? Did the Makah have stores? Did each person make his or her own clothes? Was it men's work or women's work or children's work? Did they have scissors, needles, and thread? Who would be going on the whaling expedition? How did the Makah learn to catch whales? Did they have ropes and spears? How did the people in your village make their canoes? How did they cut down the trees to make canoes?

She makes master lists of children's questions on huge sheets of butcher paper, and then she sends the children forth into the school library to begin researching answers to their questions. Eventually, the children write research papers in response to questions that particularly interest them. But she also writes a research paper along with them—bringing into class her own report on one of the questions the children asked. Throughout this teacher's learning units, students' research is activated by their own curiosity.

Activating curiosity works at the college level as well. Among the solutions developed by Cohen and Spencer (1993) to the problem of uninspired, alienated term papers in economics was their decision to switch from topic-centered assignments to problem- or thesis-centered assignments: "The thesis-less papers that I had previously received in the form of explanations of other authors' positions . . . were, in fact, rational responses to my vague instructions 'explain and comment.' In their place, I substituted more argumentative instructions, such as: 'On the basis of your reading of Sahlins (1972), argue whether or not it is human nature to have "limitless needs."' Or, 'The Physiocratic theory can be easily criticized for its errors and excessive emphasis on the role of nature. Defend the

Physiocratic contribution to the development of economic theory'" (p. 224). In Cohen and Spencer's revised assignments, students do research to solve a problem; engagement with a question thus gives purpose and direction to their work.

Teachers in other disciplines have made similar discoveries that student writing improves remarkably when it focuses on a problem rather than a topic area. The mathematician W. P. Berlinghoff (1989), for example, in describing his use of writing to teach mathematical problem solving, begins by describing two kinds of assignments that did not work for him:

1. *Write about a famous mathematician, mathematical event, or historical period.* These topics frequently invited indeliberate plagiarism in the form of an undigested patchwork from several encyclopedias or other handy references. Occasionally they provoked deliberate plagiarism from disguised sources (or commercial term-paper mills). . . .

2. *Report on an article.* A far too common result of this type of topic was five pages of "I liked it" or "I didn't like it." If the article involved any substantive mathematics, the papers became "I didn't understand it" or occasionally "I don't even know that I didn't understand it" [p. 89].

Berlinghoff's solution is to give students a complex mathematical problem and to ask them to write a narrative account of their process of trying to solve it. The entire paper, then, is driven by inquiry. (Berlinghoff's assignment is described in more detail in my discussion of exploratory essays in Chapter Five, pages 92–93.)

One cause, then, of students' poor performance in research writing is the environment of alienation that dissociates term papers from the posing of true problems. We turn next to another cause: the complexity of research writing itself.

The Complexity of Research Writing: What Teachers Should Appreciate About Students' Difficulties with Term Papers _____

After McKeachie (1986) presents his humorous account of student mores on plagiarism, he makes an important and insightful comment: "I start with the assumption that most students would rather not plagiarize. When they plagiarize it is because they feel trapped with no other way out. The trap is typically that the student feels that it is almost impossible to write a paper that will achieve a satisfactory grade" (p. 125).

I believe that McKeachie is right. Good research writing is intellectually demanding and cognitively complex. Students often turn to plagiarism because they have no other coping mechanisms. Consider, for example, what a newcomer to academic discourse has to learn before academic research writing can seem natural. I see at least eight kinds of skills that students must learn. Let us examine each in turn.

1. How to Ask Research Questions

Unless students have been nurtured by an inquiry-based pedagogy, they have had little experience in posing questions. Unfamiliar with thesis-governed writing, they do not see their own essays as responses to interesting questions, nor do they see question asking as one of their roles. To complicate the task, the nature of questions differs from discipline to discipline, and as each discipline evolves, people on its cutting edge tend to pose questions in new ways. Faculty, therefore, must not only motivate students to become question askers but also guide them toward asking discipline-appropriate questions that are interesting, significant, and pursuable at the undergraduate level.

2. How to Find Sources

Students, for the most part, are not sophisticated users of college libraries beyond knowing how to find books. Often they are unaware of other resources. Many do not understand the differences between popular magazines and academic journals, nor do they appreciate the significance of journals (as opposed to books) for scholars. Generally, they are unfamiliar with indexes beyond the *Reader's Guide* and probably know little about on-line searches, which often tend to bury users with a vast potential of information. Even if they had a good introduction to library use in a first-year composition course, they are apt to know little about the specialized resources used by specific disciplines. Teaching students how to use the library thus becomes a problematic responsibility for each discipline.

3. Why to Find Sources

Faculty need to consider what a mysterious enterprise research writing is for undergraduates. For them, the term paper has been an exercise in "using at least five sources," the last couple of which they often sprinkle in arbitrarily for padding. For the most part, their research writing is like the game of a beginning chess player who has memorized the moves of some of the pieces but has no overall sense of goals and strategies.

Thus, students need to understand, for example, two quite distinct reasons that a researcher uses a library. One reason is to find information, data, and evidence bearing on a problem—the raw material of primary sources that becomes either support for the writer's argument or the object of analytical scrutiny. But researchers also use libraries for a second reason: to position themselves in the conversation of secondary sources surrounding the topic—previous and contemporary scholars with whom the writer agrees or disagrees. Furthermore, the student researcher has to learn how scholars in different disciplines use their sources. In science writing, the conversation of different voices is usually placed near the beginning of the essay, in the "review of the literature" section. In literary criticism, however, a writer usually carries on a running argument with other writers throughout the essay. A philosophical essay might contain references to only one or two primary sources because much of the paper involves the writer's original critical analysis. A research paper in history, however, might contain copious references to primary sources. It is no wonder that academic writing, which differs remarkably from discipline to discipline, is a strange bird for students.

4. How to Work Sources into the Paper

Equally difficult for students is figuring out what to do with the sources—when to quote, when to paraphrase, when to summarize an entire argument, when simply to reference. Moreover, students need to work these quotations and paraphrases into the texture of their own prose, carrying on an argument in their own voices. The beginner, lacking a voice and an argumentative purpose, seems primarily interested in manipulating sources. Typically, beginners alternate back and forth between two strategies: the long-block-quotation strategy, in which they quote lengthy undigested chunks of text, and the extended-paraphrase strategy, in which they try to turn large chunks of source material into their own language. These strategies suggest that the writers are not in control of their sources but are simply reproducing them. We therefore need to teach students the thinking and writing strategies that lead to sophisticated use of sources. This is no small chore.

5. How to Manage Sources

Since the advent of cheap xerography, students have tended to photocopy whole articles and passages from books rather than take notes and manage a system of note cards. By not taking notes, students are less apt to reflect on their reading or make decisions in advance about what is or is not important. They also get little practice at summarizing arguments. We must observe, too, that we cannot teach students how to manage notes until they learn how the whole discourse system works—why they are using sources and how this material might be incorporated into their essays.

6. How to Cite Sources

Learning the proper formats for citing sources, though the least of concerns in the hierarchy of skills needed for research writing, is often the foremost concern for students. Judging from the number of students who come into my own institution's writing center to ask questions about bibliographic and citation formats, it is the concern they think teachers emphasize most. The wide variation in formats from discipline to discipline further complicates this problem.

7. How to Establish a Rhetorical Context, a Role, an Audience, and a Purpose

Another problem for students is understanding the kinds of roles they can play in doing a research project. Differences in role often imply differences in audience and purpose. When assigning term papers, therefore, teachers might consider discussing with students the various roles they might play in their research writing—or even specifying the role as part of the assignment. Often the writer's role and purpose depend on the nature of the research question posed. Here are some typical roles that research writers can play, each followed by some sample research questions (adapted from an original student handout on Roles for Research Writers by Jack Folsom).

Synthesizer of Current Best Thinking on a Problem. In this role, the student researches the thinking of experts on the cutting edge of some contemporary problem in the discipline and reports, in either an academic or a popular style to a lay audience, what the experts currently think.

What is the current thinking on the value of insulin pumps in managing Type I diabetes?

According to recent experts, what genetic or environmental mechanisms enable salmon to return to their original spawning grounds?

What is the current view of experts on the causes of homosexuality?

Problem-Solving Detective or Critical Analyst. Here the research question does not ask for a synthesis of current views on a cutting-edge problem. For this kind of paper, a satisfactory answer that resolves the question may sometimes be uncovered and reported. Sometimes the writer finds information that answers the question directly; at other times, the writer must apply rigorous analysis to primary sources or other data.

Dickens or Boys' Town: What was it like to be an orphan in Indiana, 1875–1920?

To what extent has the exclusionary rule handcuffed the police?

Original Field or Laboratory Researcher. Here the writer poses a field or laboratory research problem, designs and conducts an experiment or study, and reports the results in scientific format. Library research will be used primarily for the "review of the literature" section.

What is the value of a "ropes course" experience for improving team-building behaviors in work groups?

What is the effect of tank size on the survival, growth, and production of larval *gobiosoma bosc*?

What effect has a recent TV advertising campaign for product X had on buying patterns of consumers?

Reviewer of a Controversy. In this role, the writer reports the arguments on various sides of a controversy inside the discipline or field.

What are the current arguments for and against the single-payer health care system?

What are the arguments for and against creating a five-year undergraduate engineering curriculum?

Analyzer and Evaluator of a Controversy. This role is like the preceding one except that the writer must now evaluate the strengths and weaknesses of the various voices in the controversy. This extra spin makes the task much more challenging.

Examine arguments for and against a single-payer health care system. Which arguments do you find most convincing? Why?

Advocate in a Controversy. Here the writer shifts from an informative or evaluative purpose to a persuasive purpose; the paper now becomes a researched argument.

Should we permit managed harvesting of old-growth forests?

Should the United States adopt a single-payer health care system?

Analytical Thinker Positioned in a Critical Conversation. Here writers do their own analytical thinking about a disciplinary problem but must relate their views to others who have addressed the same or similar questions. These essays may use few primary sources but carry on a lively conversation with secondary sources.

How does Hamlet change in the last act?

What would be the effect on consumer credit card debt of switching from federal income taxes to federal consumption taxes?

Does the earth have rights?

8. How to Follow the Scientific Report Format

Students who must report their research in scientific format need to learn the purpose and stylistic conventions for each of the sections in a typical technical report: introduction, methods, results (findings), discussion of results, and conclusions and recommendations. Of particular difficulty for most students are the handling of quantitative data and the differences between the results section and the discussion section of a report. Students particularly need to learn the following: (1) how to display their quantitative findings in tables, graphs, and charts; (2) how to summarize and focus these data verbally in the results section, properly referencing the figures; and (3) how to analyze and evaluate these data in the discussion section, arguing that they do or do not confirm the hypothesis. (For an example of a handout explaining the format of a technical report, see Chapter Five, page 91.)

Suggestions for Teaching Research Writing ────────────

Unfortunately, there are no easy ways to attack the problems noted here. As the foregoing discussion makes clear, research writing is cognitively complex; it requires a sophisticated view of the role of research in creating knowledge and of the conversation of competing views surrounding most research questions. Telling students to follow a disciplinary style manual helps students learn only the superficial details of research formats. To teach research writing as a sophisticated process requires considerable teacher ingenuity. What is the best way to do this?

There is no universal solution, of course, but I can offer a number of suggestions that may be useful.

1. Stress the Asking of Research Questions

Help students think of their research topics in terms of a question or problem rather than a topic area. (Urge students not to say, "I'm doing a term paper on schizophrenia," but rather to say, "I'm trying to find out whether recent developments in the chemical treatment of schizophrenia are effective.") By teaching question asking, teachers can remind students of the difference between an "all about" paper and a thesis-governed paper focused on a problem. An effective way to emphasize question asking is to word your term paper assignment in the following way:

Pose an interesting problem or question, appropriate to this course, that will require a combination of library [or field or laboratory] research and your own analytical skills to answer. The quality of your research paper will depend on the quality of your initial question. I will be working with you early in the term to help you pose a productive question.

Another alternative is to give your students a problem to explore or a thesis to defend. (For further discussion of how to assign thesis-based writing, see Chapter Five, pages 87–91, especially the discussion of the generic assignment.)

2. Require a Prospectus Well in Advance of the Paper Due Date

Requiring a prospectus, which demands of your students considerable preliminary research, will help prevent an end-of-the-term rush job. Typically, a research prospectus asks students to address the following questions:

1. What research problem or question do you intend to address?
2. Why is this an interesting question? Why is it problematic? Why is it significant?
3. How far along are you in your thinking and research? What do you expect to discover? Are you ready yet to formulate a thesis statement? If so, what is it?
4. Attach a working bibliography of the sources you have used so far. Write short annotations for the material you have already read.

Such a prospectus will focus students' attention on the articulation of a problem and will reveal to you those who need early assistance. Also, the kinds of entries on the annotated bibliography will tell you something about the sophistication of their research skills. This is also a good time to check whether students know the formats for bibliographic entries in your discipline.

3. Teach the Prototypical Structure of Academic Introductions: Problem, Thesis, Overview

Most inexperienced writers have difficulty with introductions, especially academic introductions. I have found that the focus and structure of their writing can improve significantly once they learn how academic introductions work. I therefore explain that a prototypical academic introduction has three main parts or "movements." The first part, which is usually the longest, introduces the reader to the problem the paper addresses. Sometimes the writer states the problem directly as a grammatical question, but often the question is only implied. This section usually contains needed background on the problem and often reviews previous scholarship that has addressed it. Frequently the writer explains why the problem is problematic (for example, why earlier attempts to solve the problem have been unsatisfactory) and why the problem is significant and worth pursuing (some mention of the benefits, either pragmatic or intellectual, that will come from solving it).

The second movement of a prototypical introduction explains the focus and purpose of the present article. Sometimes writers state their thesis at this point; at other times, writers substitute a "purpose statement," delaying their actual thesis until later. ("The purpose of this paper is to set forth a middle ground between the two opposing theories.")

The final movement typically gives the reader an overview of the whole article, either by providing a brief summary of its argument or by forecasting its structure through a blueprinting statement ("First, I will show . . .; the second part of the paper explores . . .; finally, I show . . .").

To illustrate these movements, I give students examples of academic introductions from several different disciplines, and we discuss them in detail. Here is one such example, a particularly succinct academic introduction from a professional journal in economics; it is followed by my explanatory commentary in italics. (I have numbered the sentences to facilitate commentary).

Money and Growth: An Alternative Approach

[1] An enormous body of literature, beginning with the work of James Tobin (1965) and Miguel Sidrauski (1967), assesses the effects of sustained price inflation on the equilibrium growth path in a neoclassical setting. [2] The issue of how sustained capital accumulation, in turn, affects money's role in an evolving system of payments has received far less attention. [3] Thus, this paper takes an alternative approach to studying the problem of money and growth by developing a model in which both sides of the money-growth relationship may be examined. [*Sentences 4–9 summarize the argument to be presented.*] [10] Taking an alternative approach to money and growth, therefore, reveals that the most striking effects run not from money to growth, but from growth to money.   —P. E. Ireland, *American Economic Review*, March 1994, p. 47

Sentence 1 provides background on a general problem and refers briefly to the academic conversation this article will join. Sentence 2 states the narrower problem this article will address; the actual question is implied: "How does sustained capital accumulation affect money's role in an evolving system of payments?" Sentence 2 also hints briefly at why this issue is significant: it has received little attention and thus promises to contribute to understanding. Sentence 3 presents a purpose statement indicating that the article will address the problem of growth and money by developing a model. Sentences 4–9 provide an overview of the whole article by summarizing its argument. Sentence 10 states the argument's thesis.

Once students appreciate this prototypical structure—problem at the beginning of the introduction and thesis and overview at the end—they will better understand that their own research papers should begin with an explanation of the problem that has driven their critical thinking and research and that their paper now attempts to answer or solve.

4. Teach Your Students How to Read and Write Academic Titles

Understanding how titles work helps students learn the academic discourse system. Without guidance, students are apt to produce titles like "My Term Paper" or "The Economy." They need to see how readers of academic discourse use titles, both to select what to read and to get a nutshell sense of the whole of the article. Therefore, titles need to be brief but detailed, serving, in miniature, the same overview function as the introduction. To help students produce good titles for their own research papers, I point out three of the most common conventions for academic titles:

1. *Question.* Some academic titles simply state the question that the body of the paper will address ("Will Patriarchal Management Survive Beyond the Twentieth Century?").

2. *Summary of thesis or purpose.* Some academic titles summarize the paper's thesis or purpose ("The Relationship Between Client and Therapist Expectation of Improvement and Psychotherapy Outcome").

3. *Two-part title with a colon.* Academic titles are frequently split into two parts, separated by a colon. The most common approach is to present key words from the issue to the left of the colon and key words from the thesis to the right ("Money and Growth: An Alternative Approach"). Another common pattern is to start with an interest-arousing "mystery phrase" that does not become clear until the reader reads the article. Following the colon, the writer usually summarizes the article's key issue or thesis ("Fine Cloth, Cut Carefully: Cooperative Learning in British Columbia").

After explaining these conventions for titles, I have students write tentative titles for their own research papers using each of the conventions. This exercise, which forces a "nutshelling" of the whole, often helps students discover a better focus for their drafts in progress.

5. Provide Models

Create a file of model research papers written for your courses in the past. Attach to each one an explanation of why you admire the paper, pointing out features you particularly like. If possible, include the prospectus and all the drafts of one of the papers. You can put this file on library reserve.

6. Develop a Strategy for Teaching Library Research Skills

Another major task is to teach students how to unlock the resources of the library, including on-line searches of databases. As a general rule, generic library tours are not as effective as discipline-specific tours occurring at a "need to know" time for students. Teachers must work with librarians to develop appropriate strategies for a particular course or discipline. (I have found particularly useful Lutzker's *Research Projects for College Students: What to Write Across the Curriculum*, 1988, written by a college librarian familiar with the writing-across-the-curriculum movement.)

My own approach is to design out-of-class "scavenger hunt" projects in which students have to work in small groups to locate materials, use indexes and special reference tools, and appreciate the relevance of the retrieved information to an ongoing inquiry. My goal is for students to teach one another how to use the library. Here is an example of a scavenger hunt unit I developed for a research project on *Hamlet*. Teachers can adapt this method to their own disciplines.

Library Scavenger Hunt

Purpose. The purpose of this scavenger hunt is to awaken your appreciation of useful information and knowledge housed within an academic library. This scavenger hunt will broaden your knowledge of *Hamlet* while teaching you some of the library resources useful to English majors.

Instructions. Work with your assigned research group to complete this scavenger hunt and submit your "findings" to me. All findings are due within one week of the start of activity. You can divide up the labor among members of your group, but all group members must acknowledge that they know how to use each of the research tools. The winning group will receive a valuable "prize."

> *Task 1.* In the article you recently read by Fredson Bowers, Bowers says (in footnote 5) that Tourneur's *Atheist's Tragedy* provides "strongly corroborative" evidence in support of his theory. Read the plot summary of

Atheist's Tragedy in *Masterplots* (PN/44/M33/1968). **What to bring back:** in four or five sentences, explain how this tragedy might corroborate Bowers's thesis about *Hamlet.*

Task 2. You want to know something more about Shakespeare's use of the ghost in *Hamlet.* Find *The Concise Encyclopedic Guide to Shakespeare* (R/822.33/GM). Read entries on *Hamlet,* Hamlet, and Ghosts. Then, following the lead from the entry on Ghosts, read a plot summary of Seneca's *Thyestes* and Kyd's *Spanish Tragedy* in *Masterplots.* **What to bring back:** in a paragraph, explain how Shakespeare's use of the ghost in *Hamlet* seems to differ from these earlier uses of ghosts.

Task 3. You want to find out why Hamlet asks the players for a speech about Pyrrhus. Find *Who's Who in Classical Mythology* (REF/BL/715/ 688) and read entries under Pyrrhus (Neoptolemus), Priam, and Hecuba. **What to bring back:** in one or two sentences each, identify Pyrrhus, Priam, and Hecuba in Greek mythology. Then, in a paragraph, speculate on the connection in Hamlet's mind between his own situation and that of Pyrrhus.

Task 4. You have heard from someone that Hamlet occasionally utters obscene language. Use the on-line catalogue to locate Eric Partridge's *Shakespeare's Bawdy,* and look up "country matters" and "edge" to see examples of Hamlet's sexual innuendo against Ophelia in the mousetrap scene. See also "fishmonger" and "nunnery." **What to bring back:** explain each of these obscenities.

Task 5. You want to find out whether the soldiers' being "sick at heart" at the beginning of *Hamlet* and whether Denmark's having "something rotten" in it might be oblique references to the political and social mood of Elizabethan England at the turn of the seventeenth century. Use the Micropædia and Macropædia of the *Encyclopædia Britannica* to help you get an overview of the late Elizabethan cultural and political scene. Pay particular attention to events following the rebellion of Essex. **What to bring back:** in one paragraph, speculate on why a new fashion of melancholy and disease was finding its way into Elizabethan literature during the last years of the queen's reign.

Task 6. Using the CD-ROM *PMLA Index,* construct a bibliography of four recent articles on *Hamlet* and find them in our library. **What to bring back:** submit a printout listing the four articles; indicate on the printout where you found these articles in the library.

7. Consider Assigning an Exploratory Essay Due Before the Final Research Paper

One of the best ways to prevent plagiarism while focusing on inquiry is to require an exploratory essay, submitted several weeks before the final paper, as part of the research project. The exploratory essay, which is a first-person narrative account of the student's research process, tracing the evolution of his or her thinking, requires that students delay closure and hence explore their issues in depth. Often teachers enjoy reading the exploratory essays more than the finished research paper. (For a more detailed description of exploratory essays, see Chapter Five, pages 92–93.)

8. Consider Several Short Research Assignments or a Structured Assignment That Breaks Projects into Stages

Although the long research paper is a valuable assignment, students' writing and critical thinking skills generally develop more quickly through a sequence of shorter write-to-learn assignments such as those described in Chapters Five and Six. Erickson and Strommer (1991), for example, argue that "term papers and projects seem especially ill suited for freshmen" (p. 124). Even when an instructor's goal is to teach research writing and when students are advanced enough to undertake it, students often succeed better initially with shorter assignments that introduce them gradually to the skills of summarizing and paraphrasing, using research data, and so forth. The following kinds of short assignments are particularly useful at teaching research writing skills:

> Summaries or abstracts of professional articles (Chapter Seven, pages 128–129 and Chapter Eight, pages 145–146)
>
> Data-supplied microthemes (see pages 125–126)
>
> Analyses or evaluations of journal articles or essays comparing and contrasting two different journal articles
>
> Short arguments that require use of research data for support (see Drenk's thesis support microthemes, Chapter Five, pages 74–75)

Another approach is to devise a "structured assignment" that breaks a longer research project into incremental stages. Lutzker (1988) particularly recommends structured assignments because they pace students through the research, permit early and frequent feedback, provide thinking time, and take advantage of "the recognized efficacy of incremental learning" (p. 9).

My own typical pattern of creating a structured assignment is to mix nongraded and graded assignments due sequentially throughout the term. Here is a structure I used recently:

1. Guided-journal entries exploring possible topics and defining research problem. [Early in term.]

2. Group submissions from library scavenger hunt (described earlier in this chapter). [Early in term.]

3. Evaluative summaries of two journal articles related to the topic (graded assignment). [Week following the scavenger hunt.]

4. Prospectus (described earlier in this chapter). [Midway through term; returned quickly with comments and often followed by individual or group conferences.]

5. Exploratory essay (graded assignment—see Chapter Five, pages 92–93). [Due three to four weeks before end of term.]

6. Peer review workshop on completed rough draft of research paper. [Ten to fourteen days before end of term.]

7. Submission of a two hundred–word "abstract" of the writer's argument. [Submitted to me two days after the peer review workshop; I read and comment on abstracts and return them in twenty-four hours.]

8. Submission of final research paper (graded assignment). [Due last day of term.]

(Lutzker, 1988, pp. 9–15, provides additional ideas and advice for designing structured assignments.)

9. Consider Developing a "Walk-Through" Mini–Research Project for Your Course

Perhaps the best way to introduce new majors to research writing in the disciplines is through a walk-through project that the whole class works on together over a period of several days. The teacher develops a scenario for a fictional researcher who poses a research question. The teacher then distributes a packet of primary and secondary materials out of which the mini–research paper will be developed. With all the class using the same documents, the teacher gives short assignments in summarizing, quoting, paraphrasing, and citing material for a variety of contexts and purposes. Many of these can be done as in-class exercises. Here are some examples:

Suppose that as a researcher, you want to summarize the argument on pages 235–236 of the attached article while quoting exactly the two passages highlighted with yellow marker. Write this paragraph beginning with the following sentence: "A contrasting view of the role of labor in postwar Germany comes from . . ." Finish the paragraph, properly referencing the article and using attribution.

For the "Findings" section, you have displayed your data as shown on the attached tables, which you call Table 1 and Table 2. Write a prose passage describing these findings verbally and properly referencing both tables.

In each case, the teacher could have students share their paragraphs, comparing different versions and commenting on strengths and weaknesses. The teacher could then present his or her own version as a model. After the class has worked together on the exercises, the students put all the skills together by writing a mini–research paper using the materials already discussed. Depending on its appropriateness to the discipline, the teacher can also use the project to raise theoretical issues about the nature of knowledge in the discipline: To what extent does research uncover an objectively knowable truth? Can researchers, looking at the same data, arrive at different theses? What makes a thesis persuasive? To what extent does research writing reflect the biases of the researcher?

Conclusion: Engaging Students in Research

Although there are some generic skills of research that apply to all disciplines, the real nitty-gritty of research writing—as a process of inquiry, analysis, and argumentation—needs to be taught within each discipline. When instructors appreciate the complexity of academic research writing, particularly its strangeness to students unfamiliar with academic discourse and unaccustomed to associating writing with their own curiosity and wonder, they can better understand (but not condone) students' tendency toward plagiarism in research writing. This chapter has tried to explore some of the problems with traditional approaches to the "term paper" and to suggest better strategies for teaching undergraduate research.

Reading, Commenting On, and Grading Student Writing

CHAPTER 13

Coaching
the Writing Process
and Handling
the Paper Load

Part Three focuses on a variety of strategies for promoting active learning and for coaching students as thinkers and writers. In Part Four, we turn to strategies for coaching the writing process and for commenting on and grading student papers. As teachers, our goal is to maximize the help we give students while keeping our own workloads manageable. Chapter Thirteen offers ten timesaving strategies for coaching the writing process without becoming buried in paper grading. Chapter Fourteen focuses on ways to write revision-oriented comments that guide students to make significant, global revisions of drafts. Finally, Chapter Fifteen offers ideas for grading student writing using analytic or holistic scales or other kinds of scoring guides tailored to the individual teacher's needs and the demands of subject matter.

The goal of the present chapter is to help instructors work efficiently with their students on the development of their writing skills. Because college professors are busy people—with heavy teaching loads, many committee responsibilities, and obligations for scholarship and professional development—they have only limited time to spend on student writing. This chapter gives you ten timesaving strategies for coaching students through the process of writing an essay. These strategies will help your students produce high-quality work, while keeping your paper-grading load manageable.

The general theory behind these strategies is to get students on the right track early in the writing process before serious problems begin cropping up in drafts, to take advantage of the "summarizable" nature of thesis writing, to enlist other students in the class as first readers of drafts, to make efficient use of student conferences, and to develop timesaving methods for marking and grading student essays. Some of the following strategies, though moderately time intensive the first time you try them (for example, developing scoring guides keyed to assignments), produce materials that can be reused for years. Together, the following ten strategies will help you promote your students' growth as writers and thinkers without burying you in endless stacks of papers.

1. Save Time by Designing Good Assignments _____

One of the best ways to make efficient use of your time is to consider carefully the kinds of writing assignments you give. Much of the writing you assign can be behind-the-scenes exploratory writing, which can be integrated into a class in a variety of ways and often requires only moderate teacher time (or even none at all). (See Chapter Six for ways to use exploratory writing.)

Another highly efficient use of teacher time is to assign a sequence of microthemes that are graded using "models feedback" (Bean, Drenk, and Lee, 1986). (See Chapter Five for a discussion of microthemes, pages 79–83; models feedback is described in this chapter on page 236.)

When assigning longer papers, you can save time and frustration by steering students from the start toward thesis writing or toward an alternative that you desire. Effective assignments usually indicate the task, the rhetorical context (including audience and purpose), instruction about length and manuscript form, and a description of your grading criteria. Students always appreciate a handout sheet that explains the assignment in writing. (See pages 83–86 for further discussion of assignment handouts.) If your goal is thesis-based writing, consider giving the assignment in one of the three ways suggested in Chapter Five (pages 87–90).

Clear assignments prevent problems later on, when students might otherwise barrage you with requests for clarification or submit drafts that need complete dismantling because the assignment did not adequately steer them toward your desired goals. When you explain the assignment in class, allow plenty of time for questions and, if possible, provide an example of an A paper. This is also a good opportunity to stress the value of multiple drafts. Consider asking students to staple to their final drafts all their rough drafts, notes, and doodles (a good defense against plagiarism as well as a way to stress process).

2. Save Time by Clarifying Your Grading Criteria

The more clearly you define your criteria at the outset, the better the final products you will receive. The more students get a feel for what you are looking for, the more help they can give one another during peer review sessions. Here are two effective ways to clarify criteria.

Develop Scoring Guides or Draft Checksheets

Some teachers develop scoring guides or checksheets that can be attached to the assignment as a reminder of the criteria. The following checksheet was developed by a philosophy professor for an assignment on the film *Blade Runner.*

Draft Checksheet for *Blade Runner* Essay

This assignment asks you to defend one of the following theses: "The replicants in the film *Blade Runner* should/should not be granted minimal human rights."

1. Is the thesis being supported clearly stated in the introduction?
2. Does the draft explain the criteria a creature would have to meet in order to be granted minimal human rights? After reading your essay, could someone list your criteria?
3. Does the draft include a rationale for these criteria—that is, arguments showing why the criteria should be accepted?
4. Does the draft show how the replicants do or do not meet these criteria?
5. Does the draft include sufficient details and examples from the film?
6. Is the draft clearly written, well organized, and free from errors in spelling, punctuation, and grammar?

(For additional examples of scoring guides, see the discussion of analytic and holistic scales in Chapter Fifteen, pages 257–259.)

Hold an In-Class Norming Session

A particularly effective learning strategy is an in-class norming session in which students work in groups to reach consensus on the relative ranking of four or five student essays, ranging from excellent to weak, written for a similar assignment. After student groups have "graded" the papers, the instructor leads class discussion with the aim of clarifying his or her criteria and explaining the grades that he or she would give. (See Chapter Nine, pages 158–159, for additional discussion of norming sessions.)

3. Save Time by Using a Class Hour for the Generation of Ideas

If a writing assignment is directly linked to key concepts in the course, class time spent generating ideas for the assignment will not detract from course content. The more students can brainstorm for ideas early on, the more detailed and complex their papers will become. Here are some suggestions for stimulating rich talk about ideas.

Collaborative Small Group Tasks

When all students in the class are given the same assignment (say, to support or attack a given thesis or to respond to the same problematic question), collaborative groups could be asked to develop a series of reasons supporting and opposing the thesis or to create possible solutions to the assigned question. Later in the hour, the instructor could lead a discussion about the kinds of evidence and argumentation needed to support various theses.

An alternative is to have the whole class work together on a related topic; then, outside of class, they could apply the same thinking processes to their own topics.

Paired Interviews

Another useful strategy, especially if students are working on different topics, is to have students interview each other about their work in progress. Place students in pairs (or groups of three) and ask them to "talk through" their ideas with their partners. I guide the discussion by having interviewers ask each writer the following series of questions.

What problem or question is your paper going to address?
Why is this question controversial or otherwise problematic? Why is it significant? Show me what makes this a good question to address.
What is your one-sentence answer to this question? (If the writer hasn't a good thesis statement yet, go on to the next question and then come back to this one. Perhaps you can help the writer figure out a thesis.)
Talk me through your whole argument (or through your ideas so far). As you interview your writer, get him or her to do most of the talking; however, you can respond to the writer by offering suggestions, bringing up additional ideas, playing devil's advocate, and so forth.

During these discussions, I ask writers not to look at their drafts or notes. I do not want them reading what they have already written but rather reformulating their ideas conversationally in this new context. I generally require each student to hold the floor for fifteen to twenty minutes of active talking; the interviewer's job is to keep the talker on task by asking probing questions or playing devil's advocate.

4. Save Time by Having Students Submit Something Early in the Writing Process

I personally dislike reading students' rough drafts (I allow rewrites instead), yet I find it valuable to "check in" on their progress early in the writing process. Rather than asking for drafts, teachers can ask students to submit something else early on—something that can be read quickly and that helps identify students who need extra guidance.

Before offering some suggestions on what to ask for, let me suggest something not to ask for: outlines. Although teachers have traditionally inspected students' outlines, recent research and theory suggest that requiring outlines is not as effective as teachers imagine. First, asking for outlines early on distorts the composing process of many writers who discover and clarify their ideas in the act of writing. As discussed in Chapter Two, the "think first, then write" model implied by early outlines seriously undervalues drafting as a discovery process. The tradition of requiring outlines perhaps holds over from the days of "all about" reports ("Write a report on a famous mathematician of your choice"). It is relatively easy to make a preliminary outline of an "all about" report because the outliner, like the writer of an encyclopedia article, merely divides up a large topic area into chunks. In contrast, the outlinable parts of a thesis-governed paper often cannot be discovered until complex meanings are worked out through composing and revising.

Another disadvantage of requiring outlines is that the word *outline* bears unfortunate baggage for many students—their memories of teachers who treated outlines as finished products with their own peculiar rules about placement of periods, hierarchies of numerals and letters, and so forth. Once graded down for getting a period in the wrong place, students forever after think of outlines as foes, not friends. Finally, research in cognitive psychology suggests that the traditional outline may not be as powerful an organizing tool as the more visual tree diagram (see the discussion of tree diagrams later in this chapter).

Rather than asking for outlines, then, teachers might consider asking for one or more of the following items.

Prospectus

For long writing projects (such as research papers) for which students select their own topics, students can submit a prospectus in which they describe the problem they will address and the direction they intend to take. (For a more detailed description of what to ask for in a prospectus, see Chapter Twelve, page 207.) An effectively designed prospectus assignment can guide students toward a problem-thesis structure and steer them away from "and then" or "all about" writing.

Two Sentences: Question and Thesis

For shorter papers, students can be asked to submit two sentences: a one-sentence question that summarizes the problem the paper addresses and a one-sentence thesis statement that summarizes the writer's argument in response to the question. These two sentences can reveal a surprising number of problems in students' drafts, enabling teachers to identify students who need extra help. I require these two-sentence summaries for all of my short formal essay assignments. I can read and respond to thirty of them in less than an hour, dividing them into three piles: a "looks good" pile, a "promising but here's some brief written advice" pile, and a "come see me in my office and we'll talk" pile.

Abstracts

An alternative to asking for question-plus-thesis summaries is to ask students for 100- to 200-word abstracts of their drafts. Writing abstracts is a classic exercise for developing reading skills, especially the ability to distinguish main ideas from subordinate material (see pages 128–129). The act of summarizing one's own argument helps writers clarify their own thinking and often reveals organizational and conceptual problems that prompt revision. By asking writers to submit abstracts of their drafts, rather than the drafts themselves, teachers cut down on their own reading load while assigning a salutary exercise for students.

5. Save Time by Having Students Conduct Peer Reviews of Drafts

Another timesaving strategy is to have students review each other's drafts. Unfortunately, as all teachers who have tried them know, peer reviews often have disappointing results. Unless the teacher structures the sessions and trains students in what to do, students are apt to give each other eccentric or otherwise unhelpful advice. Peer reviews are worth the trouble only if they result in genuine substantial revision. Fortunately, there are ways to make peer reviews work effectively.

First, teachers must decide which philosophy of peer review best fits their teaching style: response-centered reviews or advice-centered reviews (a full explanation of the differences follows shortly). Writing teachers disagree on which of these methods is superior, and there seems to be no empirical research that would settle the matter. Both types have their characteristic strengths, and each approach probably works best with certain kinds of students or writing tasks. However, they require teachers to structure the review sessions differently.

Second, a teacher must decide the process for exchanging drafts. Some teachers prefer that writers read their drafts out loud to the peer reviewers—the experience of hearing one's language read aloud helps writers discover problem areas. Other teachers ask students to bring copies of their drafts for peer reviewers. Still others have students exchange copies of drafts prior to class in order to make class time more efficient. Again, no single way seems best.

Response-Centered Reviews

This process-oriented, nonintrusive approach places maximum responsibility on the writer for making decisions about what to change in a draft. Classroom procedure is as follows:

1. Divide the class into groups of four.

2. The writer reads the draft out loud (or provides photo-copies for group members to read silently).

3. Group members are given several minutes to take notes on their responses. (I ask listeners to divide a sheet of paper into three columns headed +, –, and ?. In the + column, they note aspects of the draft that worked well. In the – column, they note problem areas and any negative reactions, such as disagreement with ideas. In the ? column, they note questions that occurred while listening, such as places that need clarification or more development.)

4. Each group member, in turn, explains to the writer what he or she liked or did not like, what worked and what didn't work, what was confusing, and so forth. Group members do not give advice; they simply describe their personal responses to the draft as written.

5. The writer takes notes during each response but does not enter into a discussion. (The writer listens, without trying to defend the piece or explain "what I meant.")

6. After each group member has responded to a writer's essay, the next group member reads his or her essay. The cycle continues.

In this method, no one gives the writer advice. Respondents simply describe their reactions to the piece. Often the writer receives contradictory messages: one reader might like a given passage, while another dislikes it. Thus, the group sends the writer equivocal, ambiguous messages that reflect the truth about how real readers respond to real writing, leaving the writer responsible for deciding what to do. (For more detailed advice on conducting response-centered peer reviews, see Spear, 1988, and Elbow and Belanoff, 1989.)

Advice-Centered Reviews

This approach is more product oriented and more directive: peer reviewers collaborate to give advice to the writer. This method works best when students have internalized criteria for an assignment through norming sessions or teacher-provided scoring guides. What follows is a recommended process for an advice-centered peer review.

1. Divide the class into pairs, and have each pair exchange drafts with another pair.

2. The two students in each pair collaborate to compose a jointly written review of the two drafts they have received. I ask pairs to use a checklist like the following:

   a. Write out the question, problem, or issue that this draft addresses.

   b. Write out the writer's complete thesis statement. (Note: If you have trouble with a and b, concentrate on helping the writer clarify the problem and thesis.)

   c. Note with a wavy line in the margins all places where you got confused as a reader.

   d. Write out your assessment of the strengths and weaknesses of the writer's ideas. Assuming that the teacher is interested primarily in the quality of thinking in a paper, how will the teacher respond to the ideas in this draft? Where do you disagree with the writer?

   e. Reread the draft, looking for quality of support. Does the writer offer sufficient details to support the argument (data, statistics, quotations, textual references, personal examples)? Does the writer need to do more research?

    f. Write out at least two things that you think are particularly strong about this draft.

    g. Make three or four directive statements recommending specific changes that the writer should make in the next draft.

3. The pairs then return the drafts to the original writers, along with the collaboratively written reviews. If time remains, the two pairs can meet jointly to discuss their reviews.

Because advice-centered reviews take quite a bit longer than response-centered reviews, I usually ask writers to supply copies of their drafts to their peer reviewers the night before class so that the reviewers can read the drafts carefully and come to the review session with critiques already in mind. Because the reviews are collaboratively written by two students, they are usually well considered and thoughtful. Of course, the writer should take the reviews as advisory only and make his or her own decisions about how much of the advice to use.

Out-of-Class Peer Reviews

A variation on the above approach can be used for out-of-class peer reviews, thus preserving class time for other matters.

1. Divide the class into pairs, and have each pair exchange drafts with another pair.

2. Each pair meets outside of class to write their collaborative reviews, based on the checksheet, and they return the reviews the next day in class.

The advantage for writers in this out-of-class method is that the reviewers can spend longer than an hour on task. The advantage for the teacher is that no class time is needed.

Some General Principles for Conducting Peer Reviews

- Do not expect students to give each other very good advice about sentence structure or style. For some reason, they are not good at seeing stylistic problems in other people's drafts, and they tend to make impressionistic comments ("This doesn't flow . . ." "This sounds funny . . .").
- Train students to engage each other at the level of ideas.
- Train students to back up comments with specific examples from the draft; stress the importance of precision when giving advice.

6. Save Time by Referring Students to Your Institution's Writing Center (If Your Institution Does Not Have One, Lobby to Get One) _____

Writing centers, whether staffed by professional tutors or student peers, perform an enormous service for writers from any discipline and at any skill level. Most contemporary writing centers help students at any stage of the writing process—working with the student to clarify an assignment and brainstorm for ideas, to make substantive revisions in drafts with attention to the quality of ideas as well as organization and development, and to edit for style and sentence correctness.

At many institutions, writing centers support writing across the curriculum and are not simply places for weak or remedial writers. Nor are they "fix-it shops" where students go to get their grammar and spelling checked. Writing centers try to create for students the same kind of environment that professional writers create for themselves: a community of helpful readers who will listen to one another's ideas and respond to drafts in progress. Going to a writing center does not guarantee that the writer will immediately improve the paper, but it does ensure that the writer has talked about his or her ideas and had at least one careful reader respond to them.

If you are not sure of the kind of support the writing center at your institution can provide your students, consider calling its director for an appointment. If your institution does not have a writing center or if you would like to see your center's services expanded, make your desires known to the appropriate administrator. Writing centers are proven, cost-effective ways to help faculty members coach writing. Moreover, they help foster campuswide attention on writing as a critical thinking process central to the academic enterprise.

7. Save Time by Making One-on-One Writing Conferences As Efficient as Possible _____

The art of conferring with students on their writing requires good listening skills supplemented with the ability to provide timely, appropriate guidance. This section offers some advice on how to conduct an individual writing conference.

Distinguish Between Higher-Order and Lower-Order Concerns

Conferences are most productive if you concentrate first on the higher-order concerns of ideas, organization, development, and overall clarity as opposed to the lower-order concerns of style, grammar, and mechanics. The lower-order concerns are lower not because they are unimportant but because they cannot be efficiently attended to until the higher-order concerns have been resolved. (There is little point to correcting the comma splices in a paragraph that needs to be completely reconceptualized.) Conferences should focus primarily on helping students create good, idea-rich arguments and wrestle them into a structure that works.

Start a Conference by Setting an Agenda with the Student

Conferences work best when students are encouraged to do most of the talking—rehearsing their papers' arguments while the teacher listens and coaches. Too often, though, conferences become dominated by teacher talk. Try to avoid the tendency to tell students what to say in their papers. Although you might picture an "ideal essay" in response to your assignment, very few students are going to produce what you yourself would write. Conferences should be primarily listening sessions where the instructor asks questions and the student does 80 to 90 percent of the talking. Most students have never experienced a teacher's actually being interested in their ideas. Engaging them in genuine conversation, showing real interest in their work, respecting their ideas—these are enormous favors to a novice writer.

To establish a supportive listening tone at the beginning of a conference, the instructor can work with the student to set a mutual agenda. Here is a suggested sequence of stages for agenda setting.

Instructor	**Student**
Ask the student to explain the assignment. How would you summarize the assignment in your own words? Are there any parts of the assignment that you are fuzzy on?	Student reveals how well he or she understands the assignment.
Find out the student's expectations for the conference. How do you like your paper so far? What kind of help do you need from this conference?	Instructor learns something of the student's own assessment of the paper and attitude toward it. Instructor gets some sense of what kind of help the student wants.
Get the student to discuss his or her draft and writing process. How much work have you put into this draft? How far are you in the writing process? How much more time are you willing to put into the paper?	Student begins to feel comfortable talking; instructor gets a better sense of the student and the paper as well as of the student's own unvoiced problems with the paper. Instructor gets insights into the student's writing process.

Instructor	**Student**
Instructor reads the draft silently while giving the student a task: write out your thesis and main points; then write down the main problems you see with your draft.	Student writes in response to the writing prompt. Student must take responsibility for making an initial assessment of the draft.

As you read the draft, take mental notes that will help you focus the conference later. One suggestion is to place symbols in the margins of the draft such as + (things that are well done), * (problem areas), and ? (things you want to ask questions about). (I usually ask the student's permission before writing on the draft.) From your marginal symbols, you can see the positive elements that you want to reinforce as well as problem areas and places to ask questions about. Decide the two or three most important things to work on, beginning with higher-order concerns first. Now the conference resumes:

Instructor	**Student**
Begin with positive comments. I really like this part (be specific). You do a good job here.	Student, who sits in agony waiting to hear what you say about the paper, receives reinforcement.
Inform the student honestly of your own assessment. You are definitely on the right track here. You do a great job with Jones. But there are some places where you lose focus on your thesis, and sometimes you have too much summary of different points of view but not enough analysis and argument. You also seem to misunderstand Wheeler.	Student gets a sense of your assessment right away. Student does not have to guess what you are thinking. Student sees strengths in the draft but gets a sense of the kinds of problems you think should be worked on.
Reassure the student that it is common to have such problems with rough drafts. It's normal in a first draft to wander from the thesis. This happens to me all the time. That's why I have to go through so many drafts.	Student sees writing as a process, starts to see comments less as criticism and more as guidelines for improvement. Student feels less "dumb" and gains confidence in the value of revision.
Collaborate with the student to set an agenda for the conference. Choose a limited number of problems to work on. You don't have to solve every problem for your next draft. Should we just work on clarifying your thesis and getting your argument better organized?	In response to your initial suggestion, student might say, "But I'd also like to see more clearly what you mean by analysis rather than just summary." Student becomes involved in deciding what to work on. Instructor and student have a plan for how to spend the rest of the conference.

Develop a Repertoire of Conferencing Strategies

After setting an agenda, you begin the actual conference. How you conduct the conference depends on where the student is in the writing process. Some students need help at the very highest levels—finding a thesis and a basic plan for an argument. Others might have a good overall plan but lots of confusing places along the way. In conducting a conference, you may wish to try one or more of the following strategies, tailored to each individual case:

If Ideas Are Thin

Make an idea map to brainstorm for more ideas (explained later in this chapter).

Play devil's advocate to deepen and complicate the ideas.

Help the writer add more examples, better details, more supporting data or arguments.

If the Reader Gets Lost

Have the student talk through the ideas to clear up confusing spots.

Help the student sharpen the thesis by seeing it as the writer's answer to a controversial or problematic question (get the student to articulate the question that the thesis "answers").

Make an outline or a tree diagram to help with organization (explained later in this chapter).

Help the writer clarify the focus by asking questions about purpose:

"My purpose in this paper is . . ."

"My purpose in this section/paragraph is . . ."

"Before reading my paper, the reader will have this view of my topic: . . .; after reading my paper, my reader will have this different view of my topic: . . ."

Show the student where you get confused or "miscued" in reading the draft ("I started getting lost here because I couldn't see why you were giving me this information," or, "I thought you were going to say X, but then you said Y").

Show the student how to write transitions between major sections or between paragraphs.

If You Can Understand the Sentences but Cannot See the Point

Help the writer articulate meaning by asking "so what" questions: "I can understand what you are saying here, but I don't quite understand why you are saying it. I read all these facts, and I say, 'So what?' What do these facts have to do with your thesis?" (This helps the writer bring the point to the surface. You can then help the writer formulate topic sentences for paragraphs.)

Throughout the conference, try to make "readerly" rather than "writerly" comments—that is, describe your mental experience in trying to read the draft rather than telling the writer how to fix it. For example, say, "I had trouble seeing the point of this paragraph," rather than, "Begin with a topic sentence." This approach helps writers see that their purpose in revising is to make the reader's job easier rather than to follow "English teacher rules."

In conducting conferences, I like to have plenty of blank sheets of paper available; as the student talks, I jot down the student's ideas. At the end of the conference, I give the student my notes as a record of the conference. Sometimes the students and I work together to create either an idea map or a tree diagram. The next two sections explain these strategies.

Use an Idea Map for Brainstorming

Idea maps (sometimes called *mind maps* or *concept maps*) work best early in the writing process as a tool for generating ideas. To help a student make an idea map, you draw a circle in the center of the page and write a triggering word or phrase in the circle (usually a broad topic area, a question, or a thesis). Then, as the writer talks, you record his or her ideas on branches and subbranches that extend from the circle. As long as the writer pursues one train of thought, you keep recording the ideas on subbranches off the main branch. But as soon as that chain of ideas runs dry, you lead the writer to a new starting point and begin a new branch. Figure 13.1 shows an idea map that a student and I made for an assignment to evaluate arguments by Carl Cohen and Peter Singer for and against the use of animals in medical research.

As Figure 13.1 reveals, an idea map records a writer's emerging ideas in a visual format; notations are arranged randomly around the initial hub but hierarchically off each branch. This half-random, half-hierarchical pattern stimulates productive thinking, for it invites the writer to elaborate previously recorded ideas (by adding new subbranches off an existing branch) or to begin a new train of thought (by adding a new branch). The idea map thus stimulates open-ended brainstorming while simultaneously helping the writer discover the beginnings of an organizational structure. My goal is to have the student leave my office with idea map in hand, along with my cheery exhortation to write a draft.

Figure 13.1. An Idea Map.

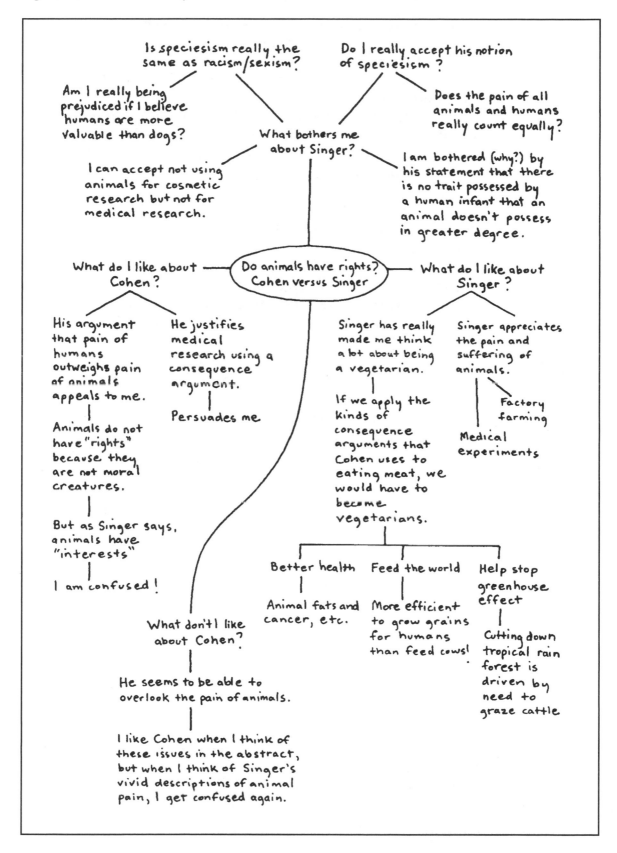

Use a Tree Diagram to Help with Structure

After generating an idea map, a student needs to develop the ideas further by writing a rough draft. At this point, most writers need some sort of plan, but how elaborate or detailed that plan is varies considerably from writer to writer. Some writers need to plan extensively before they can write; others need to write extensively before they can plan. But somewhere along the way, whether at the first-draft stage or much later in the process, writers need to concentrate on the shape of their arguments. At this point, I recommend the power of tree diagrams over traditional outlines.

A tree diagram differs from an outline in that headings and subheadings are indicated through spatial locations rather than through a system of letters and numerals. Figure 13.2 (produced by the same student who brainstormed the idea map in Figure 13.1) shows a tree diagram of an evaluative essay comparing two arguments on animal rights. The writer's thesis is shown at the top of the tree, with supporting arguments displayed vertically on branches beneath the thesis.

Although the traditional outline may be the more familiar way to represent an argument's structure, tree diagrams are often a more powerful device for planning and shaping. Their visual nature makes it easy to see at a glance both the skeletal structure of an argument and its sequential parts. Tree diagrams can also be powerful aids to invention because you can put question marks anywhere on a tree to "hold a space open" for ideas that you have not thought of yet. For example, early in his planning stages, the writer of the animal rights paper wrote a preliminary tree diagram with a branch that looked like this:

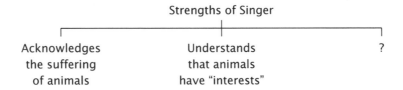

Using question marks as place markers allows the writer to visualize a large-scale structure for the paper while holding a slot open for parts of the argument still to be "discovered." The fluid, evolving nature of tree diagrams, in which branches can be added or moved around, makes them particularly valuable planning tools for writers.

I consequently use tree diagrams in student conferences to help writers with structure. Working together, we place the

Figure 13.2. A Tree Diagram.

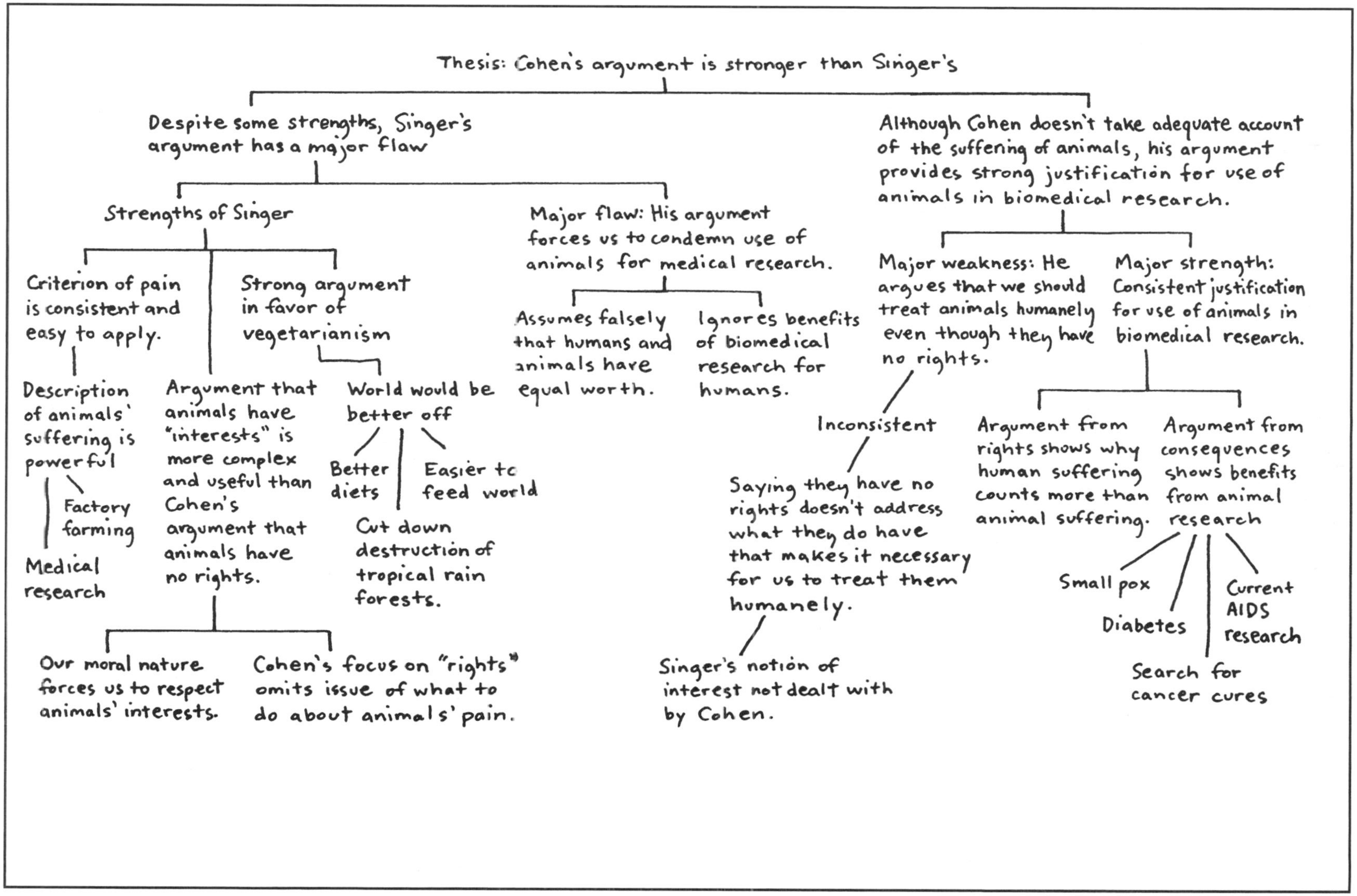

Thesis: Cohen's argument is stronger than Singer's

Despite some strengths, Singer's argument has a major flaw

- Strengths of Singer
  - Criterion of pain is consistent and easy to apply.
  - Strong argument in favor of vegetarianism
    - World would be better off
      - Easier to feed world
      - Better diets
      - Cut down destruction of tropical rain forests.
  - Description of animals' suffering is powerful
    - Factory farming
    - Medical research
  - Argument that animals have "interests" is more complex and useful than Cohen's argument that animals have no rights.

- Major flaw: His argument forces us to condemn use of animals for medical research.
  - Assumes falsely that humans and animals have equal worth.
  - Ignores benefits of biomedical research for humans.

Although Cohen doesn't take adequate account of the suffering of animals, his argument provides strong justification for use of animals in biomedical research.

- Major weakness: He argues that we should treat animals humanely even though they have no rights.
  - Inconsistent
    - Saying they have no rights doesn't address what they do have that makes it necessary for us to treat them humanely.
  - Singer's notion of interest not dealt with by Cohen.
  - Our moral nature forces us to respect animals' interests.
  - Cohen's focus on "rights" omits issue of what to do about animals' pain.

- Major strength: Consistent justification for use of animals in biomedical research.
  - Argument from rights shows why human suffering counts more than animal suffering.
    - Argument from consequences shows benefits from animal research
      - Small pox
      - Diabetes
      - Current AIDS research
      - Search for cancer cures

writer's thesis at the top of the tree. Underneath the thesis, we add the main points the writer will need to support the thesis, sometimes adding question marks for additional points that may be thought of later. Underneath each point, we brainstorm ways to develop that section of the argument (subarguments, data, details, evidence, elaboration), again adding question marks to suggest that more ideas may be discovered in the act of drafting. I then give students their tree diagrams when they leave my office, confident that they have a "map" for drafting or revision.

When Working on Sentence Concerns, Focus on One or Two Paragraphs

Having helped a writer find ideas and get them focused, organized, and developed, the teacher has done the lion's share of the work of coaching writing. Many students, of course, will have additional problems with grammar, sentence structure, and mechanics, or they may have styles that are wooden, verbose, awkward, or choppy. If you have the time and the inclination to work with students on these matters, consider helping to edit one or two paragraphs and then asking the student to scrutinize the rest of the draft in the same way. It is important that you do not become the student's editor or proofreader. Writers need to learn how to find and fix their own grammatical and stylistic problems. (That is why I also suggest not circling or marking errors when you grade papers—see Chapter Four and also Chapter Fourteen, pages 246–248, where I suggest strategies for making students find and fix their own errors.)

8. Save Time by Occasionally Holding Group Paper Conferences

Although teachers usually work individually with students, group conferences can sometimes be more lively, more productive, and more efficient than one-on-one conferences. Whenever a group of students shares a common writing problem, consider inviting four or five students at once for a group conference.

Group conferences are particularly valuable at the idea-generating stage of writing. While listening to the teacher help student A focus a paper topic, students B, C, and D start thinking of ideas for their own papers. But more importantly, students B, C, and D often come up with great ideas for A. The back-and-forth dynamics of a group conference, in which the participants collaborate to help one another, make them especially useful at the early stages of writing.

9. Save Time by Using Efficient Methods for Giving Written Feedback

Perhaps the most traditional way to coach the writing process is to place comments on students' essays. Because commenting on papers is a major part of teaching writing, Chapter Fourteen is devoted entirely to this topic. However, a few suggestions about commenting are appropriate here. I also explain two alternatives to written comments: "models feedback" and scoring guides.

Consider Commenting on Drafts Rather Than Final Products or Consider Allowing Rewrites

The best strategy for improving student writing is to make comments not on finished products but on typed late-stage drafts. (An alternative is to permit rewrites of papers so that you treat "final versions" as if they were drafts in progress.) The purpose of the comments is to provide specific advice on what needs to be added, changed, or reconceptualized for the final version. Composition research suggests that unless students do something with the teacher's comments—by making the revisions suggested—the teacher's commenting time is largely wasted. Comments, in other words, do not transfer well to later papers; they need to be applied directly to the work in progress.

My own personal strategy is not to read drafts but to permit rewrites (except for the last course paper, which comes at the end of the term). This method allows me to comment on papers as if they were drafts in progress and yet assign a grade as if they were finished products. Students who are satisfied with their grades do not rewrite (thus cutting down on the number of resubmissions I receive). I have settled on this method because it has been more effective for me than commenting on drafts. The quality of writing I initially receive is higher (students, not wanting to rewrite, try to turn in their best work on the first try), and for some students, the desire to improve their grades motivates serious revision. Whichever method you choose, the point of your commentary is to stimulate and guide revision.

Make Limited, Focused Comments and Avoid Marking Errors

Rather than commenting on everything wrong with the draft so that the student is overwhelmed with suggestions, consider limiting your comments to the major changes you would like to see in the next revision, focusing first on the higher-order concerns of ideas, organization, development, and clarity. See Chapter Fourteen for a detailed discussion of how to write revision-oriented comments on student essays. See Chapter Four for a discussion of sentence-level errors.

Use Models Feedback on Short Assignments

When students write microthemes or other short essays in response to the same assignment, consider using "models feedback." With models feedback, you do not make any comments on the papers; consequently, you can grade them very rapidly (often taking no more than a minute or two per paper). You provide feedback through in-class discussion of selected essays. If you find a good A response in your set of papers, duplicate it for the class or put it on an overhead projector. If not, write your own A-worthy microtheme as a model. The models feedback comes from a discussion of what constitutes an A response as well as a discussion of typical problem areas found in weaker papers. This discussion accomplishes two purposes: it clarifies for students the writing and thinking skills exhibited in strong papers, and it reviews and clarifies recent course material (the content part of your assignment). Often students say they learn more about writing from models feedback than from traditional comments on papers.

Use a Scoring Guide or an Analytic Scale

Scoring guides and analytic scales are discussed in detail in Chapter Fifteen. Briefly, they allow you to score separate features of a piece of writing and then sum them up for a total score. Although analytic scales cannot provide as much information as individual comments, they are more informative than a single grade by itself. They are particularly useful when your workload prevents detailed commentary on papers.

10. Save Time by Putting Minimal Comments on Finished Products That Will not Be Revised

If you have been willing to comment on rough drafts or if you accept rewrites, switch your role at the end of the process from that of coach to that of judge. You need not feel obligated to write on the finished-product version of a paper at all. Simply attach a score sheet based on your evaluation criteria and give the paper a grade.

Students always appreciate a brief end comment about your reaction to the paper or your justification for a score in a certain area, but you need not feel obligated to make extended comments. This saves time particularly with papers due at the end of a term, when students will not be revising their work.

Conclusion: A Review of Timesaving Strategies

The traditional way to coach writing is to make copious, red-penciled comments on finished student products—almost universally regarded among composition specialists as an inefficient use of teacher energy. The comments seldom lead to improvement in student writing, and the thought of grading stacks of depressingly bad student essays discourages teachers from assigning writing. This chapter suggests ten different strategies for coaching writing, aimed at improving the quality of final products while reducing the amount of commenting time teachers need to devote to papers. Here is a nutshell review of the ten strategies discussed in this chapter.

1. **Design good assignments.**

    Assign exploratory writing; consider using microthemes.

    Create assignment handouts specifying task, purpose, audience, criteria, desired manuscript form (see pages 83–86 for details).

    If your goal is thesis-based writing, consider using one of the three assignment strategies in Chapter Five, pages 87–90.

2. **Clarify your grading criteria.**

    Create a scoring guide or peer review checksheet.

    Hold an in-class norming session (see Chapter Nine, pages 158–159).

3. **Devote a class hour to generating ideas.**

    Create a small group brainstorming task.

    Have members of pairs interview one another.

4. **Have students submit something to you early in the writing process.**

    Consider asking for a prospectus, a question-plus-thesis summary, or an abstract.

    Use these to identify students who need extra help.

5. **Have students be the first readers of each other's drafts.**

   Require peer reviews (either response-centered or advice centered).

   To preserve class time, consider out-of-class peer reviews.

6. **Refer students to your writing center (or lobby to start one).**

   Recognize the value of writing centers for all writers, not just weak writers.

   Stress the usefulness of writing centers at all stages of the writing process.

7. **Make one-on-one conferences efficient.**

   Focus first on higher-order concerns (ideas, focus, organization and development).

   Begin each conference by setting an agenda.

   Develop a repertoire of conferencing strategies.

   Consider using idea maps and tree diagrams.

8. **Consider holding group conferences early in the writing process.**

9. **Use efficient methods for giving feedback on papers.**

   Comment on late drafts rather than final products (or allow rewrites).

   Make revision-oriented comments, focusing first on higher-order concerns.

   For microthemes, use models feedback in lieu of traditional comments.

   When time is at a premium, use a grading scale or a scoring guide instead of making comments.

10. **Put minimal comments on finished products that will not be revised.**

CHAPTER 14

Writing Comments on Students' Papers

Whenever I conduct workshops in the marking and grading of student writing, I like to quote a sentence from William Zinsser's *Writing to Learn* (1988): "The writing teacher's ministry is not just to the words but to the person who wrote the words" (p. 48). I value this quotation because all of us as teachers, late at night, having read whole stacks of student essays, sometimes forget the human being who wrote the words that currently annoy us. We lapse into sarcasm. We let our irritation show on the page. Perhaps nothing involves us as directly in the messiness of teaching writing as our attempts to comment on our students' essays. We know how we feel ourselves when we ask a colleague to read one of our drafts (apologetic, vulnerable). But we sometimes forget these feelings when we comment on students' papers. Sometimes we do not treat students' work in progress with the same sensitivity that we would treat our colleague's.

The best kind of commentary enhances the writer's feeling of dignity. The worst kind can be dehumanizing and insulting—often to the bewilderment of the teacher, whose intentions were kindly but whose techniques ignored the personal dimension of writing.

Imagine, for a moment, a beginning tennis class in which we ask George to give his first performance. In skill category 1, serving the tennis ball, poor George goofs up miserably by whacking the ball sideways into the fence. Here is the instructor's feedback: "You didn't hold the racket properly, your feet weren't lined up right, your body was too stiff, you didn't toss the ball in the correct plane, you threw it too high, you didn't cock your wrist properly, and you looked awkward. Moreover, you hit the ball with the wood instead of the strings. Weren't you paying attention when I lectured on how to do it? I am placing you in remedial tennis!"

Although we are far too enlightened (and far too kind) to teach tennis this way, the analogy is uncomfortably apt for the traditional way writing teachers have taught writing. Ignoring the power of positive reinforcement, writing teachers have red-penciled students' errors with puritanical fervor. These teachers have of course aimed for the right goals—they want to produce skillful and joyful writers, just as the tennis instructor wants to produce skillful and joyful tennis players. But the techniques have been misguided.

Students' Responses to Teachers' Comments

Part of the problem is that our comments on students' papers are necessarily short and therefore cryptic. We know what we mean, and we know the tone that we intend to convey. Often, however, students are bewildered by our comments, and they sometimes read into them a tone and a meaning entirely different from our intentions.

The extent to which students misread teachers' comments is revealed in Spandel and Stiggins's study (1990), in which the investigators interviewed students about their reactions to teachers' comments on their papers. Students were asked to describe their reactions to specific marginal comments that teachers placed on their essays—either what they thought the comments meant or how the comments made them feel (pp. 85–87). When a teacher wrote, "Needs to be more concise," students reacted this way:

> Confusing. I need to know what the teacher means specifically.
> This is an obvious comment.
> I'm not Einstein. I can't get every point right.
> I muffed.
> I thought you wanted details and support.
> This frustrates me!
> Define "concise."
> Vague, vague.

When a teacher wrote, "Be more specific," students reacted this way:

You be more specific.
I'm frustrated.
I tried and it didn't pay off.
It's going to be too long then.
I feel mad—it really doesn't matter.
I try, but I don't know every fact.

When a teacher wrote, "You haven't really thought this through," students reacted this way:

That is a mean reply.
I guess I blew it!
I'm upset.
That makes me madder than you can imagine!
How do you know what I thought?

When a teacher wrote, "Try harder!" students reacted this way:

I did try!
You're a stupid jerk.
Maybe I am trying as hard as I can.
I feel like kicking the teacher.
Baloney! You don't know how hard I tried.
This kind of comment makes me feel really bad and I'm frustrated!

The conclusions of this study are worth quoting:

Negative comments, however well intentioned they are, tend to make students feel bewildered, hurt, or angry. They stifle further attempts at writing. It would seem on the face of it that one good way to help a budding writer would be to point out what he or she is doing wrong, but, in fact, it usually doesn't help; it hurts. Sometimes it hurts a lot.

What does help, however, is to point out what the writer is doing well. Positive comments build confidence and make the writer want to try again. However, there's a trick to writing good positive comments. They must be truthful, and they must be very specific [p. 87].

To improve our techniques at commenting on our students' papers, then, we need to remember our purpose, which is not to point out everything wrong with the paper but to facilitate improvement. When marking and grading papers, we should keep in mind that we have two quite distinct roles to play, depending on where our students are in the writing process. At the drafting stage, our role is coach. Our goal is to provide useful instruction, good advice, and warm encouragement. At the end of the writing process, when students submit final copy, our role is judge. At this stage, we uphold the standards of our profession, giving out high marks only to those essays that meet the criteria we have set.

The Purpose of Commenting: To Coach Revision _____

When we comment on papers, I have argued, the role we should play is that of coach. The purpose of commenting is to provide guidance for revision, for it is in the act of revising that our students learn most deeply both what they want to say and what readers need for ease of comprehension; revising means rethinking, reconceptualizing, "seeing again"—for in the hard work of revising, students learn how experienced writers really compose.

As mentioned briefly in Chapter Thirteen, there are two strategies for ensuring that your comments will help stimulate revision. The first is to comment on drafts a week or so before students are to submit their finished papers. When using this strategy, I prefer to comment only on late-stage drafts, after the writers have gone through peer review. Because I do not like to read handwriting, I ask for a typed late-stage draft.

The second strategy, which is my favorite method, is to allow rewrites after I return the "finished" papers. Because not all students will choose to rewrite, this method is less time consuming for me, and the quality of the writing I initially receive is higher. By allowing rewrites, I can gear all my comments toward revision and yet feel comfortable applying rigorous grading standards because I know that students can rewrite. Moreover, the opportunity to improve less-than-hoped-for grades inspires many students toward serious revision.

From a teacher's standpoint, commenting to prompt revision, as opposed to justifying a grade or pointing out errors, may also change one's whole orientation toward reading student writing. (Recall the difference between the revision-oriented and the editing-oriented commentary on the student paragraph in Chapter Four, pages 67–69.) You begin looking for the *promise* of a draft rather than its mistakes. You begin seeing yourself as *responding to* rather than *correcting* a set of papers. You think of limiting your comments to the two or three things that the writer should work on for the next draft rather than commenting copiously on everything. You think of reading for ideas rather than for errors. In short, you think of coaching rather than judging.

General Strategy for Commenting on Student Drafts: A Hierarchy of Questions _____

Commenting effectively on drafts requires a consistent philosophy and a plan. Because your purpose is to stimulate meaningful revision, your best strategy is to limit your commentary to a few problems that you want the student to tackle when preparing the next draft. It thus helps to establish a hierarchy of concerns descending from higher-order issues (ideas, organization, development, and overall clarity) to lower-order issues (sentence correctness, style, mechanics, spelling, and so forth). What follows is a sequence of questions arranged in descending order of concern. My recommendation is to limit your comments to only two or three of the questions; proceed to lower-order concerns only when a draft is reasonably successful at the higher levels.

As you read through the following discussion, you might find it useful to have at hand one or two student papers that you are currently marking and to try out the suggestions I will make, perhaps comparing them to your current practice.

Commenting on Higher-Order Concerns

Commentary should be aimed first at the higher-level concerns of ideas, organization, development, and overall clarity. Here is a hierarchy of questions you can ask to stimulate higher-order revision. (These questions assume an assignment calling for thesis-based academic writing.)

1. Does the Draft Follow the Assignment? If the draft is not fulfilling the assignment, there is no purpose in commenting further. Tell the writer that the draft is on the wrong track and that he or she needs to start over by rereading the assignment carefully and perhaps seeking help from you. I generally return such a draft unmarked and ungraded.

2. Does the Writer Have a Thesis That Addresses an Appropriate Problem or Question? Once you see that a draft addresses the assignment, look next at its overall focus. Does the draft have a thesis? Does the thesis respond to an appropriate question or problem? As discussed in Chapter Two, thesis writing is unfamiliar to students, whose natural tendency is toward "all about" reports, toward summarizing rather than analyzing, or toward the unfocused dumping of data or information.

Drafts exhibiting problems at this level may have no discernible problem-thesis structure; other drafts may have a thesis, but one that is not stated explicitly or is buried deep in the body of the paper, forcing you to wander about lost before finally seeing what the writer intends. Frequently drafts become clearer at the end than they were at the beginning—evidence that the writer has clarified his or her thinking during the act of composing. To use the language of Flower (1979), such a draft is "writer-based" rather than "reader-based"; that is, the draft follows the order of the writer's discovery process rather than a revised order that meets the reader's needs. Thus, drafts that become clear only in the conclusion need to be revised globally. In some cases, you may wish to guide the writer toward a prototypical academic introduction that explains the problem to be addressed, states the thesis, and gives a brief overview of the whole argument. (See the discussion of academic introductions in Chapter Twelve, pages 207–209.) Composing such an introduction forces the writer to imagine the argument from the reader's perspective. Typical end comments addressing thesis and focus include these:

> I can't find a thesis here, nor is it clear what problem or question you are addressing. Please see me for help.

> Your thesis finally becomes clear by the end; for your next draft, move it up to the introduction to help your reader. Open your intro by explaining the problem your thesis will address, and then follow that with your thesis. Also, the reader needs a preview map of your argument.

3. If the Draft Has a Thesis, What Is the Quality of the Argument Itself? What are the strengths and weaknesses of the ideas? Marginal and end comments for this level address questions about ideas. Is the argument appropriate to your discipline? Is the argument logical? Is there appropriate use of relevant and sufficient evidence? Are the ideas developed with sufficient complexity, subtlety, and insight? Is there adequate awareness of and attention to opposing views? Typical marginal comments addressing these concerns might be the following:

> Interesting idea!

> Nice comparison of X to Y here.

> Good point—I hadn't thought of it in quite this way.

> Expand and explain; could you give an example?

> Aren't you overlooking X's point of view here?

> I don't see how you got from X to Y. Argument is confusing.

> This is too much a rehash of X. Move from summarizing to analyzing.

> You have covered X well but haven't addressed Y or Z.

> You need to anticipate and respond to opposing views here.

> What's your evidence for this assertion?

4. Is the Draft Effectively Organized at the Macro Level? As writers, we all struggle with organization, often producing final products organized differently from our original rough drafts. Student writers have even greater problems with organization and often need our personal help. When commenting on organization, try considering questions like these: Can the draft be outlined or tree-diagramed? What should be added to the draft? What should be eliminated? What should be moved or shifted around? Are there adequate transitions between paragraphs and sections? Are all details tied to points? Are all points supported by details? Are the purpose, point, and structure of the essay adequately previewed for the reader through a good title and introduction?

> Comment on the title, which should suggest the thesis of the piece. If the title is good, praise it. If not, suggest improvements (see pages 209–210).
>
> Comment on the opening paragraph/introduction. The opening should engage the reader's attention and, in most academic writing, set forth a problem or question that the essay will address. If the opening has a good thesis, praise it.
>
> Look at the opening sentences of paragraphs. These should be transition sentences with forward- and backward-looking elements. Praise good transitions. Point out ways to improve others. In academic writing, paragraphs typically have explicit topic sentences.

Although many students may need personal help in reaching solutions, you can draw students' attention to organizational problems by placing "readerly" comments in the margins. Typical comments include these:

> How does this part fit?
>
> You lost me in that last sentence; I'm getting confused.
>
> What's the point of this section?
>
> How does this paragraph relate to what you just said?
>
> Your introduction made me expect to hear about X next, but this is about Y.
>
> You're bouncing all over. I need a road map of where we have been and where we are going.

5. Is the Draft Organized Effectively at the Micro Level? Are paragraphs unified and coherent? Often readers first become aware of organizational problems when they get confused by the writer's paragraphing. What one often sees in student drafts is a series of short, choppy paragraphs (perhaps in imitation of the paragraphing in print advertisements or popular magazine articles) or, conversely, long paragraphs that change direction midstream so that the last part of the paragraph seems to have nothing to do with the first part. Writing teachers consider a paragraph unified if all the sentences support or develop the controlling idea, often stated explicitly in a topic sentence. They consider a paragraph coherent if the sentences link to each other without abrupt leaps or gaps in the flow of thought.

To help students notice problems of unity and coherence in their paragraphing, you can get mileage out of marginal comments like these:

Why so many short paragraphs?

This paragraph wanders. What's its main point?

This paragraph has lots of details, but I can't see their point. Add a topic sentence?

You seem to be making several points here without developing them. Break into separate paragraphs and develop each?

These sentences don't link to each other. Fill in gaps?

As an example of the kinds of paragraph-level revisions one hopes to promote, Exhibit 14.1 shows how a student revised a section of a nursing research paper in response to teacher commentary.

Commenting on Lower-Order Concerns

Lower-order concerns such as grammatical errors, misspellings, punctuation mistakes, and awkwardness in style are frequent sources of confusion and annoyance in student papers. If teachers try to note them all—especially if the teacher becomes a line editor and begins fixing them—commenting on these errors can be dismayingly time consuming. In Chapter Four, I argue for a philosophy of error that places maximum responsibility on students for learning to edit their own work. This philosophy follows Haswell's practice of "minimal marking" (1983), in which the teacher tells a student that his or her paper is marred by sentence errors and that the student's grade will either be reduced or unrecorded until most of the errors are found and corrected. To assist students, instructors can place an X in the margins next to lines that contain errors, but following the minimal-marking policy means that the errors themselves are not circled or marked.

The beauty of this policy, from a teacher's perspective, is that abandoning the role of proofreader and line editor saves substantial marking time. More importantly, it trains students to develop new editing habits for eliminating their own careless errors. Students learn to pore over their drafts with a "reader's eye," to use a grammar handbook, and to keep lists of their characteristic errors.

Exhibit 14.1. Student Writing Before and After Teacher Commentary.

Violence against women is a significant issue. Statistics vary on how many women are battered. Fifty percent of all women will experience battery at some point in their lives (Walker, 1979).

What does this have to do with nursing?

Choppy paragraphs

"One in every fifty pregnant women may be beaten, making abuse during pregnancy more common than the incidence of placental previa or gestational diabetes" (Campbell, 1986, p. 179).

Sexual frustration, mood swings, and general anxiety about the future often occur in pregnancy.

Connect to preceding paragraph?

Violence against women is a significant issue for obstetrical nurses. Although statistics vary, some researchers estimate that fifty percent of all women will experience battery at some point in their lives (Walker, 1979). There is no reason to believe that such violence diminishes when the women are pregnant. In fact, nursing research performed by Campbell (1986) estimates that "one in every fifty pregnant women may be beaten, making abuse during pregnancy more common than the incidence of placental previa or gestational diabetes" (p. 179). The causes of this abuse include sexual frustration, mood swings, and general anxiety about the future associated with pregnancy.

Students with severe sentence-level difficulties may even be motivated to take another writing course or to seek tutorial help. The point, in any case, is to make students responsible for their own editing. (See Chapter Four for a full discussion of this complex and politically charged matter.)

Even though I think it is important not to circle errors or to line-edit a student's draft, there are many helpful kinds of comments you can make on drafts to address lower-order concerns. The following questions can serve as guides for commentary.

1. Are There Stylistic Problems That You Find Particularly Annoying? Every teacher has pet peeves about style, so you might as well make yours known to students and mark them on drafts when they start to annoy you. What distinguishes stylistic concerns from grammar errors is that grammar errors are violations of the structural conventions of standard edited English. Relatively stable rules of correctness govern pronoun cases, subject-verb agreement, dangling modifiers, parallelism, and sentence completeness. In contrast, stylistic concerns involve rhetorical choices—matters of effectiveness and grace rather than right or wrong. Wordiness, choppiness, or excessive use of the passive voice are rhetorical or stylistic, not grammatical, matters.

I have my own set of pet peeves about style that I like to make known to students. (In fact, I distribute a little handout about them in my classes.) Here are my own personal top three annoyances. (I invite readers to make their own "top three" lists.)

Lazy use of "this" as a pronoun. Some writers (I think of them as lazy) try to create coherence between sentences by using *this* as a pronoun referring sometimes to a noun in the preceding sentence but more often to a whole idea. No grammatical rule actually forbids using *this* as an all-purpose pronoun (although some handbooks call the practice "broad reference" and frown on it), but its overuse can lead to gracelessness, slippage of coherence, and outright ambiguity. Here is an example:

Original Version

As a little girl, I liked to play with mechanical games and toys, but this was not supported by my parents. Fortunately, a woman math teacher in high school saw that I was good at this and advised me to major in engineering. But this turned out to be even more difficult than I imagined.

Improved Version

As a little girl, I liked to play with mechanical games and toys, but my parents didn't support such "boylike behavior." Fortunately, a woman math teacher in high school noticed my talent in math and physics and advised me to major in engineering—advice that turned out to be even more difficult to follow than I had imagined.

Wordiness. Even though I am not always able to practice what I preach, I prefer a succinct, plain style unclogged by deadwood or circumlocutions. I urge students to cut and prune their drafts to achieve economy and tightness. Here's an example:

Original Version

As a result of the labor policies established by Bismarck, the working-class people in Germany were convinced that revolution was unnecessary for the attainment of their goals and purposes.

Improved Version

Bismarck's labor policies convinced the German working class that revolution was unnecessary.

Excessive nominalization. Powerful writers express actions with verbs. In contrast, writers infested with nominalization—often contracted through unsafe intercourse with bureaucrats, psychobabblers, and educational administrators—convert actions into nouns. Instead of saying, "Effective writers express actions with verbs," the suffering nominalizer prefers to say, "For the production of a prose style that utilizes the principles of writing that are most highly regarded as effective, the expression of an action through the use of a verb is the method most highly preferred." Not only are such sentences longer and deader, but they are also less clear. (For excellent advice on how to recover from nominalization, see Williams, 1985.)

To help students overcome my top three peeves, I usually line-edit an early occurrence of a flabby passage and then ask the writer to do the same sort of thing throughout.

2. Is the Draft Free of Errors in Grammar, Punctuation, and Spelling? Although I have argued that teachers should not circle errors in grammar, punctuation, and spelling, I do not mean that these errors should go unmentioned. On the contrary, they should be mentioned emphatically, and some stick-and-carrot strategy should be applied to motivate students to find and fix them. My strategy is to write an end comment like this: "Sally, your grade has been reduced for excessive sentence-level errors. Please find them and fix them; then resubmit paper, and I will raise your grade." (How high I raise the grade depends on how successful the student is in reducing the number of sentence errors.) If I think students need extra help finding the errors, I sometimes place X's in the margin next to lines with rule-based mistakes. Another approach is to line-edit one or two paragraphs for a student and then ask the student to do something similar for the rest of the draft. If you line-edit, however, be careful to distinguish rule-based mistakes from stylistic choices. When you cross something out, for example, students often do not know if what they did was "wrong" or just stylistically unpolished. Therefore, in addition to line editing, you need to explain in a marginal comment why you made the changes.

Another strategy for helping students with sentence errors is to note characteristic patterns of errors. Shaughnessy (1977) demonstrated that what often looks like a dozen errors in a student's draft may really be one error repeated a dozen times. If you can help a student learn a rule or a principle, you can often clear up many mistakes in one swoop. Sometimes teaching a principle is a simple matter (explaining the difference between *it's* and *its*); at other times, it is more complex (explaining when to place a comma in front of *and* when not to). Even if you do not explain the rule or principle, helping students recognize a repeated pattern of error is a real service.

> Sam, you have lots of sentence errors here, but many of them are of two types: (1) apostrophe errors—you tend to use apostrophes with plurals rather than possessives; (2) comma splices (remember those from English class?).

Some Suggestions for Writing Revision-Oriented End Comments

On the last page of a student paper, a teacher usually writes a summarizing end comment. If teachers think of their end comments as justifying or explaining the grade, they tend to emphasize the bad features of the paper ("This is why I gave you a C"). But if they think of their purpose as guiding revision, their end comments can be more affirmative. A paper that deserves a C as a final product is often an excellent draft even though it has not reached finished-product standards. I sometimes tell my students that a good draft is to a final product as a caterpillar is to a butterfly: all that's missing is the metamorphosis.

In making effective end comments, the teacher needs to imagine the butterfly while praising the caterpillar. The purpose of the end comment is not to justify the current grade but to help writers make the kinds of revisions that will move the draft toward excellence. The strategy I recommend is to follow a strengths–major problems–recommendations formula: I try to write an end comment that sums up the strengths of the draft, that identifies the main problems to be worked on, and that makes a few specific suggestions for what to do next. Here are some examples of end comments that follow this formula:

> Pete, you seem to be on the right track with quite a few very promising sections, but your ideas are thin, lacking both focus and development. Please make an appointment with me (or the writing center) to work on finding a better focus and a thesis for this paper.

> Excellent draft, Sarah. Although I had trouble at first seeing your problem and thesis, along the way you present very interesting ideas. I especially liked your section on the Mapplethorpe photographs. But in many places I was lost. For your next draft, you need to do the following:
>
> 1. Rewrite your introduction so that it more clearly introduces the reader to your problem.
> 2. Work on organization. I could find your thesis, but many of your paragraphs have no topic sentences and aren't clearly linked to your argument. Also, as I have noted in the margins, many places need more development.
> 3. Rethink what you are saying about Sontag. I think you misread her argument, especially in paragraph 2.

> Paula: When this essay is good, it is very, very good. I like very much your discussion of Diem's leadership and the rise of dissent in Vietnam. Your consideration of our fears of not being taken seriously by Diem is also strong. In these discussions, you set your ideas clearly and with strong evidence.
>
> However, there are other hills and valleys here as well. You need to focus the reader on your primary concerns in an introduction. You need to expand your consideration of the military and bring in more evidence toward the end. For your revision, pay particular attention to my marginal comments, where I note the places that need more expansion and development. This is perhaps one draft away from an A.

Conclusion: A Review of General Principles

The following list summarizes the main principles of commentary discussed in this chapter.

General Procedures

1. Comment first on ideas and organization: encourage students to solve higher-order problems before turning to lower-order problems.
2. Whenever possible, make positive comments. Praise strong points.

3. Try to write an end comment that reveals your interest in the student's ideas. Begin the end comment with an emphasis on good points and then move to specific recommendations for improvement.

4. Avoid overcommenting. Particularly avoid emphasizing lower-order concerns until you are satisfied with higher-order concerns. If writing lacks focus or a thesis statement and a plan for supporting it, it is premature to worry about paragraphs or sentence structure.

5. As you read the essay, indicate your reaction to specific passages. Particularly comment on the ideas, raising queries and making suggestions on how the argument could be improved. Praise parts that you like.

6. Resist the urge to circle misspellings, punctuation errors, and so forth. Research suggests that students will improve more quickly if they are required to find and correct their own errors.

Marking for Ideas

7. The end comment should summarize your assessment of the strengths and weaknesses of the writer's ideas. Challenge writers to deepen and complicate their thought at a level appropriate to their intellectual development.

Marking for Organization

8. Use marginal comments to indicate places where structure becomes confusing.

9. Praise good titles, good thesis statements, good transitions, and so forth.

Marking for Sentence Structure

10. Although I recommend against marking or circling sentence errors, you might consider placing X's in the margins where they occur. When you return the papers, either withhold a grade or lower the grade until students who made substantial numbers of errors have reedited their work. Most students should be able to find and fix a majority of their errors. Students with severe sentence-level problems may need to seek personal tutoring.

11. Note places where sentence-level problems cause genuine unclarity (as opposed to annoyance). Marginal comments such as "Tangled sentence" or "This passage is garbled" help the writer see where problems occur.

Some Further Principles

12. Try to make comments as legible and as straightforward as possible. As anyone knows who has looked at papers graded by a colleague, teachers' comments are frequently difficult to decipher. They are often unintentional examples of first-draft writing—clear to the writer but baffling to others.

13. Whenever possible, use one-on-one conferences instead of commenting on papers. Perhaps my most frequent end comment is this: "You're making real progress. Please see me so that I can help you move to the next stage." An invitation for personal help is particularly useful when the student's problems involve higher-order concerns.

14. Finally, think of your commentary as personal correspondence with the student, something that makes your own thinking visible and permanent. Try to invest in your commentary the tone of a supportive coach—someone interested in the student as a person and in the improvement of the student's powers as a writer and thinker.

CHAPTER 15

Developing and Applying Grading Criteria

Trying to decide the relative merits of a piece of writing can lead to a tangle of problems. Given a set of student essays, instructors frequently disagree, often vehemently, with one another's assessments. Because we teachers have little opportunity to discuss grading practices with colleagues, we often develop personal criteria that can seem eccentric to others. In fact, the first half-hour of a paper-grading workshop can be demoralizing even to the most dedicated proponents of writing across the curriculum. What do teachers actually want when they ask students to write?

Answering this question is not easy. Professional writing teachers grant that the assessment of writing, like the assessment of any art, involves subjective judgments. But the situation is not entirely relative either, for objective standards for good writing can be formulated, and readers with different tastes can be trained to assess writing samples with surprisingly high correlation. But the potential for wide disagreement about what constitutes good writing is a factor with which both students and teachers must contend.

The Problem of Criteria

The extent of this disagreement was illustrated by Paul Diederich (1974) in one of the most famous experiments in composition research. Diederich collected three hundred essays written by first-year students at three different universities and had them graded by fifty-three professional persons in six different occupational fields. He asked each reader to place the essays in nine different piles in order of "general merit" and to write a brief comment explaining what he or she liked and disliked about each essay. Diederich reported these results: "Out of the 300 essays graded, 101 received every grade from 1–9; 94 percent received either seven, eight, or nine different grades; and no essay received less than five different grades" (p. 6).

Diederich discovered, however, some order in this chaos. Through factor analysis, he identified five subgroups of readers who correlated highly with one another but not with readers in other subgroups. By analyzing the comments on the papers, Diederich concluded that each subgroup was consistently giving predominant weight to a single criterion of writing. Sixteen readers were putting main emphasis on quality of ideas; thirteen on sentence structure, usage, spelling, and punctuation; nine on organization and development; nine on creative wording or phrasing; and seven on liveliness or committed voice, a factor Diederich labeled "flavor and personality." (Diederich counted one reader in two categories; hence these numbers add up to fifty-four rather than fifty-three; see his book, pp. 6–10, for details.)

Diederich's research enabled him to develop procedures through which a diverse group of readers could be trained to increase the correlation of their grading. By setting descriptions for high, middle, and low achievement in each of his five criterion areas—ideas, organization, sentence structure, wording, and flavor—Diederich was able to train readers to balance their assessments over the five criteria. Since then, numerous researchers have refined or refocused Diederich's criteria and have developed successful strategies for training readers as evaluators (see, particularly, Cooper and Odell, 1977, and White, 1992, 1994). Many of these strategies have classroom applications also, for training students as evaluators of writing greatly improves their ability to give high-quality advice in peer review workshops.

Providing Criteria for Students

Even though readers can be trained to apply uniform criteria to student essays, these criteria often vary from discipline to discipline (and from teacher to teacher), a phenomenon that often confuses students. Not only do styles vary widely across the disciplines, but there are also fundamental differences in the way arguments are structured and elaborated—a problem students feel acutely as they move through their general education courses.

To make matters more confusing for students, different teachers within the same discipline often value different kinds of writing. Some teachers, as we have seen in Chapter Three, want students to sound like professionals in the field. Others assign narratives, personal reflections, and other alternative assignments calling for voices other than the apprentice academic.

Because of such variety of expectations, instructors should describe their criteria for judging writing and, whenever possible, provide samples of successful student papers from previous classes.

Developing Criteria and Grading Scales

Criteria for writing are usually presented to students in one of two ways: analytically or holistically. The analytic method gives separate scores for each criterion—for example, ideas, ten points; organization, ten points; sentence structure, five points—whereas the holistic method gives one score that reflects the reader's overall impression of the paper, considering all criteria at once. Many instructors prefer analytic scales because the breakdown of the grade into components, when combined with the instructor's written comments, conveys detailed information about the teacher's judgment of the essay. Some people object philosophically to analytic scoring, however, on the grounds that writing cannot be analyzed into component parts. Can ideas really be separated from organization or clarity of expression from clarity of thought? Such people prefer holistic evaluation, which does not suggest that writing is a mixture of separable elements. Also, holistic grading is faster and so is often preferable when one's main concern is rapidity of assessment rather than precision of feedback.

Both analytic and holistic scoring methods can also be classified two ways: general description methods and primary trait methods. Proponents of general description argue that criteria for writing can be stated in a general or universal way (good organization, graceful sentence structure, and so forth). Proponents of the primary trait method, however, argue that criteria must be stated specifically in terms of the given writing task. For example, the criteria for a history paper detailing the origins of the electoral college would differ from those of a political science paper arguing that the electoral college should be abolished. A primary trait scale for the history paper might include criteria like these:

Does the writer make effective use of primary sources?

Does the essay explore the alternatives to the electoral college discussed at the constitutional convention?

In contrast, a primary trait scale for the political science paper might include these criteria:

> Does the writer predict the consequences of abolishing the electoral college using acceptable empirical data?

> Does the writer anticipate objections to these predictions and adequately respond to them?

Thus, a primary trait scale uses grading criteria keyed directly to the assignment. (Examples of different kinds of grading scales will appear later in this chapter.)

Developing Analytic Scales

Exhibit 15.1 illustrates a simple analytic scale using general description methods. Analytic scales normally list three or more criteria, almost always including quality of ideas, organization, and sentence structure. Many analytic scales are elaborate, with numerous additional categories and subcategories. Some analytic scales are dichotomous, meaning that the reader simply checks off "yes" or "no," depending on the presence or absence of certain features of the writing:

> Is there a thesis statement?   Yes _____   No _____

Other scales ask the reader to rate each feature of the writing along a number sequence:

> Quality of thesis statement:
>
> | Low | | | Middle | | | | High |
> |---|---|---|---|---|---|---|---|
> | 1 | 2 | 3 | 4 | 5 | 6 | 7 | 8 |

Many analytic scales weigh some criteria more heavily than others, depending on what the instructor wishes to emphasize. Thus, you might allot twenty-five points for ideas, fifteen points for organization, and ten points for sentence structure. But if you are particularly annoyed by careless spelling errors, you might give ten bonus points to papers with no misspelled words and deduct ten points for having more than, say, five misspelled words. Exhibits 15.2 and 15.3 illustrate analytic scales using primary trait criteria. Exhibit 15.2 is a scoring guide developed by an English professor for an assignment on Conrad's *The Secret Sharer.* The professor gives the scoring guide to students at the time she passes out the assignment. The scoring guide thus reinforces key features she expects in students' essays and serves as a checklist during peer review. Exhibit 15.3 is a scoring guide used by finance professor Dean Drenk to pro-

Exhibit 15.1. Simple Analytic Scale (General Description Method).

Scoring Guide for Essays

Quality of Ideas (_____ points)

Range and depth of argument; logic of argument; quality of research or original thought; appropriate sense of complexity of the topic; appropriate awareness of opposing views.

Organization and Development (_____ points)

Effective title; clarity of thesis statement; logical and clear arrangement of ideas; effective use of transitions; unity and coherence of paragraphs; good development of ideas through supporting details and evidence.

Clarity and Style (_____ points)

Ease of readability; appropriate voice, tone and style for assignment; clarity of sentence structure; gracefulness of sentence structure; appropriate variety and maturity of sentence structure.

Sentence Structure and Mechanics (_____ points)

Grammatically correct sentences; absence of comma splices, run-ons, fragments; absence of usage and grammatical errors; accurate spelling; careful proofreading; attractive and appropriate manuscript form.

---

vide feedback on his thesis support microthemes in finance (see Chapter Five, pages 74–75). His scoring guide can be easily adapted to the needs of professors in other disciplines.

Developing Holistic Scales

Samples of holistic scales are shown in Exhibits 15.4 and 15.5. Exhibit 15.4 is a holistic scale for summary-writing assignments. Exhibit 15.5 is a holistic scale for grading physics microthemes. Holistic scoring depends on a reader's all-at-once assessment of a paper based on one attentive but quick reading. Research suggests that the correlation between readers actually increases if readers read quickly, trusting the reliability of their first impressions (White, 1994). Thus, holistic scales work best in conjunction with rapid grading and "models feedback" (see Chapter Thirteen, page 236; see also Rogers, 1995, for a discussion of holistic scoring in a chemistry course).

Conducting a Departmental Norming Session

A good way to improve one's grading practices is to join a conversation with colleagues about what constitutes excellent, good,

Exhibit 15.2. Analytic Scale (Primary Trait Method).

Scoring Guide for Assignment on *The Secret Sharer*

Your essay is supposed to provide a supported answer to the following question:

> How has the experience with Leggatt changed the captain so that what he is at the end of the story is different from what he was at the beginning?

In order to do well on this paper, you need to do these things:

1. Have your own clear answer to this question.

2. Support your answer with strong arguments and textual details.

3. Make your essay clear enough for a reader to understand with one reading.

Criterion 1. Does your essay have a thesis statement at the end of the first paragraph that answers the question regarding changes in the captain?

no thesis or unclear thesis				clear thesis
2	4	6	8	10

Criterion 2. Is your thesis supported with strong argumentation and use of significant details taken from the story?

weak argument and/or lack of details as support			strong argument and good details as support	
2	4	6	8	10

Criterion 3. Is your paper easy for a reader to follow?

Paragraphing and transitions	2	4	6	8	10
Clear Sentences	2	4	6	8	10
Accurate mechanics: grammar, spelling, punctuation, neatness	2	4	6	8	10

Source: Dolores Johnson

satisfactory, and poor papers. A surefire way to stimulate such conversation is to "staff-grade" with colleagues a set of essays written in response to an assignment within your discipline. One participant selects in advance four or five essays that seem to span the range of quality from excellent to poor, duplicates them for the department, and uses them to initiate discussion. In developing criteria, instructors are advised to use a number scale that does not translate directly into letter grades. A six-point scale ranging from 6 (best) to 1 (worst) is most common. Using a numerical scale tem-

Exhibit 15.3. Primary Trait Scoring Guide for Thesis Support Essays in Finance.

Grading Criteria

Support of Theses

    A. Clarity of support: _____

    B. Logic (relationship
        of support to thesis):   _____

    C. Sources of support

        1. Quantity   _____

        2. Quality   _____

    Total microtheme grade   _____

Specific Features of Your Microtheme

_____ Grammmatical errors are numerous enough to interfere with understanding your response.

_____ The organization of your response is not clear.

_____ The logic of your support is confusing or does not make sense.

_____ Your conclusions are not warranted by your support.

_____ Your support is too imprecise or too general.

Source: Bean, Drenk, and Lee, 1982, p. 32.

porarily suspends the additional problem of variable standards for letter grades. Thus, a "hard grader" and an "easy grader" might agree that a particular essay rates a 4 on a six-point scale but disagree on how to translate that 4 into a letter grade. The hard instructor might give it a C+ and the easy instructor a B. Since standards for letter grades are a different issue from standards for ranking several pieces of writing, problems of devising criteria for writing are simplified if we separate the two issues, at least initially.

After an initial norming session in which department members reach agreement on the sample papers and develop criteria for each gradation on their scoring scale, members break into pairs to staff-grade the set of essays. Each essay is read independently by two readers, who meet periodically to compare scores and discuss discrepant grades. On a six-point scale, instructors should aim to come within one point of each other's scores. Differences of two or more points indicate a wide divergence of criteria. A departmental norming session every year or so can increase instructors' communal

Exhibit 15.4. Holistic Scale for Grading Article Summaries.

A summary should be directed toward imagined readers who have not read the article being summarized. The purpose of the summary is to give these persons a clear overview of the article's main points. The criteria for a summary are (1) accuracy of content, (2) comprehensiveness and balance, and (3) clarity, readability, and grammatical correctness.

6 A 6 summary meets all the criteria. The writer understands the article thoroughly. The main points in the article appear in the summary with all main points proportionately developed (that is, the writer does not spend excessive time on one main point while neglecting other main points). The summary should be as comprehensive as possible and should read smoothly, with appropriate transitions between ideas. Sentences should be clear, without vagueness or ambiguity and without grammatical or mechanical errors.

5 A 5 summary should still be very good, but it can be weaker than a 6 summary in one area. It may have excellent accuracy and balance, but show occasional problems in sentence structure or correctness. Or it may be clearly written but be somewhat unbalanced or less comprehensive than a 6 summary or show a minor misunderstanding of the article.

4 A score of 4 means "good but not excellent." Typically, a 4 summary will reveal a generally accurate reading of the article, but it will be noticeably weaker in the quality of writing. Or it may be well written but cover only part of the essay.

3 A 3 summary must have strength in at least one area of competence, and it should still be good enough to convince the grader that the writer has understood the article fairly well. However, a 3 summary typically is not written well enough to convey an understanding of the article to someone who has not already read it. Typically, the sentence structure of a 3 summary is not sophisticated enough to convey the sense of hierarchy and subordination found in the essay.

2 A 2 summary is weak in all areas of competence, either because it is so poorly written that the reader cannot understand the content or because the content is inaccurate or seriously disorganized. However, a 2 essay convinces the grader that the writer has read the essay and is struggling to understand it.

1 A 1 summary fails to meet any of the areas of competence.

confidence in their grading practices. For more detailed descriptions of this procedure, along with sample student essays and reader-developed scoring criteria, see White (1992). See also Bateman's discussion of scoring a set of sociology essays dealing with ethnocentrism (1990, pp. 110–116).

Determining Grades

Assigning a letter grade to a piece of writing always poses a dilemma, and I can offer no easy advice. Teachers who use analytic scales often add up each student's total score, rank the papers, and trans-

Exhibit 15.5. Holistic Scale for Grading Physics Microthemes.

6, 5	Microthemes in the category will show a confident understanding of the physics concepts and will explain those concepts clearly to the intended audience. A 6 theme will be clearly written throughout; will contain almost no errors in spelling, punctuation, or grammar; and will have enough development to provide a truly helpful explanation to learners. A 5 theme will still be successful in teaching the physics concepts to the intended audience but may have more errors or somewhat less development than a 6. The key to microthemes in the 6, 5 category is that they must show a correct understanding of the physics and explain the concept clearly to a new learner.
4, 3	Microthemes in this category will reveal to the instructor that the writer probably understands the physics concepts, but lack of clarity in the writing or lack of fully developed explanations means that the microtheme would not teach the concept to new learners. Microthemes in the 4, 3 category are usually "you know what I mean" essays: someone who already understands the concepts can tell that the writer probably does, too, but someone who does not already understand the concepts would not learn anything from the explanation. This category is also appropriate for clearly written essays that have minor misunderstandings of the physics concepts or for accurate essays full of sentence-level errors.
2, 1	These microthemes will be unsuccessful either because the writer fails to understand the physics concepts, because the number of errors is so high that the instructor cannot determine how much the writer understands, or because the explanations lack even minimum development. Give a score of 2 or 1 if the writer misunderstands the physics, even if the essay is otherwise well written. Also give a score of 2 or 1 to essays so poorly written that the reader can't understand them.

late scores into letter grades by establishing a curve or by setting point ranges for levels of grades. Other teachers, using a more holistic method, try to develop an interior sense of what an A, B, C, or D essay looks like. If possible, it is best to read through a set of papers quickly before marking them and assigning grades, trying to get a feel for the range of responses and sizing up what the best papers are like. In grading essay exams or short papers, many teachers develop schemes for not knowing who the authors are until the papers are graded. (One method is to have students use their social security numbers rather than names; another is to have students put their names on the back of the last page.) Not knowing who wrote which essay eliminates any halo effect that might bias the grade.

To avoid grading on the curve, some teachers like to establish criteria for grading that are as objective and as consistent as possible. Although this is no easy task, the following explanation, written by Cornell University English professor Harry Shaw (1984), shows how one professor makes his decision. It is as good a guide as any I know.

How I Assign Letter Grades

In grading "thesis papers" . . . I ask myself the following set of questions:

1. Does the paper have a thesis?
2. Does the thesis address itself to an appropriate question or topic?
3. Is the paper free from long stretches of quotations and summaries that exist only for their own sakes and remain unanalyzed?
4. Can the writer produce complete sentences?
5. Is the paper free from basic grammatical errors?

If the answer to any of these questions is "no," I give the paper some kind of C. If the answer to most of the questions is "no," its grade will be even lower.

For papers which have emerged unscathed thus far, I add the following questions:

6. How thoughtful is the paper? Does it show real originality?
7. How adequate is the thesis? Does it respond to its question or topic in a full and interesting way? Does it have an appropriate degree of complexity?
8. How well organized is the paper? Does it stick to the point? Does every paragraph contain a clear topic sentence? If not, is another kind of organizing principle at work? Are the transitions well made? Does it have a real conclusion, not simply a stopping place?
9. Is the style efficient, not wordy or unclear?
10. Does the writing betray any special elegance?
11. Above all, can I hear a lively, intelligent, interesting human voice speaking to me (or to another audience, if that's what the writer intends) as I read the paper?

Depending on my answers to such questions, I give the paper some kind of A or some kind of B [pp. 149–150].

Conclusion: Expecting Excellence

When students know an instructor's criteria for assigning grades—and when they have the opportunity to help one another apply these criteria to works in progress—the quality of their final products will improve gratifyingly. It is satisfying indeed to see how well many undergraduates can write when they are engaged in their projects and follow the stages of the writing process through multiple drafts and peer reviews. By setting high standards, by encouraging multiple drafts, by refusing to be the first human being to read a student's paper—in short, by expecting excellence—instructors can feel justified in applying rigorous criteria.

But it is important too that students never think of their writing as "finished." In the best of all worlds, students would be allowed to rewrite a paper if they wished to improve it further. The presence of grades should never override the more important emphasis on revision and improvement.

The point, then, of assigning writing across the curriculum is to engage students in the process of inquiry and active learning. Although one of our goals is to improve students' communication skills, writing is more than communication; it is a means of learning, thinking, discovering, and seeing. When teachers give students good problems to think about—and involve them actively in the process of solving these problems—they are deepening students' engagement with the subject matter and promoting their intellectual growth. By adding well-designed writing assignments to a course, teachers give students continued practice in critical thinking. Teachers know when their approach is working: the performance of their students improves.

REFERENCES

Abbott, M. M., Bartelt, P. W., Fishman, S. M., and Honda, C. "Interchange: A Conversation Among the Disciplines." In A. Herrington and C. Moran (eds.), *Writing, Teaching, and Learning in the Disciplines.* New York: Modern Language Association, 1992.

Abercrombie, M.L.J. *The Anatomy of Judgment: Concerning the Processes of Perception, Communication, and Reasoning.* London: Hutchinson, 1960.

Adler, M. *The Paideia Program: An Educational Syllabus.* New York: Macmillan, 1984.

Anderson, C. *Edge Effects: Notes from an Oregon Forest.* Iowa City: University of Iowa Press, 1993.

Angelo, T. A., and Cross, K. P. *Classroom Assessment Techniques: A Handbook for College Teachers.* (2nd ed.) San Francisco: Jossey-Bass, 1993.

Barnes, L. B., Christensen, C. R., and Hansen, A. J. *Teaching and the Case Method: Text, Cases, and Readings.* (3rd ed.) Boston: Harvard Business School Press, 1994.

Barry, L. *The Busy Prof's Travel Guide to Writing Across the Curriculum.* La Grande: Eastern Oregon State College, 1989.

Bartholomae, D. "The Study of Error." *College Composition and Communication,* 1980, *31*(3), 253–269.

Bartholomae, D. "Inventing the University." In M. Rose (ed.), *When a Writer Can't Write: Studies in Writer's Block and Other Composing Process Problems.* New York: Guilford Press, 1985.

Bateman, W. L. *Open to Question: The Art of Teaching and Learning by Inquiry.* San Francisco: Jossey-Bass, 1990.

Bazerman, C. "What Written Knowledge Does: Three Examples of Academic Discourse." *Philosophy of the Social Sciences,* 1981, *11,* 361–387.

Bazerman, C. "Codifying the Social Scientific Style: The APA Publication Manual as a Behaviorist Rhetoric." In J. Nelson, A. Megill, and D. McCloskey (eds.), *The Rhetoric of the Human Sciences: Language and Argument in Scholarship and Public Affairs.* Madison: Wisconsin University Press, 1987.

Beach, R. "Self-Evaluation Strategies of Extensive Revisers and Non-Revisers." *College Composition and Communication,* 1976, *27*(2), 160–164.

Bean, J. C. "Summary Writing, Rogerian Listening, and Dialectic Thinking." *College Composition and Communication,* 1986, *37*(3), 343–346.

Bean, J. C., Drenk, D., and Lee, F. D. "Microtheme Strategies for Developing

Cognitive Skills." In C. W. Griffin (ed.), *Teaching Writing in All Disciplines.* New Directions for Teaching and Learning, no. 12. San Francisco: Jossey-Bass, 1986.

Belanoff, P., and Dickson, M. (eds.). *Portfolios: Process and Product.* Portsmouth, N.H.: Boynton/Cook, 1991.

Belanoff, P., Elbow, P., and Fontaine, S. I. (eds.). *Nothing Begins with N: New Investigations of Freewriting.* Carbondale: Southern Illinois University Press, 1991.

Belenky, M. F., Clinchy, B. M., Goldberger, N. R., and Tarule, J. M. *Women's Ways of Knowing: The Development of Self, Voice, and Mind.* New York: Basic Books, 1986.

Berlinghoff, W. P. "Locally Original Mathematics Through Writing." In P. Connolly and T. Vilardi (eds.), *Writing to Learn Mathematics and Science.* New York: Teachers College Press, 1989.

Berthoff, A. "Dialectical Notebooks and the Audit of Meaning." In T. Fulwiler (ed.), *The Journal Book.* Portsmouth, N.H.: Boynton/Cook, 1987.

Bizzell, P. "Cognition, Convention, and Certainty: What We Need to Know About Writing." *Pre/Text,* 1982, *3,* 213–243.

Bloom, B. S. (ed.). *Taxonomy of Educational Objectives.* Vol. 1: *Cognitive Domain.* New York: McKay, 1956.

Boehrer, J., and Linsky, M. "Teaching with Cases: Learning to Question." In M. D. Svinicki (ed.), *The Changing Face of College Teaching.* New Directions for Teaching and Learning, no. 42. San Francisco: Jossey-Bass, 1990.

Bonwell, C., and Eison, J. *Active Learning: Creating Excitement in the Classroom.* ASHE-ERIC Higher Education Report No. 1. Washington, D.C.: ERIC Clearinghouse on Higher Education and the Association for the Study of Higher Education, 1991.

Braddock, R., Lloyd-Jones, R., and Schoer, L. *Research in Written Composition.* Urbana, Ill.: National Council of Teachers of English, 1963.

Bradford, A. N. "Cognitive Immaturity and Remedial College Writers." In J. N. Hays, P. A. Roth, J. R. Ramsey, and R. D. Foulke (eds.), *The Writer's Mind: Writing as a Mode of Thinking.* Urbana, Ill.: National Council of Teachers of English, 1983.

Bridwell-Bowles, L. "Discourse and Diversity: Experimental Writing Within the Academy." *College Composition and Communication,* 1992, *43*(3), 349–368.

Britton, J., and others. *The Development of Writing Abilities (11–18).* London: Macmillan, 1975.

Brodkey, L. *Academic Writing as Social Practice.* Philadelphia: Temple University Press, 1987.

Brodkey, L. "Writing on the Bias." *College English,* 1994, *56*(5), 527–547.

Brookfield, S. D. *Developing Critical Thinkers: Challenging Adults to Explore Alternative Ways of Thinking and Acting.* San Francisco: Jossey-Bass, 1987.

Brossell, G. "Rhetorical Specification in Essay Examination Topics." *College English,* 1983, *45*(2), 165–173.

Brown, G., and Atkins, M. *Effective Teaching in Higher Education.* London: Methuen, 1988.

Bruffee, K. A. "Writing and Reading as Social or Collaborative Acts." In J. N. Hays, P. A. Roth, J. R. Ramsey, and R. D. Foulke (eds.), *The Writer's Mind: Writing as a Mode of Thinking.* Urbana, Ill.: National Council of Teachers of English, 1983.

Bruffee, K. A. "Collaborative Learning and the 'Conversation of Mankind.'" *College English,* 1984, *46*(6), 635–652.

Bruffee, K. A. *Collaborative Learning: Higher Education, Interdependence, and the Authority of Knowledge.* Baltimore, Md.: Johns Hopkins University Press, 1993.

Calkins, L. M. *The Art of Teaching Writing.* Portsmouth, N.H.: Heinemann, 1986.

Carmichael, S. "A Declaration of War." In M. Goodman (ed.), *The Movement Toward a New America: The Beginnings of a Long Revolution.* Philadelphia: Pilgrim Press/Knopf, 1970. (Originally published 1968.)

Cashin, W. *Improving Essay Tests.* IDEA Paper No. 17. Manhattan: Kansas State University Center for Faculty Evaluation and Development, 1987.

Christensen, C. R., Garvin, D. A., and Sweet, A. (eds.). *Education for Judgment: The Artistry of Discussion Leadership.* Boston: Harvard Business School Press, 1991.

Clegg, V., and Cashin, W. *Improving Multiple-Choice Tests.* IDEA Paper No. 16. Manhattan: Kansas State University Center for Faculty Evaluation and Development, 1986.

Cohen, A. J., and Spencer, J. "Using Writing Across the Curriculum in Economics: Is Taking the Plunge Worth It?" *Journal of Economic Education,* 1993, 23, 219–230.

Colomb, G. G., and Williams, J. M. "Perceiving Structure in Professional Prose: A Multiply Determined Experience." In L. Odell and D. Goswami (eds.), *Writing in Nonacademic Settings.* New York: Guilford Press, 1985.

Connolly, P., and Vilardi, T. (eds.). *Writing to Learn Mathematics and Science.* New York: Teachers College Press, 1989.

Connors, R. J., and Lunsford, A. A. "Frequency of Formal Errors in Current College Writing, or Ma and Pa Kettle Do Research." *College Composition and Communication,* 1988, 39(4), 395–409.

Cooper, C., and Odell, L. (eds.). *Evaluating Writing: Describing, Measuring, Judging.* Urbana, Ill.: National Council of Teachers of English, 1977.

Crosser, R. L. *Instructor's Manual with Lecture Notes to Accompany Concepts in Federal Taxation.* Minneapolis/St. Paul, Minn.: West, 1996.

Daiute, C. "Physical and Cognitive Factors in Revising: Insights from Studies with Computers." *Research in the Teaching of English,* 1986, 20(2), 141–159.

Davis, B. G. *Tools for Teaching.* San Francisco: Jossey-Bass, 1993.

Dewey, J. *Democracy and Education.* New York: Macmillan, 1916.

Di Gaetani, J. L. "Use of the Case Method in Teaching Business Communication." In M. Kogen (ed.), *Writing in the Business Professions.* Urbana, Ill.: National Council of Teachers of English, 1989.

Diederich, P. *Measuring Growth in English.* Urbana, Ill.: National Council of Teachers of English, 1974.

Dillon, J. T. *Questioning and Teaching: A Manual of Practice.* New York: Teachers College Press, 1988.

Drenk, D. "Teaching Finance Through Writing." In C. W. Griffin (ed.), *Teaching Writing in All Disciplines.* New Directions for Teaching and Learning, no. 12. San Francisco: Jossey-Bass, 1986.

Elbow, P. *Writing Without Teachers.* New York: Oxford University Press, 1973.

Elbow, P. *Writing with Power: Techniques for Mastering the Writing Process.* New York: Oxford University Press, 1981.

Elbow, P. *Embracing Contraries: Explorations in Learning and Teaching.* New York: Oxford University Press, 1986.

Elbow, P., and Belanoff, P. *Sharing and Responding.* New York: Random House, 1989.

Erickson, B. L., and Strommer, D. W. *Teaching College Freshmen.* San Francisco: Jossey-Bass, 1991.

Fagen, R. R. "A Different Voice." *Stanford,* Sept. 1990, p. 41.

Faigley, L., and Witte, S. "Analyzing Revision." *College Composition and Communication,* 1981, 32(4), 400–414.

Flavell, J. H. *The Developmental Psychology of Jean Piaget.* New York: Van Nostrand, 1963.

Flower, L. "Writer-Based Prose: A Cognitive Basis for Problems in Writing." *College English*, 1979, *41*(1), 19–37.

Flower, L. *Problem-Solving Strategies for Writing.* (4th ed.) San Diego, Calif.: Harcourt Brace Jovanovich, 1993.

Flower, L., and Hayes, J. "Problem-Solving Strategies and the Writing Process." *College English*, 1977, *39*(4), 449–461.

Flynn, E. A. "Composing as a Woman." *College Composition and Communication*, 1988, *39*(4), 423–435.

Fox, H. *Listening to the World: Cultural Issues in Academic Writing.* Urbana, Ill.: National Council of Teachers of English, 1994.

Francoz, M. J. "The Logic of Question and Answer: Writing as Inquiry." *College English*, 1979, *41*(3), 336–339.

Freedman, A. "A Theoretic Context for the Writing Lab." In M. Harris (ed.), *Tutoring Writing: A Sourcebook for Writing Labs.* Glenview, Ill.: Scott, Foresman, 1982.

Freie, J. "Thinking and Believing." *College Teaching*, 1987, *35*(3), 89–91.

Freisinger, R. "Cross-Disciplinary Writing Programs: Theory and Practice." *College English*, 1980, *42*(2), 154–166.

Fulwiler, T. (ed.). *The Journal Book.* Portsmouth, N.H.: Boynton/Cook, 1987a.

Fulwiler, T. *Teaching with Writing.* Portsmouth, N.H.: Boynton/Cook, 1987b.

Fulwiler, T., and Young, A. (eds.). *Language Connections: Writing and Reading Across the Curriculum.* Urbana, Ill.: National Council of Teachers of English, 1982.

Gere, A. R. (ed.). *Roots in the Sawdust: Writing to Learn Across the Disciplines.* Urbana, Ill.: National Council of Teachers of English, 1985.

Gilligan, C. *In a Different Voice: Psychological Theory and Women's Development.* Cambridge, Mass.: Harvard University Press, 1982.

Golub, J. (ed.). *Focus on Collaborative Learning: Classroom Practices in Teaching English, 1988.* Urbana, Ill.: National Council of Teachers of English, 1988.

Goodenough, D. A. "Changing Ground: A Medical School Lecturer Turns to Discussion Teaching." In C. R. Christensen, D. A. Garvin, and A. Sweet (eds.), *Education for Judgment: The Artistry of Discussion Leadership.* Boston: Harvard Business School Press, 1991.

Gorman, M. E., Gorman, M. E., and Young, A. "Poetic Writing in Psychology." In A. Young and T. Fulwiler (eds.), *Writing Across the Disciplines: Research into Practice.* Portsmouth, N.H.: Boynton/Cook, 1986.

Gottschalk, K. K. "Writing in the Non-Writing Class: I'd Love to Teach Writing, But . . ." In F. V. Bogel and K. K. Gottschalk (eds.), *Teaching Prose: A Guide for Writing Instructors.* New York: Norton, 1984.

Grumbacher, J. "How Writing Helps Physics Students Become Better Problem Solvers." In T. Fulwiler (ed.), *The Journal Book.* Portsmouth, N.H.: Boynton/Cook, 1987.

Gulette, M. M. "Leading Discussion in a Lecture Course: Some Maxims and an Exhortation." *Change*, Mar./Apr. 1992, pp. 32–39.

Hairston, M. "Not All Errors Are Created Equal: Nonacademic Readers in the Professions Respond to Lapses in Usage." *College English*, 1981, *43*(8), 794–806.

Hammond, L. "Using Focused Freewriting to Promote Critical Thinking." In P. Belanoff, P. Elbow, and S. I. Fontaine (eds.), *Nothing Begins with N: New Investigations of Freewriting.* Carbondale: Southern Illinois University Press, 1991.

Hartwell, P. "Grammar, Grammars, and the Teaching of Grammar." *College English*, 1985, *47*(2), 105–127.

Haswell, R. H. "Minimal Marking." *College English*, 1983, *45*(6), 600–604.

Hawisher, G. E. "The Effects of Word Processing on the Revision Strategies of College Freshmen." *Research in the Teaching of English,* 1987, *21*(2), 145–159.

Hays, J. N. "The Development of Discursive Maturity in College Writers." In J. N. Hays, P. A. Roth, J. R. Ramsey, and R. D. Foulke (eds.), *The Writer's Mind: Writing as a Mode of Thinking.* Urbana, Ill.: National Council of Teachers of English, 1983.

Herrington, A., and Moran, C. (eds.). *Writing, Teaching, and Learning in the Disciplines.* New York: Modern Language Association, 1992.

Hillocks, G. *Research on Written Composition: New Directions for Teaching.* Urbana, Ill.: ERIC Clearinghouse on Reading and Communication Skills and the National Conference on Research in English, 1986.

Hillocks, G., Kahn, E. H., and Johannessen, L. R. "Teaching Defining Strategies as a Mode of Inquiry." *Research in the Teaching of English,* 1983, *17*(3), 275–284.

Hirsch, E. D., Kett, J. F., and Trefil, J. S. *Cultural Literacy: What Every American Needs to Know.* Boston: Houghton Mifflin, 1987.

Hull, G. "Research on Error and Correction." In B. W. McClelland and T. R. Donovan (eds.), *Perspectives on Research and Scholarship in Composition.* New York: Modern Language Association, 1985.

Jacobs, L. C., and Chase, C. I. *Developing and Using Tests Effectively: A Guide for Faculty.* San Francisco: Jossey-Bass, 1992.

Janzow, F., and Eison, J. "Grades: Their Influence on Students and Faculty." In M. D. Svinicki (ed.), *The Changing Face of College Teaching.* New Directions for Teaching and Learning, no. 42. San Francisco: Jossey-Bass, 1990.

Jensen, G. H., and Di Tiberio, J. K. *Personality and the Teaching of Composition.* Norwood, N.J.: Ablex, 1989.

Jensen, V. "Writing in College Physics." In T. Fulwiler (ed.), *The Journal Book.* Portsmouth, N.H.: Boynton/Cook, 1987.

Johnson, D. W., and Johnson, F. P. *Joining Together: Group Theory and Group Skills.* (4th ed.) Englewood Cliffs, N.J.: Prentice Hall, 1991.

Johnson, D. W., and Johnson, R. T. *Learning Together and Alone: Cooperative, Competitive, and Individualistic Learning.* (3rd ed.) Englewood Cliffs, N.J.: Prentice Hall, 1991.

Johnson, D. W., Johnson, R. T., and Smith, K. A. *Cooperative Learning: Increasing College Faculty Instructional Productivity.* ASHE-ERIC Higher Education Report No. 4. Washington D.C.: George Washington University, School of Education and Human Development, 1991.

Keith, S. "Exploring Mathematics in Writing." In P. Connolly and T. Vilardi (eds.), *Writing to Learn Mathematics and Science.* New York: Teachers College Press, 1989.

Kenyon, R. W. "Writing *Is* Problem Solving." In P. Connolly and T. Vilardi (eds.), *Writing to Learn Mathematics and Science.* New York: Teachers College Press, 1989.

Kirkpatrick, L. D., and Pittendrigh, A. "A Writing Teacher in the Physics Classroom." *Physics Teacher,* Mar. 1984, pp. 159–164.

Kolb, D. A. *Learning Style Inventory.* Boston: McBer, 1985.

Kolln, M. "Closing the Books on Alchemy." *College Composition and Communication,* 1981, *32*(2), 139–151.

Kroll, B. "Cognitive Egocentrism and the Problem of Audience Awareness in Written Discourse." *Research in the Teaching of English,* 1978, *12*(3), 269–281.

Kurfiss, J. G. *Critical Thinking: Theory, Research, Practice, and Possibilities.* ASHE-ERIC Higher Education Report No. 2. Washington, D.C.: ERIC Clearinghouse on Higher Education and the Association for the Study of Higher Education, 1988.

Larson, R. L. "The 'Research Paper' in the Writing Course: A Non-Form of Writing." *College English,* 1982, *44*(8), 811–816.

Lunsford, A. A. "Cognitive Development and the Basic Writer." *College English,* 1979, *41*(1), 38–46.

Lunsford, A. A. "Cognitive Studies and Teaching Writing." In B. W. McClelland and T. R. Donovan (eds.), *Perspectives on Research and Scholarship in Composition.* New York: Modern Language Association, 1985.

Lunsford, A. A., and Ede, L. *Singular Texts/Plural Authors: Perspectives on Collaborative Writing.* Carbondale: Southern Illinois University Press, 1990.

Lutzker, M. *Research Projects for College Students: What to Write Across the Curriculum.* Westport, Conn.: Greenwood Press, 1988.

MacDonald, S. P., and Cooper, C. R. "Contributions of Academic and Dialogic Journals to Writing About Literature." In A. Herrington and C. Moran (eds.), *Writing, Teaching, and Learning in the Disciplines.* New York: Modern Language Association, 1992.

MacGregor, J. "Collaborative Learning: Shared Inquiry as a Process of Reform." In M. D. Svinicki (ed.), *The Changing Face of College Teaching.* New Directions for Teaching and Learning, no. 42. San Francisco: Jossey-Bass, 1990.

Machlup, F. "Poor Learning from Good Teachers." *Academe,* Oct. 1979, pp. 376–380.

McKeachie, W. J. *Teaching Tips: A Guidebook for the Beginning College Teacher.* (8th ed.) Lexington, Mass.: Heath, 1986.

Mahala, D. "Writing Utopias: Writing Across the Curriculum and the Promise of Reform." *College English,* 1991, *53*(7), 773–789.

Maimon, E. P. "Talking to Strangers." *College Composition and Communication,* 1979, *30*(4), 364–369.

Maimon, E. P., and others. *Writing in the Arts and Sciences.* Framingham, Mass.: Winthrop, 1981.

Meacham, J. "Discussions by E-Mail: Experiences from a Large Class on Multiculturalism." *Liberal Education,* 1994, *80*(4), 36–39.

Meisenhelder, S. "Redefining 'Powerful' Writing: Toward a Feminist Theory of Composition." *Journal of Thought,* 1985, *20,* 184–195.

Meyers, C. *Teaching Students to Think Critically: A Guide for Faculty in All Disciplines.* San Francisco: Jossey-Bass, 1986.

Meyers, C., and Jones, T. B. *Promoting Active Learning: Strategies for the College Classroom.* San Francisco: Jossey-Bass, 1993.

Morton, T. "Fine Cloth, Cut Carefully: Cooperative Learning in British Columbia." In J. Golub (ed.), *Focus on Collaborative Learning: Classroom Practices in Teaching English, 1988.* Urbana, Ill.: National Council of Teachers of English, 1988.

Mullin, W. J. "Qualitative Thinking and Writing in the Hard Sciences." In P. Connolly and T. Vilardi (eds.), *Writing to Learn Mathematics and Science.* New York: Teachers College Press, 1989.

Myers, G. "The Social Construction of Two Biologists' Proposals." *Written Communication,* 1985, *2,* 219–245.

Myers, G. "Reality, Consensus, and Reform in the Rhetoric of Composition Teaching." *College English,* 1986a, *48*(2), 154–174.

Myers, G. "Writing Research and the Sociology of Scientific Knowledge: A Review of Three New Books." *College English,* 1986b, *48*(6), 595–610.

Myers, I. B., and McCaulley, M. H. *Manual: A Guide to the Development and Use of the Myers-Briggs Type Indicator.* Palo Alto, Calif.: Consulting Psychologists Press, 1985.

National Conference on Undergraduate Research. *Conference Program and Abstracts.* Kalamazoo: Western Michigan University, 1994.

Noguchi, R. R. *Grammar and the Teaching of Writing: Limits and Possibilities.* Urbana, Ill.: National Council of Teachers of English, 1991.

Norman, D. A. "What Goes On in the Mind of the Learner." In W. J. McKeachie (ed.), *Learning, Cognition, and College Teaching.* New Directions for Teaching and Learning, no. 2. San Francisco: Jossey-Bass, 1980.

Paul, R. W. "Dialogical Thinking: Critical Thought Essential to the Acquisition of Rational Knowledge and Passions." In J. B. Baron and R. J. Sternberg (eds.), *Teaching Thinking Skills: Theory and Practice.* New York: Freeman, 1987.

Perry, W. G., Jr. *Forms of Intellectual and Ethical Development in the College Years.* Troy, Mo.: Holt, Rinehart & Winston, 1970.

Pinkava, B., and Haviland, C. "Teaching Writing and Thinking Skills." *Nursing Outlook,* 1984, *32*(5), 270–272.

Ramage, J. D., and Bean, J. C. *Writing Arguments: A Rhetoric with Readings.* (3rd ed.) Needham Heights, Mass.: Allyn & Bacon, 1995.

Rogers, C. *On Becoming a Person: A Therapist's View of Psychotherapy.* Boston: Houghton Mifflin, 1961.

Rogers, M. L. "How Holistic Scoring Kept Writing Alive in Chemistry." *College Teaching,* 1995, *43*(1), 19–22.

Rose, B. "Writing and Mathematics: Theory and Practice." In P. Connolly and T. Vilardi (eds.), *Writing to Learn Mathematics and Science.* New York: Teachers College Press, 1989.

Rowe, M. B. "Using Wait Time to Stimulate Inquiry." In W. W. Wilen (ed.), *Questions, Questioning Techniques, and Effective Teaching.* Washington, D.C.: National Education Association, 1987.

Schroeder, C. C. "New Students—New Learning Styles." *Change,* Sept./Oct. 1993, pp. 21–26.

Schwalm, D. E. "Degree of Difficulty in Basic Writing Courses: Insights from the Oral Proficiency Interview Testing Program." *College English,* 1985, *47*(6), 629–640.

Shaughnessy, M. P. *Errors and Expectations: A Guide for the Teacher of Basic Writing.* New York: Oxford University Press, 1977.

Shaw, H. E. "Responding to Student Essays." In F. V. Bogel and K. K. Gottschalk (eds.), *Teaching Prose: A Guide for Writing Instructors.* New York: Norton, 1984.

Shook, R. "A Case for Cases." In P. L. Stock (ed.), *Forum: Essays on Theory and Practice in the Teaching of Writing.* Portsmouth, N.H.: Boynton/Cook, 1983.

Slavin, R. E. *Cooperative Learning: Theory, Research, and Practice.* Englewood Cliffs, N.J.: Prentice Hall, 1990.

Sommers, N. "Revision Strategies of Student Writers and Experienced Adult Writers." *College Composition and Communication,* 1980, *30*(4), 378–388.

Spandel, V., and Stiggins, R. J. *Creating Writers: Linking Assessment and Writing Instruction.* White Plains, N.Y.: Longman, 1990.

Spear, K. *Shared Writing: Peer Response Groups in English Classes.* Portsmouth, N.H.: Boynton/Cook, 1988.

Spellmeyer, K. "A Common Ground: The Essay in the Academy." *College English,* 1989, *51*(3), 262–276.

Steffens, H. "Collaborative Learning in a History Seminar." *History Teacher,* 1989, *22*(2), 125–138.

Steiner, R. "Chemistry and the Written Word." *Journal of Chemical Education,* 1982, *59,* 1044.

Sternberg, R. J. "Teaching Intelligence: The Application of Cognitive Psychology to the Improvement of Intellectual Skills." In J. B. Baron and R. J. Sternberg (eds.), *Teaching Thinking Skills: Theory and Practice.* New York: Freeman, 1987.

Swartz, R. J. "Teaching for Thinking: A Developmental Model for the Infusion of Thinking Skills into Mainstream Instruction." In J. B. Baron and R. J. Sternberg (eds.), *Teaching Thinking Skills: Theory and Practice*. New York: Freeman, 1987.

Tedlock, D. "The Case Approach to Composition." *College Composition and Communication*, 1981, *32*(3), 253–261.

Tobias, S. "Writing to Learn Science and Mathematics." In P. Connolly and T. Vilardi (eds.), *Writing to Learn Mathematics and Science*. New York: Teachers College Press, 1989.

Voss, J. F. "On the Composition of Experts and Novices." In E. P. Maimon, B. F. Nodine, and F. W. O'Connor (eds.), *Thinking, Reasoning, and Writing*. White Plains, N.Y.: Longman, 1989.

Walvoord, B. E., and McCarthy, L. P. *Thinking and Writing in College: A Naturalistic Study of Students in Four Disciplines*. Urbana, Ill.: National Council of Teachers of English, 1990.

Welty, W. M. "Discussion Method Teaching: How to Make It Work." *Change*, July/Aug. 1989, pp. 40–49.

White, E. M. *Comparison and Contrast: The California State University Freshman English Equivalency Examination*. Vols. 1–8. Long Beach: California State University, 1973–1981. (Available through ERIC, 1111 West Kenyon Road, Urbana, IL 61801)

White, E. M. *Assigning, Responding, Evaluating: A Writing Teacher's Guide*. (2nd ed.) New York: St. Martin's Press, 1992.

White, E. M. *Teaching and Assessing Writing*. (2nd ed.) San Francisco: Jossey-Bass, 1994.

Wiener, H. S. "Collaborative Learning in the Classroom: A Guide to Evaluation." *College English*, 1986, *48*(1), 52–61.

Wilen, W. W. (ed.). *Questions, Questioning Techniques, and Effective Teaching*. Washington, D.C.: National Education Association, 1987.

Williams, J. M. "The Phenomenology of Error." *College Composition and Communication*, 1981, *32*(2), 152–168.

Williams, J. M. *Style: Ten Lessons in Clarity and Grace*. (2nd ed.) Glenview, Ill.: Scott, Foresman, 1985.

Williams, J. M. "Two Ways of Thinking About Growth: The Problem of Finding the Right Metaphor." In E. P. Maimon, B. F. Nodine, and F. W. O'Connor (eds.), *Thinking, Reasoning, and Writing*. White Plains, N.Y.: Longman, 1989.

Yoshida, J. "Writing to Learn Philosophy." In A. R. Gere (ed.), *Roots in the Sawdust: Writing to Learn Across the Disciplines*. Urbana, Ill.: National Council of Teachers of English, 1985.

Young, A., and Fulwiler, T. (eds). *Writing Across the Disciplines: Research into Practice*. Portsmouth, N.H.: Boynton/Cook, 1986.

Zeiger, W. "The Exploratory Essay: Enfranchising the Spirit of Inquiry in College Composition." *College English*, 1985, *47*(5), 454–466.

Zinsser, W. *Writing to Learn*. New York: HarperCollins, 1988.